The **DAY**
is **BORN**
of **DARKNESS**

The **DAY**
is **BORN**
of **DARKNESS**

by **MIKHAIL DYOMIN**

Translated from the Russian
by TONY KAHN

Alfred·A·Knopf · New York · 1976

ISBN: 0-394-49166-1

Library of Congress Catalog Card Number: 75-36783
Manufactured in the United States of America
First American Edition

The **DAY**
_is_ **BORN**
_of_ **DARKNESS**

Part I

You and I are like midnight expresses,

Exchanging whistles in the dark;

Just a moment in the stillness,

Flashing fires, and we part.

—FROM A THIEVES' SONG

In the evenings, before they sound the retreat, the prison
draws into itself and settles down. Deep in its bowels a secret
life begins. This is the hour the prison telegraph starts to stir.
Every evening, a barely audible series of taps worms its way
through the thick stone walls, bearing back and forth calls,
curses, and appeals, the words of despair and the rhythms of
dread.

I sit on my bunk beneath the little window, looking up at
the caged sky beyond the grate. There, in the blue, a
transparent July sunset smolders into darkness. Someone taps
me on the shoulder and whispers in my ear.

"Hey, Chuma, you got a call."

"Who?"

"The Gypsy. From seventy-two."

The Gypsy is one of my partners; we'd been arrested and
detained together at the Konotop train station. We often
exchanged news like this, tap for tap. This time the message
was brief.

"The tribunal meets tomorrow. . . . They say our case is in
court already. . . . Sit tight. They'll call us in the morning."

A pause. Then he started tapping out a line from an old
tramp song. " 'I'm dying, yes, I'll die.' " And then: "They got
a new edict on the books. You hear about it? This time, they
say, the sentence is hell. . . . Hope to God they're wrong!"

Edict? I shrugged my shoulders. No, it was news to
me—probably just the same old scuttlebutt life around here
was so full of. I didn't have much faith in prison rumors. I
should have this time. That very day, so quiet and so clear, a
dire new government edict—"*Ukaz* 6/4/47"—had in fact been
issued. It inaugurated the brutal postwar reign of terror. Along
with thousands of other prisoners I was to share its disastrous
consequences. . . . But that's for later. Finding myself a place
on the bare boards of the bunk, I waited for tomorrow and the
hour of our trial.

The night guard pattered down the hall. Opening the

"feeder" (a little hole bored into the door for passing food), the head guard glanced into the cell.

"Retreat," he said hoarsely. "Everybody quiet!" Wheezing and squinting, he stood there and stared. Then, with a crash, he slammed the bolt home.

The day withdrew, one of many days I'd be spending behind bars. The streaming sunset faded beyond the grate and yielded to the darkness. A dim and dusty lamp captured by a rusty net beneath the ceiling flared up, painting the faces of the men a deathly yellow.

The crowded cell got ready for sleep, tossing and turning, smelling of sweat and despair. We were all awaiting trial here; for many of us the coming morning would be a turning point.

A quiet, steady tap resounded in the corner. Six knocks: an *f*. . . . Then one: an *a*. . . . A quick series followed, ending on *i*. . . . Then a *t*. . . . *F-a-i-t.* The *h* was missing.

I moved to the corner and put my ear to the wall. Suddenly a cold drop of water struck me in the face.

So that's what it was. The moisture of the prison, trickling away. At night, while men slept, the prison itself had begun to speak.

"Fait!" I wiped the moisture from my eyelashes. "What's there left for me to believe in now?"

Once again I remembered the Ukrainian border town of Lvov, the most "Western" and free of all postwar Soviet cities. Full of contrabandists, Ukrainian nationalists, and black market profiteers, Lvov had had its reasons for attracting me. I'd decided to make my way west, to relatives in France who'd left Russia after the Revolution. Armed with the addresses I'd need in Lvov, I'd fallen in with one of the countless underground bands of Ukrainian terrorists in the town. The *benderovtsy*, as they were called, were supposed to have ferried me across the border, but the Cheka had begun a roundup and I'd been forced to leave town on the run.

I traveled the country roads on foot, faint with the heat and hunger; there wasn't a bit of food in that impoverished backwater, even if I'd had the money to pay for it—which I didn't. Stealing and begging were out of the question, too; you couldn't so much as approach a farmhouse without being greeted with hostility and suspicion and driven off.

I drank stagnant pond water; I ate grass, even nettles. (If you turn back the stinging outer side of the leaves, they are perfectly edible, with a taste like fresh cucumber.)

At first, I steered clear of the train stations, but after a while I couldn't hold back. In the darkness, at a crawl, I dragged myself to a platform and hid beneath the planking for long stretches at a time, waiting for a train. Eventually I met up with my partners. For two weeks we traveled the local rails, making a little money; I grew stronger. That's when the ridiculous affair I was now caught up in occurred. Not far from Konotop, on the platform of one of the cars of the night train, we met up with two profiteers carrying colored Rumanian shawls and ladies' underwear to the Poltava markets. We helped ourselves to a piece of their merchandise and late that night were detained by the railroad militia on a charge of railway larceny.

I recalled it all now in an agony of insomnia, as the night dragged painfully along. The cell was fast asleep. Except for a remote rustle, some snoring, and a hasty whisper in the far corner, it was quiet. Suddenly I caught some strange snatches of conversation: "Pull. . . . No, not like that . . . from the bottom. . . . Listen, scum, that's mine!" I got up, looked around, and made out some vague shadows in the corner.

The *shkodniki* were harbored there: petty crooks and market swindlers—citizens of the criminal world, but far from its elite. In the prison table of ranks, they held a lowly, almost insignificant place. Something was clearly bothering them. A moment later I shouted: "Hey, what's happening?"

"The *fraier* here's croaking," they answered. A *fraier*—an outsider—not one of them. "Giving up the ghost."

"What in the hell are you waiting for? Call the guard!"

"Later. We're divvying up his stuff right now."

I couldn't believe it. "You're going to leave him naked?"

"Hell no. We got him covered," one of the *shkodniki* said, moving off. He was holding a new striped cloth jacket. He looked it over and grinned. "Good piece of material. Why leave it to a stiff? It's all the same to him. The way things are going, any kind of clothes would do for him, like a box."

When they carried the *fraier*'s body out of the cell, I got a good look at his face: young and freckled, with high cheekbones. The face still hadn't lost its color and the expression was strangely unperturbed.

Just before dawn I fell into a deep sleep full of feverish dreams: a thicket of nettles surrounded me and the dead boy turned his freckled face my way. "You can't pass here," he muttered, pointing to the thicket. "We're both naked. It stings. . . . Ah, if only we had our clothes! With clothes, we could—" I awoke, roused by the shout of the guard.

"All right, get your clothes and out into the hall!"

There were quite a few of us headed for trial that day. They counted us out in the hall, lined us up in pairs, and led us to the prison yard, flooded with sharp sunlight. A tall black van was waiting for us, snorting and fuming: the infamous convict "raven."

It was Saturday, the day for parcels and meetings. Not far from the gates, a bit to the side of the raven, some women who'd come from the outside were gathered in a crowd. One of them, a redhead with high cheekbones, looked strangely familiar to me. I had the feeling I'd seen her somewhere before. There she stood, holding a saucepan full of steaming soup close to her stomach. Suddenly her arms trembled, her face sharpened, her eyes widened and turned glassy. I followed her stare and realized with a start who she was and what had happened.

Somewhere in the crowd she caught sight of the new striped jacket that had once belonged to her son. Looking further, she recognized the rest of his things on other strangers—the shirt, the pants, the shoes.

A dark tremor crossed her face but she didn't scream or rush forward. Her mouth stayed tightly shut, her lips white. There she stood, her eyes fixed on us, her whole face turned to stone. Only her hands moved, trembling more and more, dropping lower and lower, spilling the soup she'd brought her son into the dust.

"WE'VE ALL GOT UKAZES"

The trial was short and sweet; the whole procedure took no more than an hour. After the prosecutor's charge—he insisted that the sternest measures be taken—our defense counsel, if you can call him that, stepped forward. We'd met him for the first time in the hall of the courtroom a half-hour before the session: a backwoods lawyer who, as he himself insisted, had undertaken our case merely as a matter of duty. Feeble, narrow-chested, and balding, he paused for a moment, looking at us out of the corner of his eyes. Then, with a shrug of his puny shoulders, he began:

"I really don't know how to proceed. . . . I'm obliged to defend them, of course, as a matter of duty. . . . But, frankly, I'd rather not. These are clearly not Soviet citizens, but renegades—yes, and criminals, the spoor of an alien environment. . . . In all honesty, how *can* they be defended? Look at those faces: the clear traces of cretinism, the undeniable evidence of bad genes and of every conceivable vice."

The judge noticeably revived at these words and carefully wiped his glasses. His jurors, distributed on either side of him, exchanged brief remarks. Then they all began looking intently at us as if to examine the traces of cretinism the orator had just pointed out.

What a fine little defender, I thought in consternation. I'd never seen anything like him.

Meanwhile, a vague rumble was building in the hallway. From the back rows a woman boomed out in a bass: "You call that a lawyer? It's a cop with a change of clothes! Cut out the dirty tricks and give 'em a real defense!"

"Silence!" the judge announced, slamming the top of the

table with his fist. "Or I'll order this courtroom cleared! Now then—" He turned weightily to the speaker. "Proceed. Only be brief."

"What more can I say?" Our hopeless defender spread his arms. "Everything, it seems to me, is perfectly clear. One can, of course, discover some mitigating circumstances: their youth, for example, the clear immaturity of this one"—he poked a finger in my side—"and the generally difficult conditions of life for all the defendants. The war, a homeless youth, the slum world that raised them"—for some reason he pointed at me again—"were a far cry from Soviet social ideals. Naturally, it did nothing to train them for work or provide them with any positive examples. It is therefore incontestable that stern discipline and unremitting, obligatory physical labor will be both useful and normalizing."

With that he sat down, wiping his moist bald spot with his palm. The session was adjourned and the court retired to confer.

"With a little luck he might even tie the noose around our necks," the Gypsy whispered, bending toward me. "What an ass."

"We'll see," I said. "We'll see. Whatever happens, we won't escape the *ukaz*."

I was right. We didn't get off the hook. In compliance with the new code, my two comrades (the Gypsy and another nicknamed Scarface) were sentenced to ten years' imprisonment. For me, the youngest of the group, it was six years in camp "with stern isolation" and three years' exile "in remote places."

Six plus three—nine years in all without my rights—and a stern regime to boot. I felt my insides turning cold.

As they were leading us out of the courtroom, we caught sight of the "plaintiffs," the profiteers who'd sent us to camp in the first place. They were headed there, too, by the way. Their cheeks unshaven, their hands in chains, they looked miserable —just like us, in fact. The court had availed itself of their testimony and then turned right around and charged them with profiteering.

Scarface laughed at them. "Still feeling crafty? That's what you get from looking for sugar in shit!"

The Gypsy was more philosophical. "Hey, you bastards," he said reproachfully, "aren't you ashamed of yourselves? We played fair with you. We didn't lift all your stuff, just a piece. . . . And you couldn't wait to rat. What's the point of being honest anymore? Where are you going to find a pure conscience these days?"

He spoke as if his heart were breaking, with a wave of his arms and a thunder in his voice like iron. The world had lost the meaning of honor and he was crushed, crushed to the bottom of his soul. The escort cut him off. He ordered the Gypsy to shut up and keep moving. And so, in silence, we headed for the raven.

The raven was packed with prisoners and buzzing like a beehive. Partitioned on the inside into narrow little sections— boxes, they called them—it looked exactly like a huge, harassed beehive that never housed a single drop of honey and never would. The box I went to was full of the *shkodniki* who'd stripped the dying boy the night before. Stalin's new *ukaz* concerned them, too; they'd all received ten-year terms. A lot longer than mine. And to give you an idea of how low I'd sunk, the news of their misfortune relaxed all my tensions.

"Ten years!" someone shouted behind my back. "A nightmare! And for what? For a little white lie, for playing dolls, that's all!"

"White lie" is the term crooks have for a petty market swindle. Some of the swindles are quite interesting and clever. Take, for instance, the "purchase" of a watch.

Drawing up to the counter, the buyer carefully selects a watch. He looks it over, hoists it to his ear, keeping it hidden in his palm out of the salesman's view.

"Hey," the buyer says suddenly, "it's stopped. It's dead. . . . No, wait, it's going. It's going, sorry, it's going."

The watch, in fact, has already "gone"—straight from the swindler's palm into the hand of an accomplice who's stolen up from behind and dissolved back into the crowd.

"Well," the client says a moment later, "guess I'm off."

"What about the watch?" the salesman asks.

"What watch?" The swindler acts surprised. "Oh . . . that. Look, I changed my mind. The thing's a piece of trash; I wouldn't even take it for nothing."

He spreads his hands—the palms are empty. The startled salesman screams bloody murder, but he can't prove a thing. Indignantly, the "buyer" demands to be searched in the presence of witnesses and then walks away free as a bird.

One of the most widespread market activities is "playing dolls," an affair born of consumer shortages. It's a pretty straightforward business. Under the counter people are offered an assortment of scarce goods rarely if ever found in the stores: imported dresses, expensive cuts of cloth and so forth. The merchandise usually comes wrapped in newspaper and tied with heavy rope. It's taken out of the bag, shown on the sly to the prospective buyer (tearing back a corner of the newspaper, the dealer gives the buyer a chance to feel the material), and then quickly stashed away. There are cops everywhere, after all, a man's got to be careful! The dealer gets a little nervous and suggests they move someplace else a little more secluded. That's where the deal is consummated. The bundle's taken out of the bag again; the wrapping and twine on the outside, the little torn edge of the paper, they all coincide to a T. It's all there. Only, it isn't. The real merchandise has been replaced by a "doll" filled with torn rags.

It was the doll that had finally been the undoing of the *shkodniki*. They'd snared themselves an experienced, hair-splitting buyer who'd checked out the bundle right on the spot and called a cop.

Now they bemoaned their fate, the authorities, and the new code, all at the top of their lungs. The *ukaz* had nearly tripled all the sentences. "How is a man to live?" they grieved. "How is a man to work?"

In the neighboring box sat a quiet, gray, gentle little old man who'd been arrested for cannibalism and sentenced to twenty-five years hard labor. Judging by the stories, he'd started his business during the final year of the war. Quite a few people (people, in essence, like myself) were wandering through the Ukraine at the time, fleeing the authorities. The gentle old man would shelter and hide them and, after an overdose of home-brew, polish them off as they slept by hammering a heavy shoemaker's awl right into their skulls. Then he would neatly cut up the bodies and bury the bones in the garden. From the fingers and cartilage he'd make gelatin; the meat would go for cutlets. In the course of two years (from 1945 to 1947) he sold the cutlets at train station markets and was discovered only by accident, when his neighbor's pigs uprooted the bones in his garden. So many bones turned up, in fact, that the investigator first thought he'd uncovered the forgotten remains of a communal grave, a story the old man himself persisted in telling. But here again the bones betrayed him. They were too smooth, too cleanly picked—and had been boiled.

He conducted himself like a model prisoner (the authorities were always holding him up as an example), and now he sat all alone in his own box, as quiet as a mouse, keeping his thoughts to himself.

Somewhat more vocal were the two political prisoners in the corner. Both of them had been sentenced to twenty-five years, the maximum penalty. Realizing they had nothing left to lose, they had started sounding off fearlessly, at the tops of their lungs.

"A country of informers and scum!" You could hear the bass booming from the darkness. "Just think what they've done to Russia!"

I recognized the voice. Aaron Brovman. We'd spent several days together in the Office of Preventive Detention where people were sent immediately after arrest.

A gifted linguist and great philologist, Brovman had been a department head at Kharkov University after the war. Later, frightened by denunciations and growing anti-Semitism, he'd fled the university for the provinces and his relatives in Konotop. There he took a job at a secondary school and lived for a while in peace, teaching the history of literature. He didn't escape denunciations here either, though, and his beloved science finally did him in. On one of his exams he flunked an untalented student who couldn't tell a knight of the realm from a night on the town. The good-for-nothing's parents demanded a re-examination. Brovman refused. They offered him a bribe and he kicked them out. A denunciation followed, and soon after, the philologist was nabbed on suspicion of seditious and premeditated activity. At the trial, along with a number of other crimes, he was accused of morally corrupting his students with depraved bourgeois culture, including the works of Céline, Kafka, and Joyce.

His companion in misfortune, a former soldier, was also the victim of a denunciation. Shocked by the severity of the sentence, he spent the whole journey cursing the laws.

"What laws?" Brovman asked loudly. "Soviet laws? Don't kid yourself. The whole system is founded on lawlessness. And the most scandalous miscarriages of justice! Take a look at our sentences. Monstrous!"

Then, as if in answer to his remarks, someone in a distant box started to sing:

"My long, long sentence takes me northward,
We've all got ukazes. They've thrown the book.
Look, my beloved, deep in my eyes now,
It may be the last time you'll look."

"Quiet!" the guard shouted. "No singing or loud conversations on the train. Don't you know the rules?"

"Where are they taking us, anyway?" I got interested.

"To the train station," the guard replied, rattling his keys. "To where ninety-nine weep for each man that laughs—and he's the head of the regime!"

"What times," Brovman spoke out. "Bad enough they made a regime, now they've even dreamed up a special post. 'The Head of the Regime.' Who's that? Isn't it Josef Vissarionovich himself?"

So. That, in a nutshell, was our "beehive": a noisy bin of sin and nightmares. The very nightmares that had come to torment my Russia in her postwar years and spread across her frail and massive land.

COLD MOUNTAIN

Twenty-four hours later I found myself in the Kharkov Central Distribution Prison—the largest deportation center in the Ukraine. It dominates the whole town; you can see it from miles away. Gloomy and bulky, it rests on an elevation the people of Kharkov have christened "Cold Mountain." And with good cause.

Railroad tracks to every nook and cranny of the state originate here. That's why it's a deportation prison. Like a gigantic pump, it tirelessly shunts masses of human beings from the south to the north and the west to the east . . . to the Far East, that is, and the distant north.

The transports move in a continuous stream from warm climes to the taiga, the deadly snowy tundra, and the coasts of freezing seas. The very thought of it can chill you to the bone.

For all that, Cold Mountain does have its "warm" spot: an exotic cell, usually located in the corner, at the very top, called "India." The name arose from a sense of irony. After all, a prison has its sense of humor too, even if a cruel one. India is the appointed home of the aristocracy of thieves.

The prison authorities try not to admit thieves into the general cells, preferring to detain them separately, nearer the spotlights and machine guns of the watchtower. The sorting process begins immediately after the arrival of a convoy. They line up the prisoners in the corridor, order them to strip to the waist, and inspect them carefully for traces of a tattoo—the one sure-fire method the authorities have of identifying a thief. Almost everyone in the underworld carries a tattoo as a kind of caste mark and evidence of his chivalry and foppery.

"A painted one," the corridor guard says, fishing out the

showoff from the ranks. "A colored one. Come on, move it, over to your own kind!"

"Roosters to the roosters, and lobsters to the side." That's the way they described the procedure. I was shunted over to the "roosters" the second I took off my shirt. The guard spotted an ace of clubs on my shoulder, squinted, and waved his hand: "Move it!"

My partners were luckier. The Gypsy had no tattoos and Scarface carried the sign of an anchor and Naiad on his hand, a design popular chiefly among sailors. Besides, he was dressed for the part in a sailor's striped vest and bell-bottomed pants (a favorite outfit among the rabble of Odessa).

"Sailor?" the guard asked.

"You got it," Scarface barked, sticking out his chest.

"How'd you get here?"

"Fist fight in port."

"Hooligans, huh?"

"Nope." Scarface dropped his glance. "A little misunderstanding. I'm ashamed of it myself."

"Okay," the guard said. He could, of course, have verified the statement, but he was too lazy to go to the office, dig through some papers, and come up with the official list. "You got a good-for-nothing mug. Can't say I trust it, but . . . okay."

On my way out I looked at my friends with envy; they'd managed to get into the general cell and that, as everybody knew, was a bed of roses. A cell full of quiet, unintimidated people who got parcels.

A word about those parcels, by the way. According to a prison tradition, thieves have the right to one-third of all the grub that comes into the cell from home because, unlike the outsiders—the *fraiers*—they're a homeless breed without families or even a place to perch. There's no one around to spare them a moment's thought (except, perhaps, for the Ministry of Internal Affairs); and so they worry about themselves.

"A crafty breed": that's what the prisoners call themselves, and they have a point.

An experienced prisoner (in this case, an inhabitant of India) is in fact as wily and resourceful as a beast at bay. He is hounded into bondage and stripped of his most elementary possessions. All the same, by circumventing every ban, he manages to get everything he needs.

Here a sliver of glass covered on one side with soot becomes a mirror—or even a periscope. Fastened to a chip of wood or a pencil and thrust through the peephole in the door, it can give the thieves a full view of the corridor and any approaching guards.

A vital kind of security. Especially in the case of cards. All cards found during a search are confiscated without question. Still, no matter what, the game goes on. The prisoners' cards are no more than about four centimeters long, and made out of the most varied materials (birch bark in the main camps, cigarette filters or corners of white paper in the detention cells). The carefully prepared strips are pasted together and placed beneath a press so that they will be thick and stiff.

Prisoners make glue out of bread, chewing it up and forcing it through a thin rag. This is the famous all-purpose prison glue, with a thin viscosity and the tensile strength, when dry, of a bone. Prisoners use it not only for cards, but for making chessmen, toys, even smoking pipes. The secret of the glue has been known in Old Rus since time immemorial, and passed down from generation to generation. At one time or another the Decembrists used it, the convicts of Sakhalin, even the Populists and Bolsheviks. Every textbook on the history of the Party, for instance, has some mention of Lenin's famous "inkpot," made of bread and filled with milk. You won't find milk in Russian prisons anymore—not these days, at least— but the prisons themselves stand indestructible, as a kind of guarantee that the secret will never die but will be passed on to our most distant descendants and serve them well.

But let's get back to the cards. Once the strips have been glued together, they're marked by suits and given values. There are two colors, of course, red and black. Colors made in prison of blood and soot. The blood isn't hard to come by, but for soot you need a fire. Matches, as a rule, aren't normally found in a cell. (The authorities are extremely reluctant to distribute them among the prisoners, and then only in carefully limited numbers.) All the same, the prisoners solve the problem with remarkable simplicity.

First you need some cotton (not the medicinal kind, but the raw gray fabric cotton used for lining padded jackets and peacoats). A scrap of cotton extracted from the lining is rolled tightly and carefully into a kind of wad. Next, the wad is placed on a level spot on the floor and rolled until the cotton starts to steam. You can use anything you like to roll with: a board, the sole of your shoe, just as long as you do it swiftly, strenuously, and with a sharp and steady rhythm. I knew specialists who could get a fire going after a minute and a half or two, and not just from cotton, either, but even from dry moss!

I remember how amazed I was the first time I saw the process in my youth, in Butyrsky Prison. I felt as if I'd suddenly been dropped out of civilization into an ancestral world of caves and savagery.

This gloomy world knows no pity; here man's most basic instincts reign supreme. Delicacy, gentleness, helpfulness—all the attributes of educated society are nothing more than detriments, clear and shameful signs of weakness. And one must not be weak! To survive here, to withstand, you have to fight for your life and win a right to it. You have to love life imperiously and with a rage.

Imperiously and with a rage. . . . It was a precept I'd adopted long ago and was to observe steadfastly all through the years of my wanderings. Who knows, perhaps because of it, I lived to tell my tale.

Life in India was lean (no parcels came our way) but far from uneventful. We amused ourselves as best we could.

The card game would begin immediately after breakfast: 450 grams of bread—our daily ration—a piece of sugar, and a muddy bowl of codfish and cabbage soup. Sitting in the corners and under the bunks, the convicts would play without restraint and for any kitty they could find: clothing, soup, and sugar. The only thing you weren't allowed to play for was bread.

I didn't play myself. I'd given it up a long time ago, while still in Groznyi, after a memorable incident with a fellow named Khasan. Sitting stark naked beneath a Caucasus sky, I'd vowed that night never to take another card in my hand. Never! And I kept my word. In memory of that pledge the ace of clubs was etched into my shoulder.

After a lunch of soup and watery kasha, they'd lead us out into the exercise yard. That's when they'd air out the room and subject it to a search. These searches—*shmony,* they were called—were a constant feature of our lives that rarely turned up anything. We weren't the kind to be caught; we'd safely hidden all our contraband—razors, cards, and mirrors.

Everything I'm describing is, in essence, a prelude, an introduction essential to what follows. Still, I do have to digress a little with a word or two about architecture. Prison architecture, that is.

Russian prisons conform to a standard evolved during the reign of Catherine the Great—a woman, as everyone knows, celebrated for her advanced ideas and distinguished by her love of the arts. She wrote little plays; she composed elegies. And spent a good deal of her time and energies on the construction of prisons—a field in which she enjoyed enormous success. It was here, in fact, that her brilliant artistic talents burst into full flower. The Empress' literary efforts have not withstood the test of time; her dungeons, however, have been preserved in full. They've become classics of their kind, transformed into an image that remains, in a sense, the sole relic of her reign.

Almost all of our prisons bear the impress of the classic Catherine standard; they are tall, monumental, and laid out in the shape of the letter П. The exercise area is in dead center, as if at the bottom of a deep, stone well, satisfying all the demands of security. This arrangement has not stopped prisoners from drawing some advantages all their own. All the windows of the building that overlook the yard have no "muzzles" (the special metal shields attached to the bars from outside). The prisoners take their walks in full view of the entire complex and can therefore call back and forth between the different cells, collecting notes and tobacco thrown down from the windows. The practice is prohibited, of course, but that rarely stops anybody. They have a name for it here: the open postal system. There's another, secret one, reserved for special needs. But more of that later.

After circling the yard for the appointed period, stocking up on news and something to smoke, we'd return to our overcrowded shelter, which, after the walk and the intoxicating drafts of fresh air, would seem even more congested than before. Dinner came next (the same old soup of rotten fish and cabbage), followed a little while later by the sounds of the retreat. Evening would settle in—the most difficult and tormenting time of all.

Extraneous noises and movements were now prohibited; you were supposed to sleep, which nobody wanted to do. (Later, in the north, we'd long for sleep; it would become as dear a commodity as bread, even dearer . . . but that was in the taiga and the camps. Here we were fed up with it.)

The bustle of the day would fall away like so much foam and, in the stillness, an anguish born of despair would revive. You had to fight it off somehow and break free of the curse of the mood. That's when the "novéls" would come to our rescue. "Novél" is a term coined by the thieves for every kind of oral narrative and tale. They'd pronounce the word incorrectly on purpose, ironically, with a stress on the second syllable as if, in one stroke, to establish both its connection with and its independence of literature.

They were curious creations, whimsical mixes of folkloric traditions and bookish romance. The widest possible selection of works, including even the classics, would be grist for them. I managed to hear (and myself relate) stories based on Dickens, Dostoyevsky, Mérimée, and Leo Tolstoy. Little remained of the originals, of course, except for the general outline.

Along with serious literature, the prisoners would make use of cheap novels. The choice here was especially wide and its incorporation into the thieves' own folklore made for the uniquely bloody quality of the tales.

"At twelve midnight exactly," the narrator spins his tale in a resounding whisper, "along the dark streets of the city of Paris, at a speed of one hundred and twenty kilometers an hour, a mysterious carriage rushed by with lanterns doused. A man sat inside in a black raincoat, a half-mask, and a wide-brimmed hat. It was none other than Rocambole himself, the terror of the population, the king of the dens, the Atman of the infamous and merciless gang of the Jack of Hearts. The carriage drew to a halt before one of the medieval castles. Rocambole stepped out, pressed a hidden button in the wall, and disappeared into the ground. . . ."

Practiced storytellers and "novélists" are at an amazingly high premium in prison. They're paid great attention, pampered, and fed. "Doctors of depression" the convicts call them. And they're right. I was a "doctor" myself, although not for long. After exhausting my resources and retelling everything I'd ever read a few times, I dried up and retired. Besides, I didn't have a taste for bloody plots.

A fellow named Stilmark, though, was a specialist in the field; an older man, lean and sluggish, he had no relationship whatsoever with the convicts. He was there for political reasons and had joined our crowd quite by accident, as a result of a quarrel with a guard for which he was now being punished.

Stilmark quickly made himself at home in India. An educated and clever man, he realized what the score was and quickly became one of our most popular novélists. His imagination was truly inexhaustible. He'd drag out the adventures of Rocambole, for instance, night after night, dropping his hero into the most amazing circumstances, countries, and epochs. He knew no obstacles in this regard, not even Soviet Russia. The Russian variant would go like this: "Our thieves knew Rocambole well. He often traveled on business to Odessa, that Russian Marseilles, where he lived under the assumed name of Semka Rabinovich. Many even thought that was his real name!"

Descriptions of traditional castles and dungeons, nightmarish intrigues and deadly combats would follow. And always in abundance. Stilmark was no miser when it came to that. He knew his audience well.

And so we whiled the time away, waiting for the convoy. Our quiet life, though, soon ended suddenly and irreversibly, with the appearance in our cell of a new prisoner.

THE ORIGINS OF THE BITCH WAR

He appeared late at night and stood on the threshold, carefully surveying the cell: a short, thickset man, with a square face full of scars. He took a knapsack from his shoulder and, dragging it by the strap along the floor, walked nonchalantly to the window.

Even when they don't know each other personally, thieves are quick and telling judges of character. They go by the gestures, the intonations, and other sharp, if subtle, signs. Even, to some extent, by the way a man comes into a cell. Everybody has his own style of entering. A man there for the first time will hesitate a long while at the door, peering like an animal at bay. The stinking prison twilight frightens him, the pale smudges of faces and those intense, inflamed, and hungry eyes. A man with a little more experience behaves more courageously. He comes in, looks for a free place (usually right by the doors) and quickly settles down on the bunk or underneath it.

A professional convict conducts himself with self-assurance, as if he owned the place. Prison is his home. He spends half his life here and he knows the system. The small fry usually huddle by the doors, cheek-by-jowl with the communal washtub and toilet. The true aristocracy reside on the other side of the cell, near the window, which is precisely where the stranger headed.

He knew his worth; every action said so. Slowly moving our way, he tossed his bag on the bunk and, bending toward my neighbor (an elderly pickpocket named the Redhead), unceremoniously said: "Come on, move it!"

"What?" the Redhead drawled threateningly. He raised himself on his elbow. "The hell with you. Get out of here."

He was performing a time-honored ritual. If the threat took effect and the fellow went away, he clearly didn't belong there. If not, it would mean the bunk was his. The stage was set, and his answer followed at once.

"Now, now"—the newcomer grinned—"no need to get nervous. Who's here mostly? Thieves?"

"Yes."

"Any chance I've come to the wrong place?"

"Nope, you've got it right."

"Then what's the problem? Move it!"

He said it quietly, lazily even, but there was a special power in his voice and the Redhead sensed it; slowly he moved off, straightening out the place as he went.

Later, lying on his bunk and lighting a smoke, the newcomer introduced himself properly. His nickname was the Goose. His specialty: locksmith (an apartment thief). He'd been arrested on an *ukaz* and sentenced to twelve years. He did night work in Kiev and had been born in Rostov.

The Redhead, now on perfectly good terms, chewed on his cigarette and said: "A Rostov tramp . . . it's an old city, all right. Noble, too. Almost like our Odessa."

"What do you mean 'almost'?" The Goose shrugged his shoulders. "Makes me laugh to compare them, even. There's never been a time they haven't called Rostov the papa. Think about it! Papa!"

"So? They call Odessa the mother."

"That's the whole point," the Goose mumbled. He stretched himself with a crackle and readjusted his knapsack at the head of his bed. "That's just the point. That's what she's famous for."

And, yawning, he quoted the words of an old, old song:

> *"Odessa is famed for her whores,*
> *Rostov is known for its tramps,*

> *Moscow looks after the Holy Faith*
> *And Sevastopol, sailors and scamps."*

The day began as usual: breakfast, cards, a walk. Everything in order and nothing prophesying disaster. We'd barely returned when the telegraph got working. It was the Gypsy tapping—for me.

"I'm sending you a *ksiva*," he signaled. "Look for it in the mailbox. Don't forget!"

"What's up?"

"Too long to explain," he answered evasively. "Anyway, it's serious business."

In our jargon, a *ksiva* is a note, a piece of information, any kind of document. The "mailbox" is the communal toilet in the prison corridor. Twice a day (before breakfast and just before the retreat) the different cells are led there by turns to relieve themselves. The box is reserved for special, top secret communiques and remains, in that sense, one of the safest places we had.

There are any number of secluded spots in the box. Even though obliged to by regulations, the guards hardly relish the idea of digging around in any of them and, as a result, the correspondence almost always reaches its intended destination.

By evening I had already read my *ksiva*. "Here's what's up," the Gypsy wrote. "You've got a Vitka Gusev in the cell. I saw him today on the walk. He's probably passing himself off as an honest thief, a purebred, but don't you believe it. Don't let him near you, and tell the others the same. The Goose is a stoolie—a bitch. I met up with him in '45 in Gorlovko, in a uniform no less, all dolled up with medals and a lieutenant's bars. I'll stand by my word; you can quote me on it. Besides, there are other people who know about him too. It grieves us and insults us to look on your cell and see, among its worthy thieves, scum of that sort, believing in God knows what and praying to God knows who."

I read the note twice. The second time I read it aloud.

When I finished, the cell fell silent, pricking up its ears. All eyes turned to the Goose.

He was rolling a cigarette; his fingers suddenly fumbled, spilling the tobacco on his knees. Slowly, very slowly, while the cell waited, the Goose gathered it up and poured it into his open palm.

Then he lighted up, took a deep drag, and raised his face to us. It was composed (the moment of weakness had passed). Only his right eyebrow, cut by a scar, trembled slightly.

"So?" he said. "The Gypsy and I met. What about it?"

"You were in the service?" they asked him.

"I was."

"With a uniform on?"

"What else?"

"You had decorations?"

"Sure I had 'em," he said. "Military decorations!"

He lightly touched his right brow, drew his palm across his cheek (it was streaked with a wide, dark, slanting scar), and, with a characteristic smile, continued: "They're all marks of the war. Big deal. Almost all of Rokossovsky's army was made out of prison camp convicts like me. No, brothers"—he shook his head—"I'm no bitch."

"What's a bitch?" asked one of the thieves. He had a bald, prominent forehead and they called him Vladimir—or Lenin for short. "What's a bitch?"

"A bitch?" the Redhead grumbled. "Anyone who renounces our faith and betrays his own kind."

"But I didn't betray anyone," the Goose shot back at him. "I was in the army, that's all. I fought the enemy!"

"Whose enemy?" Lenin screwed up his eyes.

"What do you mean, whose? The enemies of the Motherland, of the State."

"This State some friend of yours?"

"No, but there are times when—"

"You listen to me, you bastard," said Lenin. "You're a third-time loser already, thanks to that State of yours. You telling me you can't figure it out?"

"Figure what out?"

"The difference," said Lenin. "The difference between them and us. If you're in shoulder straps—"

"I haven't been in uniform in a long time!"

"Doesn't matter. I'm speaking generally. About the rules. If you're in shoulder straps, you're not one of us. You're under their rules, not ours. At any moment they could order you to guard the prisoners and you'd do it. If they ordered you to guard the storehouse, you'd guard it. And if, all of a sudden, some thieves decided to get into that storehouse and lift a thing or two, what then? You'd have to shoot them, right? That's the rules!"

"That's all theories," the Goose muttered, looking around.

"It could happen in the real world."

"Well, in the real world, I did my shooting at the front, in a war. I don't see what's wrong with that."

"We do," Lenin said firmly. "A real thief doesn't have to serve the authorities. Any authorities!" He moved, raising his voice. "Am I right?"

"Right!" they answered him.

"Right," he repeated weightily. "That's the law."

And the entire cell picked it up in a rumble.

"But the law's unfair," the Goose cried. He said it breathlessly, scraping his collar with his nails, and then jumped down from his bunk. "In other words, if I spilled my blood for the Motherland—"

"You can't have it both ways," Lenin told him. "If you spilled it, then live by it. By their rules, but don't be a thief. Don't sneak into our ranks. Honor the criminal code!"

I was silent all through the conversation. In the depth of my soul I sincerely sympathized with the Goose. He was right, in his own way. What was happening seemed preposterous and unfair. But the ones who defended the thieves' law were right, too.

The Redhead now spoke, bending toward the Goose. "Yesterday, remember? You had your doubts; you said you'd come to the wrong place. Well, you were right."

"Okay," the Goose hissed and took his knapsack down

from the bunk. "The wrong place, eh? Then, let's look for another."

And he walked right out of India. Not alone, though, At the last moment, when he was already at the door, knocking and calling for the guard on duty, three more people came up to join him.

"What do you want?" he shouted back at them. "Or did you spill blood, too?"

"Of course," they answered.

He was halfway out when he stopped and turned around. "Remember, thieves. There are a lot of us. We're not afraid of blood. And there'll be some yet. Plenty of it!"

Suddenly he looked sharply at me and smiled, his dark face broken by the glint of his teeth: "And you, my little friend. Remember this. Whoever crosses me doesn't live to regret it."

There was so much hate in his face and voice that I involuntarily shuddered and stepped back.

SOLITARY

Soon after the Goose left, the guards burst into the cell and conducted a search. This time they found everything they'd been looking for. There wasn't a trick or a secret of ours they didn't know.

We'd hidden all our sharp-edged objects—the razors, the needles, the mirror—in the bread. A special ration was usually chosen for this, donated by the most successful gambler among us, who possessed more than enough bowls of soup and kasha. (In doing so, he repaid society, as it were, for his own wealth and good luck at cards.) The bread would be torn into pieces and the scraps—containing our treasures—left in the most conspicuous spots: on the shelf, the window sill. That was why the authorities never paid them any attention. This time, though, all the pieces of bread were painstakingly gathered and removed. The ropes, threads, and pencils (also prohibited) had been hidden in the cracks beneath the threshold of the door. In the past, the guards had never once looked there; this time, they did.

"It's the Goose's doing, the bastard," the Redhead whispered to me. "He sold us out!"

"Maybe it wasn't him," I said with some doubt.

"Balls." The Redhead brushed it aside. "What's the difference anyway? He's their head man—the Atman of the Jack of Hearts gang!"

"What're you two whispering about?" the older guard asked us suspiciously.

"Nothing," I said. "Just discussing the weather."

The insolence wasn't to his liking. "You're asking for it," he grumbled. "Out with it!"

"I'm not talking to you," I objected with a smile. "Don't butt in where you don't belong." I was sorry the second I said it. It was a risky business calling the attention of the guards to yourself, especially in my case. I had some playing cards hidden in the back of my cheek and even though you couldn't see them from the outside, they still made it difficult to speak. The older guard, apparently, sensed it.

He came up, looked me over for a minute, and barked out an order: "All right, open your jaws!"

And then, without even waiting for me to do it myself, he stuck his fingers in my mouth, tearing my lips. His fingers were salty and rough, reeking with sweat and tobacco and some other vile smell I couldn't identify. Choking back a sudden wave of nausea, I drew away, but it was too late.

"Aha!" he said, looking at the well-thumbed little strips of paper, "so that's how you do it!" He wiped them off, nodding as if in reply to some thought of his own. "I was right, after all."

And then, grabbing me by the shoulder and pushing me to the door, he said: "It's solitary for you." So, cards had been my undoing again, and not even for a game.

The darkness was heavy, almost palpable. It swirled about me and flowed like dark water. There was no lamp. (This was a special isolation cell of the kind I'd heard about ever since I was a kid.) Light usually came in through the window, from a deep socket facing the sky. But even the sky betrayed me now. It was dark and painfully empty. Carefully groping along the walls, I examined the cell, found myself a relatively dry corner, curled up on the sticky cement and fell into a light sleep.

I woke up suddenly, without any idea of how long I'd been asleep. Time had died, the world had lost its solidity. Only one thing was clear: the night had not yet ended. The same thick darkness prevailed behind the window and in the cell.

But the darkness was full of sounds, both small and near (the babble of water drops, the rustling of wind in the window), and large and palpable (people pacing and remote, intermittent voices in the corridor). It was the voices, in fact, that had awakened me. I raised myself a little and listened carefully. Suddenly I recognized the characteristic intonations of the Goose's full, husky bass. He was discussing something with the guard and—even more surprising—talking with all the assurance of an equal.

The bolt thundered, the door opened wide, and in the blinding yellow light the Goose's stocky figure loomed on the threshold.

"Well, well," he said, leaning against the doorpost, "still alive, scum?"

"I'm alive," I answered, desperately trying to figure out what he was doing here. They'd apparently decided to plant him with me.

"Well, breathe while you can," he said slowly, drawing out the words.

He took a pack of Belomor cigarettes from his pocket and flicked his nail against the bottom. Two cigarettes popped out. He caught one of them in his teeth and held it in the corner of his mouth. The other he offered to me.

"Go ahead."

"No," I said with an effort, turning my eyes away.

"Of course, I forgot," he smirked, returning the pack to his pocket. "You're not supposed to take a smoke from bitches, right? Whoever's outside the 'law' isn't a person, right?"

I said nothing. He took a drag and the thick smoke swirled around his face. He spat. He spoke: "That's why I hate you, you bastards!"

"Listen, Goose," I said. "You're wasting your time. Our law is eternal, you won't change it."

"But that's exactly what I plan to do: to change the hell out of it and do away with the whole lot of you."

The light was pouring into my eyes and blinding me; the Goose's figure, looming in the doorway, seemed about as flat to me as a tin plate.

"You're not a thief anymore," I said, looking at that silhouette. "You're a nobody! Why don't you just crawl off to some corner and leave us alone! You'd be better off that way!"

"Not a chance, brother. Like we say in Rostov, 'Go find yourself another fool.' "

He stepped past the threshold, beyond the border of the light. I saw his face clearly now, and I didn't like it. His eyebrows were drawn tight, the slanted scar on his cheek trembled and slowly turned crimson. "You get to be the aristocrats, while I break my back pushing a plow like a beast and eating watery cabbage soup with the rest of the stiffs. No, sir, go find yourself another fool! I want the same things as you. Look at the life you lead. It's a cinch. Everybody afraid of you, everybody respecting you and splitting his spare food with you."

"Take another look," I said. "I'm sitting here in solitary on three hundred grams of bread and water and you're roaming the halls like you lived here. Come to think of it, Goose, why?"

"What do you mean why?"

"How come you're flying around free as a bird?"

"They like my looks."

"Pretty fast work, man. What'd you buy them with? Or was it the other way around?"

"Figure it out for yourself." He faltered for a moment. Suddenly, his voice rose to a scream of rage. "Who the hell cares! The main thing is I can do anything—anything I want! And I'll crush every last one of you without mercy. Starting with you!"

I tensed myself and pushed my back against the wall. He was a lot stronger and he wasn't alone. There was a guard in the hall. Plenty of guards, in fact.

As soon as the thought crossed my mind, a guard in a blue uniform service cap appeared in the doorway, right behind the Goose. He said something to him, jerked him by the sleeve, and pulled him back into the corridor, sharply slamming the cell door behind them.

"Not with me," I heard, "not on my watch! You wanted to talk? Okay, you talked. That's enough for now."

Clinging to the door, I strained to catch every word: the Goose's undecipherable mumbling, broken by hoarse shouts, and the clear-cut replies of the guard.

"Who? The Captain? . . . I don't know. . . . Let him order me personally. Officially. That's the only way. Enough. Go on, Gusev, move!"

What's happening? I wondered, pacing back and forth in my cell. The night was already drawing to a close. Sleep was the last thing I wanted, though.

In the morning, the food dispenser, an elderly convict with a bony, bristled face, looked in the feeding hole and handed me my ration: a sticky chunk of bread half the length of his palm and a mug of cloudy, steaming water.

"Take it," he said. "And listen, brother, that's all you get for today. And in the evening some hot water, nothing more."

Then, looking around and lowering his voice, he asked:

"Want a smoke?"

"God!" I said quickly. "Do I! I don't have any strength left."

"I understand, brother." He nodded. "Here, take it, give yourself a treat."

And with a conspiratorial wink, he threw a fat cigarette, tightly rolled out of newspaper, into the cell. In a whisper, he added: "Don't smoke it!"

The feeding hole slammed shut. Waiting till the racket quieted down in the hall, I picked up the cigarette, turned it in my fingers, and inspected it carefully.

Afraid of spilling even one little flake, I carefully undid it and poured the tobacco into my pocket. Then I spread out the crumpled scrap of paper and on the inside, between the printed lines, made out some tiny scribbles in pencil:

"You don't know me, but I want to help you. As a matter of conscience. I got wind the Goose talked about you with the Head of Internal Security. The Captain said the thieves were a party to themselves and had to be destroyed. That's it, brother—you're done for. If not today, then tomorrow; they'll come for you again. They've already gotten to one of your men and made him renounce the faith. God spare you the same. They spent the whole next day wiping up the blood in the cell. Save your own skin. Fake some sort of illness or go on a hunger strike. They won't touch you in the infirmary."

HUNGER STRIKE

So that's where things stand, I thought. I quickly rolled the butt again, got myself a light, and sat back, savoring the sour smoke and growing tipsier with each drag. My head might have been spinning, but my thoughts were clear, and as I smoked, I mulled over what had just happened. The split in the criminal world and the war with the bitches, it seemed to me, were a direct continuation of the international war that had just ended.

Any number of thieves had participated in that slaughter, fighting fiercely and heroically. But the Motherland, victorious, had turned her back on them. Demobilized and returned to a peaceful life, the former thieves once again found themselves renegades on the outskirts of society. In short order they sank straight back to the bottom. And even there, in the pit, they couldn't find themselves a place. They became outcasts among their former comrade thieves, taking on the shameful name of bitches—betrayers.

In declaring war on us, the Goose had said, "Remember, we're not afraid of blood." He'd been telling the truth: the war had exposed them to blood and fire and their training now stood them in good stead with the troops of Stalin's secret police in their struggle with us, the criminal underground of the country.

The Chekists called the underworld a party. And they were right. Not a political one, of course, but a tightly organized unit all the same, actively at war with the establishment.

It was no accident, then, that the authorities had now begun to give the bitches their full support; it was with men like the Goose that they hoped to destroy the outlawed party from within and chop it into bits.

With men like the Goose. . . . I remembered those hands and that face: warped by rage, convulsed and gasping. I suddenly realized that the Goose was playing a double game. Strange that the Chekists hadn't seen it. He wasn't fighting the underworld at all (as the authorities had planned); he just didn't happen to like some of our terms.

Rejecting the old law, he wanted to create a new one of his own, still a criminal one, but one more in line with his own interests: a law that could help restore his former rights and privileges and strengthen his position in the underworld. For the sake of his own privilege, the Goose would stop at nothing. He wasn't afraid of blood; I was the one who had to worry about that. He'd said so himself: there was nothing he couldn't do. Here in solitary I was defenseless. He was sure to come, if not today, then tomorrow. What nightmares lay in wait for me?

Basically, I'd made the decision long ago to leave the underworld, to "tie up" and start a new life. When the time came, I would do it irrevocably, but not the way the Goose wanted it, not by debasing myself or betraying my friends. And, even more to the point, not now. How could I leave the thieves at a time like this, in the opening days of a violent bitch terror, with a time of great bloodletting, as the Goose had prophesied, clearly on its way?

I'd smoked my cigarette down to my lips. Even so, I couldn't get enough of that bitter-sweet, venomous smoke. I went to the door and called for the guard on duty.

"What is it?" he asked, opening the feeder.

I shoved my ration at him. "Take it!"

"What?" He eyed the bread and knit his brows and looked right back at me. "Think they didn't weigh you out enough?"

"The hell with that," I said, "I'm just refusing to eat."

"Don't be a fool," the guard grumbled. "I don't want to hear any more about it. I'm sick and tired of your tricks."

He backed off and tried to slam the feeding hole shut. I jammed it open with my elbow, though, and threw the bread into the hall.

"There," I said, "you understand now? I'm going on a hunger strike! I want you to give me a pencil and a piece of paper; I'm going to write a notice to the head of the prison."

"You threw it away," he said reproachfully. "You threw the bread away, you parasite! People on the outside are breaking their backs for a little portion like that!"

He grumbled and cursed in the hall for a while, but finally he got me the paper.

I quickly wrote a note and then, for greater effect, decided to sign it in blood. I ripped the skin of my arm by the left elbow with my teeth and, dipping my little finger in the wound, wrote my name, thick and bold, on the bottom of the paper: "Dyomin."

Every morning, like clockwork, a guard, who'd replaced the food dispenser, would bring me my ration, and every morning I'd refuse it. It wasn't easy, but I got what I was after. From that moment on, no one disturbed me. On only one occasion during the entire time did I hear an indistinct rumble on the other side of the door—a whisper, a quiet wheezing, and the shuffling of footsteps. The spy hole opened a crack. Through it, someone watched me in silence, looking long and hard, as if aiming at a target.

I felt a cold tremor of anxiety; for a second, my breathing stopped; shivers ran up and down my spine. Trying to control myself, I walked toward the door and bent down, bracing myself for action. What was I planning to do? It's hard to say. I didn't have any strength left. Only one desperate thought drove me on: to meet my fear head on, to fight to the end.

My years of wandering had taught me a thing or two. Now I recalled the lessons of my stay in the Caucasus and Rostov and the portside dens of Odessa. I was weak and sick and unfit for a pitched battle, but I braced myself all the same. Whatever happens, I thought, they won't take me easily.

As it turned out, my fears were groundless. The feeding hole closed with a click, and footsteps shuffled off into the distance; at the end of the hall the echoing voices disappeared. And once again silence, for a long time.

I'd gotten what I was after. I'd saved my neck for a while, but at a price. The first four days had been the most tormenting. The main thing to do in a hunger strike, in fact, is to hold out during that first stretch.

I was exhausted by thirst (I did get water, luckily, but not much), I roared and writhed with the colic that constantly sucked at my belly. After a while, the sensations started to fade and a strange, feverish exhaustion settled in. I would lie motionless for long periods of time now, my eyes closed in oblivion. In the darkness, pictures of the past would flare up and splinter, all of them connected with food, its agonizing images, its thick and juicy colors. For some reason, the most frequent and distinct of my recollections were of times I'd passed up the chance to eat well.

God, what a fool I'd been. How little I'd valued my good luck at the time.

Once again I saw the Dagestan village: a small, crowded canyon settlement resting in the rough hands of the mountains. I'd spent a night there once in a house belonging to the local *baryga*—a speculator and fence for stolen goods. Cunning and rapacious in his business dealings, the old man was the very model of cordiality at the table. He treated me to his meat and wine with an open hand. His table groaned beneath the weight of a steaming lamb, *khinkali* (a kind of Caucasian meat dumpling), and tempting, glossy pieces of fatty sheep's bottom.

The host, a heavy man with a loose and crimson face, devoured his suet with slices of lamb as if they were bread. He bit off the tail, rolling his eyes in sweet delight. Then, breathing heavily and grumbling, he'd gnaw into the flesh of the lamb. The whitish grease, mixed with sweat, would bubble on his lips and flow lazily down his chin, congealing in the flabby folds of his skin.

Looking at him and those jellied jowls, I'd suddenly felt a heavy wave of nausea. Quickly lighting a cigarette, I'd gotten up, walked over to the window, and turned my back on the food. I couldn't face it; I simply didn't have the fortitude.

Roughly the same thing had happened to me in Turkmenia. Out of the darkness my memory fashioned the outlines of the poplars, the waving thickets of the shrubs above the splashing irrigation ditch, the clay-walled cottage at the edge of the village.

An old friend of mine lived there, Izmail the *planakesh* (an Eastern term for opium smoker). On the evening in question, Izmail had set a *toi*—a feast in honor of three recently arrived Afghan contrabandists. They sat on rugs and brightly colored pillows in the heart of the room, munching fruit and sipping green tea.

I'd dropped in quite by chance without any thought of staying. Izmail had other ideas. "You'll leave," he said, "and offend us. I won't forgive you. Please stay. We'll drink tea; later, there'll be flat cakes to eat with honey and butter and yogurt. And then, pilaf and, ah, what pilaf that will be!"

He winked and gave me a smile. Bunching his fingers in a pinch of pleasure, he raised them to his lips and smacked them loudly and voluptuously.

"Pilaf like you've never had before, by the beard of the

Prophet, I swear it! Can you smell it? It's already on the boil!
Soon it will be ready. Please, sniff!"

"You tempt me, Izmail," I said, catching the aromas that
wafted through the house and drew my strength away. "But
the boys are waiting for me. You know that yourself. And I've
got a broken-winded, unreliable horse. As it is, I hope to God
I can make the trip before morning."

"You'll make it." He waved the sleeves of his robe. "Worse
comes to worst, I'll give you a horse of my own."

"Well," I said, "since you put it that way, I accept."

I went outside to the yard—into the cool, light blue, moonlit
night. I unsaddled my horse, gave him some grain, and headed
back for the house through the rear door. It was then I
chanced upon the women's quarters.

No one was allowed there without permission; in matters of
this sort Moslem men have strict—and, if you ask me, fully
justified—rules. I knew the ways of Asia and, embarrassed,
hastened to withdraw.

But I couldn't help seeing what was going on there. It was
hot and filled with smoke. The dishes rattled and female forms
darted back and forth. In the corner beside the oven a dried
up, hooked-nose hag had taken her place. (Izmail's mother,
perhaps? His eldest wife?) She was sitting on the floor, leaning
against the wall, her legs spread shamelessly wide. Her dress
was turned up; from beneath the corner of her dirty undergar-
ment I could see her wrinkled, emaciated thighs, interlaced
with blue veins. From a trough she raked out a viscous lump
of dough and, with a smack, slapped it on her thighs. She
kneaded it there, smoothing it out with her fingers, and, after
preparing the pancake, tossed it on the burning, hissing pan.

Good God, I shuddered, what a kitchen! They make the
food under their dresses. Imagine what they do to their
precious pilaf? I left immediately, telling Izmail that I was in a
rush and that, unfortunately, there was no way I could wait
without letting my friends down.

For a long time afterwards, the nauseating image of that old
lady dogged my steps. Now I remembered her with an almost
tender emotion.

Shrinking in the corner on the slippery cement, I lay thinking of all the roads I'd ever traveled in my country. Where hadn't I been? And wherever I'd gone, I'd come up against the eccentricities of local habits and cuisine. Among the Kamchadals and Yakuts, for example, the fat of fish and seals is considered a delicacy. As a special kindness to visitors, they often heat the premises to such a degree that you have no other choice than to strip to the bone; you feel like you're at the baths—a bath, that is, steeped in the stench of fish fat.

Many dwellers of the taiga take great pleasure in drinking milk mixed with fresh deer's blood. Overlooking anything else about it, the drink is unusually beautiful. I didn't value it properly at the time.

My recollections would grow dim and mingle with the nonsense of my dreams. Monstrous, teeming gorges would surround me through the nights. I would dream of winds laced with the smell of fat and blood, and sands that turned to quicksand, orange as a dish of fat and lamb, surrounded on either side by rising heaps of dough, thick blocks, viscous landslides, and smoking mountain ranges baked through and through by the sun.

Like an endless filmstrip it would roll before me—strange, uneven, skirting the thin line between reality and delirium.

YOU CAN SLEEP SAFE AND SOUND

At the end of the eighth day I received a visit from the senior local security chief, Captain Kireev—the very captain the Goose had referred to in his recent conversation with the hall guard, the one mentioned in the note. He was the ideological support of the bitches, and one of the instigators of the bloodbath that had just begun. He was also my most dreaded foe.

I realized all this in a flash as he crossed the threshold of my cell and called me by my name. I rose at once, barely

overcoming my feverish stupor and the spinning in my head.
"We have read your statement," the Captain spoke confidingly. The delirium was over; reality had stepped in.
"You sure took your time about it," I said slowly, moving my parched mouth like a man out in the cold.
"That's the way it goes." He shrugged his shoulders. "I had other things to tend to a little more important than this."
He was tall and red-haired, with a fresh complexion. I confess that startled me. For some reason I'd imagined he'd be different: gray-haired, perhaps, wrinkled. And vicious. A new generation, I thought. Beria's tribe. SS types. The worst of all. No mercy from them. Fascism always relies on the keen, the athletic, and the young.
"Yes," he repeated, "there were other matters. But let's return to your announcement. Why did you feel it necessary to sign in blood, by the way? That was, you'll agree, a cheap trick." He frowned. "A silly melodrama. Where did you suck it from?"
"I didn't suck it," I objected. "I've been spitting it. Could even be a form of tuberculosis."
"Or a form of fear, maybe?"
The Captain came closer and bent down, playing with his eyebrow a little. "Out with it, now. In the open."
"First," I said, "let's smoke. Okay?"
He opened a little case and extended a cigarette, providentially clicking the lighter. After giving me a chance to savor the smoke, he said, "Now, then, if we're going to be open about it, you're dying to get to the infirmary because of the Goose, right? You're afraid he'll make good on his threat, show up again, and . . . get persuasive."
Get persuasive! So that's what they called it around here, I thought, peering into his well-groomed, well-fed face. The bastards, they've already managed to coin their own terminology.
"Admit it," the Captain continued to press, "it's all on account of him, isn't it?"
"I had my reasons," I answered evasively. "Lots of them. You read the statement. You know. I'm ill—"

"Yes, yes, I'm familiar with all that," he interrupted me impatiently. "But the main reason . . ."

"Well, let's assume it was the Goose. So what?"

"So now there's nothing to be afraid of anymore. The Goose has gone. He left three days ago."

"What?" I was dumfounded. "Where to?"

"Deportation."

"Where?"

"My, how you revived," the Captain muttered with a laugh. "You even got your color back."

He was silent. Then, casually, he asked: "What do you want to know, the route?"

"Of course."

"Can't help you there. I don't have the authority. Anyway, what does it matter to you? The main thing is, he's gone. To the north. You can sleep peacefully now."

"Peacefully?" I gave it some thought. "Hardly, Citizen Superior. Hardly. One man's gone, another'll take his place. What kind of guarantee is that?"

"Guarantee? You've got my word," he said with authority. "And, believe me, it's dependable. But in return you've got to give me a guarantee of your own."

"What kind?"

"First of all, an immediate end to your hunger strike." He said it slowly, separating and rapping out the syllables: "Im-me-di-ate! Furthermore, a promise to keep it quiet. Not a rustle. And no demonstrations."

With a convict's animal instinct, I caught his hidden confusion, his unexpected weak spot. So, he wanted everything hushed up. But why?

"Not a rustle, you say, but you're too late for that already," I said.

"Then end it," the Captain announced, "or we'll take action. We'll start force-feeding you through a hose. You have any idea how that's done? And if that's not enough"—there was a metallic ring in his voice—"we'll slap a second sentence on you, for provocation."

"But what if the provocations are coming from you,

instead?" For an instant I felt a hot wave of hate swell inside me. "Remember, if I have to, I can take some measures of my own."

"Your own?" He screwed up his eyes. "How interesting. What can you do?"

"I can write! To the Procurator's Office, to the Supreme Soviet, to the Minister himself! I'll tell them everything that's going on here!"

"Swine!" Kireev shouted. He was finally speaking his own language now. "Do you think, do you really think that's going to help you?"

"I don't know. Maybe it will, maybe it won't. It doesn't matter." I brushed it aside. "One thing's for sure: it'll hurt you."

During the conversation I'd been sitting on the floor, resting my shoulders against the damp cement wall. The Captain had been bending over me, his palms on his spread knees. Now he straightened up and approached, his face growing dark.

One look and I realized I'd been right! They had made a muddle of things. Without a doubt, the Goose's departure was part of it. Of course! He had been thirsting for blood and, by all indications, had gotten it. More than they'd bargained for, apparently. Someone had been maimed or killed. Killed, most likely. And maybe more than one. But this wasn't a northern prison camp; you couldn't just draw up a document on a dead man with the classic formula, "Shot during work detail, while attempting escape."

Besides, on the highest levels the authorities disapproved of unscheduled deaths; a Soviet convict, in principle, should be forced to labor, to dig in, to build Communism! Death was too small a punishment, an inadmissible luxury. And if he must disappear, then it should be according to plan, on orders from above. The bureaucracy likes its bit of order in everything. And it tolerates negligence and arbitrary action from no one.

"I wouldn't try to scare me if I were you," I said. "It's not worth it, Citizen Superior, sir."

"I'm not scaring you." He spat it out. "I came to you

in good faith and you insist on being stubborn. Watch out."
The conversation continued for some time. Sooner or later,
though, I realized I'd have to compromise. It was high time to
end my exhausting hunger strike. My excitement had yielded
to weakness and nausea. Stubbing out the butt of my cigarette,
I waited a moment and then said: "You're looking for peace
and quiet, right? Okay, transfer me to the infirmary and
you've got it."

"Done," the Captain said. "We'll transfer you. But—you
promise?"

"My word."

"Good, it's settled then."

And once again he became benevolent and polite.

"Everything will be taken care of. You'll rest in the
infirmary and recover. Only, remember, not for long. You'll be
transferred within three days. I trust you'll manage without
. . . excesses?"

"You can rest assured." I smiled weakly. "I don't plan to
stick around."

The internecine war in the Kharkov deportation center proved
to be so violent and brutal that at first even the authorities
were stunned. Especially the local ones. For a time the prison
administration lost its head and refused to assume any
responsibility. That was when the local security chief had
come to call. In the event of a scandal, I could have been a
very damaging witness. It was essential they get rid of me, and
the sooner the better, which Kireev could do only if I ended
my hunger strike and announced a full recovery.

The administration's hesitation, incidentally, didn't last
long. Soon after my meeting with Kireev, instructions came
from Moscow—special orders from Beria that put everything
in order. The carnage, as it were, was given its proper legal
limits as part of the general state of terror; the upheaval was
contained. Luckily, this all happened after I'd left the prison.
If I had stayed on at Kharkov an extra week or two, I might
never have come out alive.

THE ORDEAL

I left the prison late one August night toward dawn, under brilliant skies alive with shooting stars. High up in the blue they exploded noiselessly one by one, falling slantwise to the ground. They flew over the sleeping earth, over the huge mass of the town, over the disordered throng of convicts mournfully making their way to the train.

They say that you can wish on a falling star. I remembered that as they started counting us out and leading us to the train (these weren't passenger cars, by the way, but cattle cars, a sure sign we'd be heading far). With anguish and hope I turned and made a silent appeal to the skies. A prisoner's prayers are brief, as a rule, and his wishes simple and direct. In that hour, under the slanting streams of the meteor shower, we all had the same thoughts and dreams.

We wanted to survive the deportation in one piece. We wanted fortune to send us an easy lot and a bearable life in that far land they call the Gulag system. No map has marked the borders of that country; no guidebook records the roads that lead there. Fenced off from the adjacent world by forbidden zones and barbed wire, it exists in the backwoods, a dark secret on the other side of civilization. No guidebook records the roads—but the prisoners know them well. They know that deportation is not just a distant journey, but a path full of brutal and fatal consequences, a way of the cross, leading to another life and other shores.

Driven along by the mallets of the guard and finding ourselves a place in the dark womb of the train, we each held the same prayer in our heart: "Lord, save and preserve me: from misfortune, oh Lord, from the uranium mines of Norilsk, from the peat marshes of Mordovia, from the wet pits and snowbound mine fields of Kolyma."

During my hunger strike, as I later learned, they'd deported some of the people in India. My partners, the Gypsy and Scarface, had left for the east. I was never to lay eyes on them again. What happened to them and where? Did they live to see freedom or did they lay their bodies down in some hole and sink without a trace? Siberia is vast and stern and full of dark corners from which few ever return.

Of all my old acquaintances, I met only three on the long trip there: the Redhead, Lenin, and another called the Maiden, a blue-eyed youth with the face of an angel. He'd been arrested for some "wet deals"—murder, that is—and sentenced to twenty years, a fact that, apparently, didn't bother him in the least. Stretching out on the bunk and crossing his arms behind his head, he'd usually sleep soundly for long stretches at a time. When he'd wake he'd lazily hum some sentimental songs. From morning till night Lenin and the Redhead would play cards.

I'd write verse, if you could call it that. Actually, I still wasn't old enough then for serious poetry and generally gave it little thought. Songs were more to my liking—"thieves' music," the rich and heart-rending folksongs of the prisoners. With their strong traditions and deep social roots, these songs reflect the life of the criminal world and record the story of Soviet prison camps since their very beginning. They contain, in fact, nothing less than the entire history of today's forced-labor Russia.

It is a history that begins with the Solovki. The first massive concentration camp was born at the start of the twenties on the Solovetsky Islands, an archipelago set in the White Sea that once belonged to a famous monastery. The monks are gone now from the islands and convicts take their place.

Countless songs have been composed about the Solovki. "They shipped us off to distant lands," is the story one of them tells, "Water, marshes all around, / And for crimes long since atoned for, / We're jailed on monastery ground."

"Crimes long since atoned for"—not a careless line. The origin of the first all-Russian concentration camps coincided with the first "quarantines," the name given, at the dawn of the Soviet regime, to the epidemic massive repressions that periodically rocked the entire country. The legislation of those years established the possible criminal liability of individuals who had committed no specific offense but who, as the Penal

Code put it, "represented, in view of their past activities, a decided social threat," a phrase intended to cover a multitude of sinners, all of them thieves! During these quarantines, thieves would be apprehended for no apparent reason. Even those who had tried to tie up and leave the criminal life didn't escape arrest.

This all found expression in the songs. Here's how they'd sing of it in Odessa:

> *The thunder rumbles,*
> *The quarantine comes;*
> *They say all Odessa is teeming with thieves.*
> *Crooks everywhere,*
> *Not a second to spare!*
> *The critical moment has come!*

At the end of the twenties a mutiny erupted at the Solovki, followed by a massive group escape. Several sailboats inherited by the camp from the monks were seized. The rebels headed out to sea, crossed the demarcation line, and landed in Norway. Unfortunately, their desperate flight ended unhappily. The Norwegians refused to grant them asylum, and returned them to the Soviet authorities.

Nonetheless, the event seriously unsettled the government. Clearly, a camp as near the western frontier as the Solovki had proven its unreliability. Little by little the camp was broken up and the inmates transferred, most of them to the construction site for the White Sea–Baltic Canal, a track extending hundreds of kilometers through the marshes of Karelia. They couldn't have devised a more terrifying camp if they'd tried. Strips along the construction site such as Voita and Medvezhegorsk have been preserved in the folksongs forever:

> *Bear Mountain lies along the canal.*
> *How many thieves there have fallen!*
> *They stood us on stumps,*
> *They stripped off our clothes,*
> *They beat us and buried us*
> *From night until dawn.*

That was only the beginning. All of it—the first quarantines and the camps—was but a rehearsal, an early test of strength in the grammar school of terror.

Soon, throughout the Soviet Union, in the outermost districts of the mainland, gigantic administrative camps sprang up: the secret principalities of the Cheka, the countless states of the sinister country of Gulag. The largest by far was Dalstroi, which included parts of Yakutiya, Kolyma, and Chukotka, embracing far more territory than all of Europe combined. More songs have been dedicated to Dalstroi, and Kolyma especially, than to any other place:

> *The stormy seas raging,*
> *The fog thickly spread,*
> *Magadan, Magadan,*
> *Capital of Kolyma,*
> *Magadan rises ahead.*

The camp motifs, however, are but a small part of the entire range and variety of this folk music. Along with the prison and concentration camp lyrics (in essence laments for freedom) there are tramp lyrics, wanderers' songs, and the genuine songs of the criminal world, based largely on descriptions of the life-styles and crafts of the thieves.

These works can be divided into different "professional" categories, so to speak, such as the songs of the *maidanniki* (train robbers), the ballads of the "bear hunters," or safe-crackers, the couplets and quatrains of the pickpockets, and the songs of the murderers.

"In my lonely life," one of them goes, "How many men have I killed? / Who is to blame, my dark-eyed one, / That I loved you more than life itself? / I have a blouse I earned with blood / And a fur coat made of fox; / You'll walk about in the finest silks / And go to sleep on down."

The couplets of the pickpockets are just as colorful and expressive, even mischievous at times. Here, for example, are some lines addressed to a *fraier* just picked clean of his purse:

> *You had it coming, don't complain;*
> *Next time you go shopping, don't look at the planes.*

Others are full of a mournful lyricism:

> *To love a young lady you have to have money,*
> *And I've chosen myself a dangerous path.*

No less diverse is the repertoire of the train robbers, with songs celebrating trains, train stations, and the vast expanses of the Motherland:

> *A steam engine flies through the green, open spaces,*
> *It flies and no one knows where.*
> *I was called, my boy, a rogue and a swindler,*
> *And I bade my freedom forever good-by.*

That last song was one of my own. I had long been attracted to folk poetry and tried my hand at all of its different forms. Most of all, I'd been drawn to the poetry of wandering and the open road.

The profession of the train robber may well be the most romantic of all and, while I was at large, it was the one I chose for myself. Thanks to it, I traveled our country from one end to the other, dedicating most of my songs to my wanderings. Almost all of them were written in captivity, during deportation, on the road, through the long hours of enforced and agonizing inactivity, in the penal quarantines, or in the silence of the infirmaries.

That was only natural, of course. Creativity demands concentration, a renunciation of the bustle of one's daily life. And what greater renunciation than in the cold cell of a prison or a deportation train?

That's the way it had always been. And now, smoking on my train bunk and listening to the booming rhythm of the wheels, I whispered the words of a new song to myself:

"Here we lie," I muttered, "Gloomy and mute, / Looking at the incarcerated sky. / A smoky evening lies beyond the windows of the car, / This distant journey cures me of my love. / The way is hard, a winding and sorrowful path . . . / In the shimmering darkness, / In the rumbling of the train, / Forget the past forever / And, like a hunted animal, / Flee from your despair."

The words seemed to come unbidden, by themselves. All the same, the song had its snags and the going was rough. The thoughts were uneven, the feelings confused. For the time being, I couldn't completely renounce the world outside. A war was going on out there, poisoning the very air I breathed. Besides, I had other, more compelling reasons.

When we parted on Cold Mountain, Captain Kireev had said: "The Goose has gone. You can sleep safe and sound." The fact was I still had another enemy, one even more dangerous to me in some respects than the Goose, more dangerous if only because he was at my side, not as an enemy, but as a brother in arms, a party comrade. And an old comrade at that!

The man I'm talking about is Lenin. Stocky and bald, with a wide, prominent brow, he fully earned his nickname. And not on his appearance alone. He was unusually shrewd and experienced. He knew every one of our rules and procedures by heart and would address our general gatherings with skill and great conviction. He was considered "authoritative," a hard label to come by, and one that meant as much, in essence, as being a member of the Central Committee.

Generally speaking, the criminal world is structurally quite similar to the Communist Party, with the same kind of solidarity and unquestioning submission to regulations. There is a difference, though. Unlike the Communists, criminals are organized along deeply democratic lines, without leaders or dictators of any kind. The only place you'll ever find leaders is among the bandits and gangsters, criminal professions not usually accorded much respect. Armed thuggery, as the true thief sees it, is crude work demanding neither tact nor talent. It's no wonder the word "gangster" is spoken with disrespect in the Russian underworld. Thieves have no dictators. They do, though, have their own form of ruling center, a kind of legislative committee composed of the worthy and the authoritative—the group to which Lenin belonged.

Long ago and (in my opinion) without any justification whatsoever, Lenin had started badgering me. He'd call me an intellectual—a term which on his lips sounded highly questionable and vile. Every time he'd talk to me he'd make a wry face, as if to insinuate we shared some dark, unspeakable secret. But what kind? There was never a time I didn't feel his enmity and suspicion, never a time I didn't catch his strange, sidelong glances at me, filling me with an instinctive anxiety.

This won't end well, I'd feel. No, it won't. Sooner or later, something has to break.

BLOOD AND FOAM

It wasn't an easy deportation. It dragged on for fourteen days. Our convoy passed through Central Russia, through the Urals, past Chita and Khabarovsk, landing, at long last, at Vanin Bay (on the coast of Tatarsky Strait). That's when we knew where they were taking us. The Vanin deportation center was well known throughout the Far East as the principal transshipping base for Kolyma.

From here on—up to Magadan itself—the prisoners were taken by sea in the close, stinking confines of a ship's hold. First we were ordered to disembark. The escort counted off the prisoners, lined them up, and led them to the gates of the deportation center.

The head of the convoy then left with his lists to consult with the watch guard. The transfer of the group to the local administration lay ahead—a long and tedious procedure. Stretching our legs and shrinking from the early cold, we gathered by the living quarters and eyed the people there. You could see their dark figures loitering behind the barbed wire, the outlines of the distant barracks, and the breaks in the roofs, colored by dawn.

Suddenly the crowd stirred and rippled with an indistinct murmur, like the rustling of woods in bad weather. Elbowing his way up from the rear ranks, the Redhead appeared. Disheveled, his dark face troubled, he drew near me and said in a low whisper: "We're in a bad way, Chuma, this is a bitches' zone!"

"How did you find out?" I asked him quickly.

"No mistake about it. The guys here recognized someone. Looks like they saw the Goose." He shivered, his eyes opened wide. "So look out for a little action."

"Ay-yai-yai," muttered a stoop-shouldered and dour thief nicknamed the Wood Goblin. "What next, eh?"

I'd met the Goblin on the road, not long ago. They'd put him in our car in the Urals, in Sverdlovsk, and he'd spent the whole trip gloomily avoiding any conversation. Now, suddenly, he spoke up.

"Listen, it looks bad for us. Walking in there is like walking into a trap. There's no way we're going into that zone. Absolutely no way!"

"That's what Lenin says, too." The Redhead nodded.

"How many thieves are there in all?"

"Enough." The Redhead winked. "A big levy, thirty cars. And five thieves in each one, no less. Count 'em for yourself."

"That's power, all right," the Goblin said. "That'll give the authorities something to think about, whether they want to or not."

"They're not too crazy about thinking," somebody said. "They'd rather shoot."

"I doubt it," the Goblin answered after a while. "They won't have the guts to shoot right out in the open, in front of the entire transport. Besides, what's the provocation? We're not revolting. We'll ask them to put us in quarantine, off to one side."

And so, when they finally got around to leading the prisoners in through the gates, the thieves bunched together, took a firm stand, and announced they weren't going into the general zone.

The guards were thrown into confusion. There was a burst of machine-gun fire. Apparently, one of the soldiers had either decided to give us a scare or been frightened himself. But he shot over our heads, right at the gleaming edge of the sun rising behind the barbed-wire fence.

Just as abruptly, the shooting stopped. The Goblin had been right. The Chekists hadn't dared take reprisals in full view of the deportation contingent.

"All right, the hell with you," the head of the transport announced after some prolonged discussions. "You don't want to be with everyone else? Then we'll lock you in quarantine. But first it's the sanitary treatment for you. That is, unless you crooks are scared of a little hot water?"

We headed eagerly for the baths. Tearing off our sweat-soaked, salty clothes and getting a supply of soap from the guard, we made a dash with a stomp and a hoot of laughter for the stuffy semidarkness.

Our bodies thin and white, our faces black, we were a strange sight. The sharp contrast made us look unreal, like vague apparitions, bony ghosts in dark masks come to haunt the prisoners' bath.

Sitting on the bench, I washed and gave myself a careful inspection—my thin chest, the sharp bows of my ribs, my sunken stomach. The hunger strike had left its marks on me, picking my bones and laying me waste. I'd saved myself from the Ukrainian bitches, only to land in the hands of the Far Eastern ones. And we still had no clear idea what dangers lay ahead.

"What's there to worry about?" I suddenly heard someone say. "A swarm of bitches. Big deal. Are we supposed to be scared of that?" The words sounded like an answer to my thoughts. And I immediately turned around.

Clouded in steam on a neighboring bench, several figures had gathered. Among them I noticed the Redhead (and flaming red he was, with thick patches of freckles from his head to his toes!), the Maiden's soft profile, and Lenin's hilly bald spot.

Two fellows I didn't know were also sitting there. One of them, leaning over a small washtub, was soaping his head. The other, who was also all lathered up, sat smoking, his legs crossed like a Tatar, sucking away at his damp cigarette butt and thinking out loud in a bass: "So what if there are a lot of them? There are quite a few of us too, thank God!" His high-cheekboned, pock-marked face twisted into a smile. "Why do we have to hide in quarantine under lock and key? We're going to be in quarantine long enough as it is!"

"Right," the one who'd been washing his head said with a snort. "Do what you want, but I'm for the general zone. If we're going to stand firm together, the whole crowd together, then—"

"How do you know what'll happen out there?" Lenin asked him in a quivering voice. "They'll pull us apart into separate barracks and the first night out crush us like rabbits!"

"Ah," the pock-marked man brushed it aside and spat out his butt. "You're running scared."

"And you're a real hero, I see," the Redhead said abruptly, "but what's your courage all about? You're up to something, Pockface. . . ."

The conversation had apparently been going on for quite some time. People were getting nervous and angrily interrupting each other.

I got distracted. It was my turn to take the boiling water and I splashed my way to the faucet. The seething water was running unevenly, spurting and burning my hands.

I stood there, hopping around, trying to balance the heavy oaken washtub. Suddenly, from behind my back, I heard a muffled scramble and a violent burst of swearing.

The very next instant I caught sight of Pockface. He was running, dodging blows and making a break for the doors.

Someone raised his hand against him from the side. He darted back and, with a short, strangled cry, slipped and crashed backwards on the wet floor.

Apparently the fall had hurt his leg. He picked himself up and tried to stand. He couldn't.

The Maiden appeared. How that angel face of his smiled! Little dimples trembled on his cheeks, his blue eyes were clear and unperturbed. Taking the washtub out of my hands (it was already half full of boiling water) he walked over to Pockface and, bending low, said: "So, you were off to the bitches, eh? To your own kind?"

And he flung the water in his face.

I turned around and shut my eyes. When I opened them, I saw a heap of shining bodies swarming before me. I caught sight of the Maiden again, repeatedly beating the fallen man with the edge of the heavy washtub.

A heavy, oppressive silence followed, broken only by the choking, fragile voice of the Redhead: "It's done."

"And the other one?" they asked him.

"Him too," the Redhead answered. "Oh God."

The crowd thinned out and scattered to the sides. Pushing and shoving, the people made a run for the dressing room to put their clothes back on.

You could see the Pockface now. He lay perfectly still, one of his hands stretched toward the door, the other, stiff and twisted, covering his face. Blood flowed from his shattered skull, mixing with the soapsuds and turning them scarlet. For a second I thought the Pockface had moved, but he was dead. It was only the foam, bubbling and sliding.

THE MARTIAN

The incident had a lot of repercussions. A special investigative commission from the Vladivostok procurator's office appeared, and the "Case of the Group Killing in the Bath" was underway. Three of the men who had taken part in the slaughter were dispatched in irons to the inner prison. Each of them now faced a "make-weight"—a heavy new additional sentence. The rest were sent to the Intensified Regime Barracks instead of the quarantine zone.

Lenin and I stayed awake most of that night, talking.

"How did it all happen?" I asked, recalling the murder with a shudder of disgust: the squirming bodies, the bloodied foam. "Why them? Because of what they said? Because of some doubts?"

"I don't get it myself." He knit his brows thoughtfully. "If Pockface hadn't made a break for it, probably nothing would have happened. Oh, a little yelling, maybe, even a few blows. Big deal! But he made a rush for the doors, and that's what started it all."

"A mess," I muttered.

"Sure," he agreed with a yawn. "Not much good in it. But then, God works in mysterious ways."

"Leave God out of this!" I shouted.

"All right, God or the Devil, it's all the same to me. I'm a simple, uneducated man. Anyway, that's got nothing to do with it."

"What does, then?"

"The fact that these are bad times we're living in." He looked at me, screwing up his eyes. "Am I right, Mr. Intellectual?"

"Right."

"Right," he repeated it slowly. "Well, when there's a war on, every doubt smells like a betrayal. Who knows what Pockface had on his mind? Do you?"

"No." I shrugged my shoulders. "How could I?"

"Well, neither do I," he said. "Nobody knows. And that's just what we *do* have to know: what a man stands for, and who you can afford to turn your back on."

"Easier said than done," I objected. "How in the hell do you figure out what a man stands for, anyway?"

"There are ways," Lenin said. "Ways and words. And acts. You can tell. Take you, for instance. . . ."

"What about me?" I asked him, suddenly on my guard.

I had the constant feeling that Lenin, little by little, was going after me, circling, making loops, plotting his moves. And the circles were getting closer all the time. "Just what *do* you have to say about what I did?"

"Nothing substantial yet. Only details. Take that bath, for instance. What did you do there?"

"Nothing."

"That's my point!"

"All right, then," I shot back. "What about you? What did you do?"

"Why me?" He spread his arms in surprise. "I was in the corner, off to one side."

"And so was I. Look, there were a lot of people there. Whoever could, did something. I didn't manage."

"Right, right, the Maiden did it. But he got the tub of boiling water from you."

"So? He snatched it away from me."

"No, my friend, you gave it to him yourself. Even if I was in the corner, I saw it all." Lenin moved closer and breathed in my face. "You didn't have the guts, you didn't want to take the chance, you wanted somebody else to do the dirty work!"

"Why are you telling me all this?" I asked him quietly. "You want to accuse me of something? Then let's have it!"

"It's not that easy." He smiled. "But you're right. I've got my suspicions."

"Then out with them!" I got up and looked straight into his icy, round eyes. "Let's see your hand, damn it! What do you suspect me of?"

"Not being one of us."

"Then who do you think I am?"

"Who the hell knows? A Martian. From another world! Not our world, anyway."

"You still have to prove that," I said. "You know the rules. Without incriminating facts . . ."

"We've already got some of those," he said. "You say your mother was a whore and your father was a Rostov tramp, right? That you grew up in a thieves' den, correct?"

It was true. At one point I had said all of that. And more than once.

"I said that," I admitted, studying him and bracing myself for his next move.

"Then where did you get all that stuffing of yours? All those educated, intellectual things? Where did *they* come from? Who taught you about books and writing songs? Your old man, the tramp? Your mother, the whore? Pretty cultured upbringing you had there. . . ."

I lost control for an instant. The blow had landed much too

quickly. But it was too late to keep quiet. I knew that my best defense was to attack. "How do *you* know, maybe I'm a genius! A kind of Maxim Gorky. You ever hear of him? He grew up in dens, too. But even if I had dreamed it all up, so what?"

"If you dreamed up one thing, what would keep you from dreaming up another? And all the rest of it, too."

"You don't have any right to accuse me of that! A lot of people know me—by my acts, when I was on the outside! You're whistling in the dark, Lenin, you can't prove a thing. As it is, I could accuse you of working for the bitches by trying to undermine thieves like me."

"You're clever," he said slowly, "real clever. One of these days I'd really like to have it out with you, brother."

"So who's stopping you?" I said.

Lenin hadn't been far from the truth. I really was a Martian— a stranger here. But I couldn't admit it.

The time had finally come to look at the past. A long, watery road lay before me, hundreds of nautical miles. Our ship would have to pass through the Tatarskiy Strait and the Straits of La Pérouse, round the misty shores of Japan and the windy rocks of Sakhalin. And then, out across the Sea of Okhotsk: gray, murky, and bristling with the hard frost of an early fall.

Once there, the ship would still have a long way to go. Rising to the sixtieth parallel, it would quiver and creak, tossing in the foam, tumbling in the salty breakers. What better time then than now to recall my youth and childhood in full detail?

I want to tell you the story of my wanderings, of how my family was shattered and destroyed, of how it all began.

Part

And so, without a father to support me,

I left my home and went into the streets,

A path that soon would lead me straight to prison,

Branded with the name, and fate, of thief.

—FROM A THIEVES' SONG

If my prison camp life can best be drawn in coal and India ink, my childhood and youth call for rich highlights and bright hues. I need only close my eyes for an instant to see the pines near Moscow rising in my mind, the transparent blue branches stitched with sunshine, the orange trunks and the white sand. . . .

My earliest years passed to the murmur of those pines in the suburban settlement of Kratovo, an extensive community belonging to the All-Russian Society of Old Bolsheviks and Former Political Convicts, comprised of the families of ex-revolutionaries, veterans of the underground, and heroes of the Civil War.

One of the main figures in this society was my father, Evgeny Andreevich Trifonov. I see him clearly, as if he were alive. I see him smiling, knitting his eyebrows, the little lenses of his pince-nez agleam. I see him in sadness and in anger (his face would grow hard, then, and angular, as if hewn out of stone). I see him strolling down the streets of the settlement, energetically and a bit pigeon-toed, like a cavalier, driving the heels of his army boots into the dust.

A veteran officer, he disdained civilian dress with its coats and ties and wore nothing but an army uniform all his life. And so he remains forever engraved in my memory: the field shirt, the Battle Order of the Red Banner (he had a medal with the number 300 on it), the creaking belt, the holster on a strap.

It is the belt, perhaps—wide and yellow, its metal buckle stamped with a glittering star—that I remember best of all. He'd beaten me with it more than once—for the window I broke with my slingshot, for the bonfire I set in the woodshed playing Indians. . . . Frail, small, and lop-eared, I'd walk away from the flogging gripping my burning rear with both my hands, and for a long time afterward my bottom would bear the crimson impress of a five-pointed star. Soon, though, all my grief and injured pride would fade away. I was never able to feel very insulted by my father for long. After all, he was teaching me the way!

"It was your fault," he'd say with a laugh, "so grin and bear it. You're a Cossack, all right. Hang in there and someday they'll make you an Atman."

And more: "Don't be afraid of a beating. Don't you dare be scared. Remember, it won't kill you."

And again: "Learn how to handle a blow. Be fearless, and if you do get into a fight, don't cry and don't run. Defend yourself the best you can. And above all, don't ever be afraid! It's one thing to use cunning in a fight, but don't ever be a coward."

He'd talk to my brother Andrey and me a lot like that. Most of all, to me. Maybe because I had a habit of getting into more trouble.

"What are you teaching that boy?" Ksenya would sometimes ask him. This dark and delicate woman had taken the place of a mother for us. Quite unlike the stepmothers you read about in fairy tales, she cared for us, took pity on us, and raised us the best she could. "If you ask me, talking about fighting only spoils the children."

"Nonsense," my father would answer, smoothing his closely trimmed red mustache with the side of his hand. "One of these days it's going to come in handy for him."

"But when? And why?" Ksenya would be amazed. "Life's quieted down a bit, thank God. You measure everything by your past, but it'll never come again. You'd do better to talk about literature and books."

"All right." My father would laugh and rumple my hair. "We'll talk about literature. Compare it to fighting and you get a paradox. Qualities essential in the first case are absolutely out of place in the second. Mutually exclusive, you might say. A fight calls for malice and cunning, and art—creation—for kindness itself."

This was the period of my first experiments with verse. For some reason my poems were surprisingly gloomy back then, full of pathos and a satanic pride.

One of them accidentally fell into my father's hands. It began like this:

I stand above all others on this earth;
I never shall forget these days of glory.

My father gave my scrawls a long, hard look. I watched his
face. The more he read, the harder and squarer it became. I'm
in for it now, I thought uneasily. But no, he didn't lay a hand
on me. In fact, he said nothing at all. He turned around with a
frown and, walking to the window, stood there for some time
in silence, chewing on his cigarette and drumming his fingers
on the pane.

My brother and I grew up without a mother. Our parents had
separated long ago, at the beginning of the thirties. My mother
remarried and lived somewhere in Moscow, and my memories
of her during this period are dim at best. During the years
spent in Kratovo, I saw her only three times. She'd arrive
unannounced, without my father's knowledge, and our meetings would be brief, tormenting, and sad.

She never came alone, but in the company of a tall, silent
man who parted his hair on one side. I'd look up at him the
way you'd look at a tree from ground level, throwing back my
face. Foreshortened like that, he'd seem immeasurably large to
me, with a strangely narrowed, sleeky smooth top.

"Shura," my mother would say, snuggling up to him, "isn't
it a charming landscape, just like one of Levitan's!" A smile
would tremble at the corners of her mouth and her cheeks
would gleam with tears. "The river, the fir trees, the pine-
scented breeze. It's good for the children here."

My father would find out about the visits from his friends
upon his return from Moscow in the evening, on the nine
o'clock electric train. On one occasion I overheard a conversation he had with his dacha neighbor, a stocky, elderly
Ukrainian working in the Military Procurator's Office.

"So, she was here again, eh?" my father asked, leaning
heavily against the fence. "With him?"

"With him." The neighbor nodded and fell silent, relighting
his pipe. Then, almost in a whisper, he added, "Listen,
Zhenya, we've been friends for a long time, you and I; we've

known each other ever since 1905. We were in hard labor together, we went through the war, right?"

"Right," my father agreed, "but what are you driving at?" He laughed and carefully rubbed his pince-nez. "You've got something to say?"

"Yes, I do. A question, actually. Forgive me, brother, but tell me, how did you let it all happen? From the very beginning, eh?"

"What could I do about it?"

"Why didn't you give that old fop the boot the second he showed his face around here? Why didn't you break him into a hundred little pieces? I've seen you work a saber. Remember, back near Rostov. . . ."

"That was a battle," my father said slowly in a hoarse voice, barely containing a sigh. "Things were different back then. Anyway, it doesn't have anything to do with him. Just her."

"That's true," the neighbor said, puffing thoughtfully on his pipe. "Things were different in the war. She needed you back then, that's what it's all about! I don't care what you say, in her situation, landing a commissar like you was salvation itself. You saved her neck! And then you helped her relatives and wrangled them a visa for Paris. . . ."

There were other conversations and gradually, piece by piece, the picture of my parents' life emerged. It was a very romantic tale. I'll try to lay it out as briefly as I can, not to let the theme grow out of hand and carry me far from my story. Someday, perhaps, I'll devote a separate book to it. For the time being, I have a different task before me. And so, a few words about my father.

A Don Cossack by birth, he left his native village while still a young man for the town of Rostov, where his luck turned sour and he began his wanderings. For a while he was associated with the "grays," an old Rostov term for free peasant bandits. Soon after, he joined the Bolshevik underground, largely through the help and contacts of his brother Valentin, who had also left his Cossack village as a youth. In 1903 Evgeny Andreevich entered the ranks of the Russian Social Demo-

cratic Workers Party. Two years later he had already taken
part in the armed Rostov uprising and commanded the
Cossacks on the Temernitsky barricades. He was then just
twenty years old. The uprising was crushed, however, and the
brothers were caught and imprisoned in the Novocherkassk
military prison. After the trial Valentin was sent to Tyumen in
the Trans-Ural Territories, while Evgeny, sentenced to fifteen
years hard labor for the murder of a police officer, left in irons
with a party of prisoners on a deportation train bound for East
Siberia.

It was there, behind bars, that he began his education as a
poet. He composed a book of verse entitled *Wild Intoxication*,
which would later bring him fame and remain perhaps the
only example of the prison and penal-servitude lyric at the
start of our century. Isolated poems in this genre were, of
course, no rarity back then—you could find them among the
works of many poets—but the distinction of composing an
entire book of them, a special collection, was his alone. As I
write these lines, I can't help thinking how much his fate and
mine have in common. My wanderings also began in the
south, on the Don, among Rostov tramps and prisoners. I, too,
passed through the same hard-labor deportations, on the very
same trains. We spent the same number of years in the taiga
and my first collection of poems, published in Siberia, also
consisted of verses written primarily in prison and exile.

Wild Intoxication took more than four years to write, in the
forests and blizzard-blown mines of my father's captivity. Not
long before his release (thanks to an amnesty declared in
honor of the three hundredth anniversary of the House of
the Romanovs) he sent his poems to his brother, Valentin
Trifonov, by then in Petersburg.

He wrote on narrow strips of paper, in a clear, small hand.
As a child I used to love to creep into my father's office, comb
through his archives, and uncover those marvelous sheets.
Yellowed and decrepit, they all bore an oval lilac stamp
reading: "Inspected, Alexandrovsky Central Forced Labor
Prison."

Few of these missives, sad and pensive, derisive and

austerely businesslike, ever survived. "Destroy all the dates beneath the poems," he advises his brother in one of them, "and when you're finished, send the manuscripts off to Gorky." The manuscripts, however, never reached their destination. The February Revolution broke out—hardly a time for poetry or literary discussions. Valentin was in the underground, working for the Party, while Evgeny was already on the road to Petrograd. There, in the capital, he became head of the city workers' militia and a member of the staff of the Red Guard, joining the ranks of the famous "Initiative Five" that was busy preparing the take-over of the Winter Palace. After the overthrow, he headed for the front as the military government commissar for the South Russian Territories.

As everybody knows, the civil war began in the south of Russia and enveloped the Cossack Don from the very start. The commander-in-chief of the White Armies at the time, under Atman Krasnova, was General Svyatoslav Denisov, my mother's uncle. The Red Cossack units were headed by my father.

Commissar Trifonov and General Denisov met on the field of battle without the slightest inkling of how soon they'd be related. Even if they had known, however, the enmity between them would have been no less fierce or irreconcilable. A good deal has already been written on this war; there's no need to repeat it. I will only note that the battles were long and the victories inconclusive. At long last, though, the White Army quavered, the front rolled back, and the city of Novocherkassk, capital of the All-Powerful Troops of the Don, was firmly taken by the Bolsheviks.

The staff of the military commissar set up shop in a spacious private residence formerly owned by the Novocherkassk notary Vladimir Apollonovich Belyaevsky. The Belyaevsky family was already in an advanced stage of dissolution: Vladimir Apollonovich's daughters Varvara and Vera had died suddenly of typhus, and he soon took to his bed himself as a helpless paralytic, never to rise again.

Elizaveta Varlamovna, his wife (or widow, rather), evicted by the authorities from the main quarters of her home, took shelter upstairs in the garret, where she lived with her two surviving daughters, Tatyana, the oldest, and Lika, the youngest.

I've often tried to imagine what their life was like back then. Surely it must have seemed like a bad dream: their gentry nest transformed into a barracks echoing with the rumble of voices, the rattle of sabers, the clatter of staff typewriters that never stopped, day or night. Once in a great while messengers from the front would burst into the courtyard on snorting, dust-covered chargers bearing uniformly comfortless dispatches. The anti-Soviet ranks were falling farther and farther back.

And so the Belyaevsky ladies lived, until a new disaster struck. In the fall of 1919 Lika ran away from home; Evgeny Andreevich Trifonov had carried her off, in the night, on a Cossack cart.

The event created a great stir in Novocherkassk. The union of a Red commissar and a girl of the gentry, the niece of Denisov himself, was a scandal that took everyone by surprise. And no wonder. Revolutions cannot abide half-tones; they must ruthlessly divide the world into two opposing camps. My mother and father had committed a kind of apostasy against the very class ideals of the age.

Their betrayal had required the greatest secrecy. As events later revealed, Evgeny Andreevich's sister, Zinaida Boldyreva, who lived in Novocherkassk next door to the Belyaevskys, had been a party to it all. It was at her home that the lovers had met and planned their escape. My father took my mother to his native Cossack village in the steppes, where they waited in hiding for the uproar and the rumors to subside.

Before long they left the area for good. The war was thundering from one end of the country to the other now, and my father was soon caught up in it. He commanded the Ninth Cavalry Division of Budenny's Red Cavalry; he escorted the "golden train" in the Far East, bearing money captured from Kolchak; he fought in Central Asia against the counterrevolutionary robber bands. This Central Asian campaign was his last; the civil war ended and a life of peace returned.

In the mid-twenties my father moved to Moscow. The war

had ended, but he still knew no rest. Not that he ever courted it. A professional soldier, he served, as before, in the army, training the troops. At the same time, he returned to his writing, publishing books under the pseudonym of Evgeny Brazhnev.

All his life he had pursued literature, even though he rarely had the time. He was never able to take up his pen except in fits and starts. Still, he wrote a good deal during the postwar period, including a biographical novel, *Worker's Blood Is Pounding*, a play, *Four Stages of the Train*, and two books on the civil war, *The Burning Path* and *In the Bonfire's Smoke*, each of them true to his own personal experience and the tenor of his times: bloody, fierce, and never to come again.

What was my mother's life like during these years? What can I say of her? A woman's world, as a rule, isn't as rich in external events. Her destiny is different, concealed, and strange.

After running away from home she lost almost all her ties with her relatives. Elizaveta Varlamovna cursed her in her wrath and wouldn't forgive her for a long time to come. They met in Moscow, but only briefly. In 1925, after many ordeals, my mother's grandmother and aunt finally received their long-awaited visas and left for France where they were to remain forever.

I was born a year later. My very earliest childhood recollections are connected first with Finland and then with Moscow. In neither case, though, are they very strong or sure. The image of my mother stands before me shrouded in a fog; it diminishes, recedes, and disappears. She abandoned us, as I've already said, at the start of the thirties. Immediately thereafter my father married Ksenya and moved with us to Kratovo.

I close my eyes and once again see that distant suburb near Moscow. The hillsides, the haystacks, the dandelions by the road, the dewy border of the pine forest strewn with light and shade, the orange tree trunks, and the white sand.

I grew up there, building cities in the sand and thinking

nothing of the changes. Life seemed tranquil and secure. How could I have known that it might fly apart at the very first puff of trouble?

DISASTER

The summer of 1937 was hot and windy. Sandstorms whirled through the streets of the settlement, swaying the tops of the pines and whipping the telegraph wires to a piercing whine. The wind dragged the lilac clouds from behind the cover of the woods and seemed to shepherd them on high. Shaggy and laden with moisture, they would swell and darken the sky. Often, in the evenings, a thunderstorm would burst over the settlement.

The ringing sheets of rain would fall beyond the windows of our home. From time to time, to the crackling of the thunder, the twilight would swing open and melt away and, just as suddenly, thicken and close back in, the darkness increasing with each new wave of the storm.

On one such evening my father came home late—tired, soaked, and unusually gloomy.

"Good God," said Ksenya, taking the heavy wet overcoat from his hands, "what happened to you? You look awful! Have you had anything to eat?"

"No," my father answered. "I don't feel like it. . . . I'll have some vodka."

"What happened?"

"Valentin's been arrested," my father said. "There are strange things doing in Moscow."

His voice dried up and he seemed to choke for a second. Then, with a strong, abrupt movement, he tore open the tight hooks of his collar.

"Valentin?" Ksenya gasped, turning pale.

"Yes. Today."

He noticed me then (tousled and barefoot, I was looking out from my room) and suddenly said, sharp and loud:

"What's going on here? You, go to bed! On the double!"
Then, with a heavy tread, he walked down the hall.

I had trouble getting to sleep that night. Light poured in
through the crack in my door and I could hear their anxious,
muffled voices and Ksenya's sobs.

I learned a new word that night: terror.

"I was at the Academy, preparing a report," my father was
saying. "Suddenly, I got a telephone call. About Valentin.
Come to the Central Committee, on the double. When I got
there they told me: 'Looks like your brother is an enemy.'"

"But how?" Ksenya was dumfounded. "What kind of
enemy could he be? A well-known revolutionary. A great
diplomat. Living in the Government Home. No, there must be
some mistake."

"The Government Home," my father said slowly. Suddenly
I imagined his usual sullen smile. "That place is half-empty
already. Valentin wasn't the only one they took, not by a long
shot! It's terror like the country's never seen before."

"But why, why?" Ksenya couldn't quiet down. "Where is it
coming from?"

"From the top, of course."

"Wait. You said the top. But that's where the people who
were arrested come from."

"There's still the Politburo," my father said harshly. "And
Stalin."

"Stalin knew Valentin, didn't he?"

"Yes. He'd met him at one point in the underground, even
lived with him for a while, in Petersburg, in a conspirator's
apartment."

"You mean to say he doesn't believe . . ."

"I mean to say there isn't anyone he believes. No one and
nothing! That's the most frightening thing of all! And he's
making a special point of persecuting people he knows
personally."

"My God, my God," Ksenya muttered. "What next? Then
they could arrest you, too."

"They could."

My father fell silent. A glass tinkled. You could hear the liquid gurgling from his bottle.

"Of course they could," he repeated. He put his glass down with a knock and struck a match.

"The fact is, some unpleasant things have already started happening to me."

"Don't you dare keep anything from me." Ksenya's voice trembled and fell to a whisper. "Tell me everything. All right?"

"All right. Here's how it stands. A purge of the command cadres is going on right now. A list of suspects has already been drawn up and, according to some of the stories I've heard, my name's on it, too."

He fell silent again, tapping his finger on the edge of the table.

"Strange lists, too, by the way, including just about all of the old Lenin Guard."

"Who is this Stalin, anyway," Ksenya suddenly asked in a ringing voice. "A madman? What?"

"Keep it down," my father said. "I don't know. I don't know anything. But it doesn't take much to see what it's leading to. If the terror isn't brought to a halt, it'll be my turn soon. Sooner or later, they'll get to me and take me away. That's the only thing I can see happening. I'm no different than the others."

Suddenly he stood up and, rushing down the hall on tiptoe, threw his overcoat over his shoulders.

"Where are you going?" Ksenya asked in a frightened whisper.

"To Nikiforov," he explained sullenly. "I want a word or two with him about Valentin. If I'm right he's in Butyrsky. The commandant of the prison there is an old friend of Nikiforov's. They served together in the Special Services Department. I'll drop by and ask him; maybe he knows something or can ask around. . . ."

"It's two o'clock in the morning! They're all sound asleep by now."

"Asleep?" My father laughed. "Look for yourself. Out the

window. The only people sleeping nowadays are fools—or informers."

He left. I woke up Andrey. We leaned against the window, frozen in amazement.

The quiet night street was bathed in light. The thunderstorm had passed and the sky was clear; light-blue, milky Northern lights swarmed above the rooftops, twinkling in the branches of the pines and mingling with the lights of the settlement.

All of the windows in the neighborhood were brightly lighted. And in the glowing squares (orange, white, and green) loomed shadows, the unsteady silhouettes of people on the move. It was all very beautiful and terrifying.

No matter how he tried, my father couldn't learn a thing about Valentin. His older brother had sunk without a trace. And never reappeared. Where and when did he die? Under what circumstances? Probably, like many before him, he was shot in the basement of Lubyanka immediately after arrest. Maybe, though, it happened differently. Maybe he died under torture, slowly and in torment, lying somewhere wracked with pain, his kidneys broken and vertebrae shattered. What did he think of in his final hour? What visions came to call before he died? The blue waves of the Don? His native village? His family? Or was it the winding roads of the Revolution, sprinkled with blood—the Revolution: his former flame and present darkness. . . .

My father rushed about Moscow, feeling like a man in the desert, in the unpeopled steppe. His official inquiries went unanswered, and trusted friends, to whom he might have turned for help, grew fewer and fewer every day. Soon there were hardly any left at all. Most of them had perished; the others had learned the art of survival and gradually turned their backs on him.

He had fallen into disfavor. The word was out. His affairs were going poorly, his future was in doubt. Tired of all the inner torments, my father submitted an official report requesting a transfer to Spain, where many of his old comrades were still fighting in the mountains of Guadalajara and the entrenchments of Valencia and Aragon. His request was denied. It was then he decided to go on leave; they released him unconditionally and at once.

Strange days now began for all of us—sleepless, spectral, full of anxiety.

My father would spend every night in his den, smoking and pacing the floors in his squeaking shoes.

He was waiting for the ax to fall. He knew they might arrest him at any moment (they came, as a rule, at night) so he didn't sleep. He didn't want to be taken by surprise. He wanted to share his brother's fate and meet disaster with dignity.

And disaster was near; it wandered somewhere beyond the threshold and any incidental sound—the rustle of tires on the street, a noise on the stairway, the jingle of a bell—reminded him of it and carried its smell. Tight-lipped and bound in his military belts, he paced till dawn with a heavy, measured tread, his hands clasped behind his back in the old prison style. He had acquired the habit in the detention cells of Nicholean Russia. Almost thirty years had come and gone since that time and yet, here he was again, right at the very start.

Once, rising by chance before dawn, I caught the sounds of a quiet, rather muffled bass; it was my father, reading to himself from his first book, *Wild Intoxication.* He was recalling his youth.

" 'From the window to the doors,' " he recited thoughtfully, " 'six paces in a tiresome circle. The night draws on, slow, cold, and dreary. It's quiet in my cell. Nothing but my footfalls, along the sounding flagstones, to measure off the minutes. And there's nothing to remind me of where I once had been. Was there once a time before this? Is there anything on Earth? These walls, these stones! This filth and freezing darkness, welling in my heart . . .' "

Suddenly the stairway outside began to squeak. A minute later the bell rang deafeningly.

My father fell silent in mid-sentence. Then I heard his slow, measured tread. To this day those paces still echo in my memory. The lock clicked, the door flew open, and on the dimly lighted threshold a stocky figure in an overcoat appeared. My father looked intently and drew a deep breath. It was our neighbor, a worker in the Military Procurator's Office.

"Don't tell me *you're* after me," my father asked. A gloomy smile came to his face and then faded.

"Zhenya, don't talk like that!" the man answered in a distressed voice. "God forbid. We don't have anything to do with that. We're no agents. I just happened to notice you in the window, so I decided . . ."

"Something wrong?"

"Yes. Boredom. Forgive me, brother. Listen, I've got a little bottle of pepper brandy with me. You won't object, eh?"

"Well, what the—" my father said, scratching the tight collar of his field shirt. "All right, come on in. Only be quiet. Don't wake up the rest of the house."

"I'm not sleeping," Ksenya suddenly spoke up. She entered from the bedroom, closing her robe as she went. "Come into the den. I'll scare up something to eat."

She said it quietly, matter-of-factly, but in her eyes and face, in the nervous movements of her hands, in everything she did, you could catch the signs of a hidden, still active terror.

That's how we lived out those days. And we weren't alone. The entire settlement was sick with panic and insomnia. Thunderstorms roared and frothed above us, the wind raged, the days yielded to one another. Not the days so much as the nights, actually—all time back then was measured in nights. Every home waited for disaster to strike and in every window you could see the glimmers of anguish and the dying flickers of hope. The colorful squares (orange, white, and green) burned bright and uneasy and then faded, one by one. The settlement was slowly perishing. A wave of arrests rolled through Kratovo, sweeping over the houses and submerging them in darkness. It advanced on us, leaving fewer and fewer windows glimmering in the night.

At long last my father's turn came. Not by arrest, though. No, he died without any help, on his own, of a heart attack. He had worn his military uniform all his life, and he died in it, meeting his attack the way he would have any onslaught on the field of battle.

Years later, after I'd grown up and seen enough of the world on my own, I had a good chance to observe how people who have the time prepare themselves for death. It happened on the Kara Sea, during an equinoctial gale, which in those latitudes can be unusually long and fierce. Tattered and out of control, our doomed trawler was being carried toward the Taymyr Rocks. Luckily, we were spared, but there was a moment when disaster seemed unavoidable.

That was when the sailors gathered in the crews' quarters and began to change their clothes. Carefully, with a certain gloomy solemnity, they put on clean shirts and ties and took out their parade uniforms from their trunks. They were performing an ancient seaman's ritual, and as I looked at them and changed dress myself, I suddenly recalled my father.

I remembered how every night, as darkness fell, he would dress up in his parade uniform, carefully clean his shoes, tighten his shoulder belt, and strap on his weapon, trimmed in gold and stones and inscribed with his own name. Back then, in Kratovo, I confess I was quite amazed by it all. Now at last I understood what it had all been about. He had been performing the very same ritual as the sailors, preparing for his own annihilation.

I was to remember those nights in Kratovo my whole life through—the troubled whistling of the wind beyond the windows, the rain-drenched darkness, the glowing, slowly dying Northern lights, the resounding, sleepless pacing of my father, and Ksenya's desperate shout:

"Who is this Stalin, anyway? A madman? What?"

Often now I would catch myself wondering if my father's untimely death hadn't been a blessing after all. He was never to know the full consequences of the terror. And thank God! He would never have been able to reconcile himself to what was going on; he would not have endured it or wanted to live any longer himself. Steel yields only to a point and then it breaks—suddenly and forever.

Apparently back there, in that suburban community near Moscow, he had already sensed that break within himself.

WHEN YOU CHOP WOOD, THE CHIPS WILL FLY

After my father's funeral, our Kratovo family fell apart. Ksenya became ill and took to her bed; she never recovered from the shock and didn't survive him long. Soon after, my brother and I moved to my mother's place in the city.

We left Kratovo late in the fall. The telegraph lines droned and whined and a low, cheerless sun rolled above the fences, casting long, pale shadows along the deserted streets of the settlement. It looked as though the entire community had died out. Everything now seemed alien and comfortless. The gardens and farmsteads had gone to ruin, the houses were all boarded, and a sad emptiness now reigned in our old home as well.

I recall our first evening in Moscow; my mother's tears and her rapid, confused words: "Chop wood and the chips will fly," she is saying, "and here we are—the chips!" She paces the floor, wrapping herself up against the cold in her shaggy shawl. "Everything's destroyed and done to dust. No one's left—not even Shura. Do you remember, the one I came to Kratovo with? He's disappeared, too, and might as well be dead."

"How come?" I was at a loss. "Where did he go?"

"Arrested," Andrey volunteers from the corner. (My brother is a big boy already; he's finishing seven-year school; he smokes on the sly and knows real grown-up words.) "They probably just nabbed him—picked him right up."

"Of course not." My mother brushes it aside. "Shura's abroad now, in America. A nonreturnee. He left me. And what can I do, all alone? How can I live another day, how am I supposed to feed you? I don't know, I don't know. What can

I do? Go to work? But that's dangerous: all those question-
naires. I'd have to explain everything in detail. And where
could I go?"

She throws her hands up in dismay. "I don't know how to
do anything, I don't know how. . . . No, there's no way out,
no way out. . . ."

And suddenly, with a weak, halting movement, she turns to
the large looking glass on the wall. She stares at it and fixes her
hairdo. And carefully, with the tips of her fingers, touches her
cheekbones and her lips.

And still another evening—a long and agonizing winter night.
Settling down by the window, I leaf through a thick volume of
Vazara, killing time. I am all alone in the apartment. My
brother is off somewhere (lately he's taken to vanishing from
the house). My mother is gone, too, living in another place
now with her new husband.

I am bored and crackle through the pages, looking dejectedly out the window. It's already late. The frost-covered
windows are flooded with a thick, frozen blue. There in the
swirling darkness I see the clustered rooftops of Moscow—the
white curves and sharp corners, the frosty spires of the towers,
the wadded haze above the chimneys.

Suddenly there's a knock at the door. It must be Andryusha,
I think, or Mother, perhaps. She's completely forgotten about
us; so many days have passed since she's been by.

I burst into the anteroom, unlock the door, and see a
stranger before me. Removing his hat and shaking it free of
snow, he steps across the threshold and politely inquires if he
may please see Elizaveta Vladimirovna?

I explain she isn't here; that she lives at another address.
"Who are you? A friend of Mother's?" I ask him.

"You might say so, yes," he replies. "Yes, of course. Mainly,
though, I'm a friend of the man who used to live here. You
remember him, don't you?"

"No, not especially," I answer slowly. "I saw him once a
long time ago, but he isn't here either."

"I know," the stranger sighs. "I know."

Dry-faced and quick, he pushes past me into the room and sits down in a creaking chair.

"He may not be here, but the rest of us stayed, all his old friends. And friendship, my boy, is a great thing! I, for one, think of him often, as do the others, no doubt. . . ."

He looks at me carefully and smiles, screwing up his eyes.

"After he left, someone visited you. Someone came to see your mother and talked about him, right?"

I shrug my shoulders and say nothing. Mashing a cigarette with his fingers, the guest tries to cheer me up.

"Don't be afraid, my little man, speak up. What's the matter with you? Why, we had lots of friends in common—Anisimov, for example. . . ."

He gives me a few other names. I don't recognize any of them and tell him so.

"All right." He nods his head. "All right, I'm not insisting."

He lights up, takes a drag, and rounding his lips into a circle, puffs out a ring of whitish smoke.

"Well, what about the letters?" he asks. "Any kind of notes or messages come from him? Why do I want to know? Simple curiosity, you know, how he's doing there, what's happening with him in America. You mean to say he hasn't written a word about himself all this time? Not even a little piece of news?"

"I don't know," I tell him. "Go ask my mother. I told you already, she doesn't live here anymore."

"Well, thanks," he says, getting up to go. "I'll be sure to do that. She doesn't come to see you too often, that it?"

"It all depends," I answer with a sharp and sudden sense of injury. "Sometimes she disappears for weeks. You wait for her, and wait . . ."

"Ay, ay, ay." He lays his stiff, dry palm on my head. "That's not good. What kind of a woman is she? And such excellent children. Are you going to school?"

"You bet," I say, adding with pride, "the Repin Art School."

"You want to be an artist?"

"Uh-huh!"

"And your brother?"

"He hasn't made up his mind yet. He likes to travel, though."

"Well, well," he mutters, "excellent children."

The guest heads for the door. And suddenly, half-turning, he adds: "How do you get by here, anyway? Who cooks for you, at least? Don't tell me you do it yourselves?"

"Of course not. A houseworker comes by."

"A houseworker?" He falls to thinking for a second and his eyes narrow. "What's her name?"

"Nastya."

"Nastya," he repeats, "and her last name?"

"I don't know."

"What's with you, my friend?" The guest smiles sparingly. "No matter what I ask you, you don't know the answer. Who was in the house? You don't know. As for the letters, the same thing. And you want to be an artist? A man of art must be observant and notice every little detail."

We say good-bye. For a long time afterwards I have trouble sorting out my feelings. The unexpected visitor intrigues me: there's something interesting about him, something unusual and alienating, that gives rise to an instinctive watchfulness.

And so, at the age of twelve, I meet my first investigator and learn what an interrogation is.

Time flows swiftly, the days flash past. I've already turned sixteen.

Meanwhile, all about me, a war is raging. The capital is darkened, gripped by panic, hunger, and fire. My school has been evacuated, but I still continue my studies, attending the workshop of Dmitry Stakhevich Moor.

This honored illustrator and poster-maker is no longer young; deep wrinkles now plow through his soft and flabby face; the gray mane of his hair rests on the collar of a workman's shirt. From time to time he is wracked by fierce coughing fits from which he takes a long time to recover. He is far from well, but as energetic as ever. He works day and night, filling the rush orders of the war press, drawing for *The Windows of TASS*.

I help him as best I can, but basically I'm still an apprentice, looking on. I study the laws of drawing, the secrets of line and shade. Sometimes, during the breaks, he speaks to me of the meaning of art.

"Painting's a luxury," he wheezes. "Drawing's a necessity! And that's the heart of it. Graphics serves the people directly, day in, day out. Any of the objects around us can be rendered with its help. A drawing of wallpaper and fabrics, the painting on a cup, the form of an ashtray, and the jacket of a book—everything, literally everything, is rendered by our craft. We lend things their beauty and put order in the world. The world is chaotic, unformed, and evil. Where would it be without us?"

The world is unformed and evil—the old man got it right. Personal experience had already taught me as much.

My whole life, even then, had been compounded of misfortunes and losses. Nothing but losses. I contemplate the fact, holding a notice in my hands of Andrey's death.

He had left for the front at the start of the war and now he was dead. Dead on delivery, in his very first battle. "He died a valorous death," the official letter says.

The lines ripple and darken before my eyes. Impetuously I crumple up the paper. Then, on second thought, I smooth it out again and, folding it neatly, hide it away in the side pocket of my jacket.

I'm alone now in the world. And it is unformed and evil, with precious little chance of ever getting any better.

The slow wail of a siren starts up beyond the window, an air-raid warning. I turn off the light and quickly pull the shade. Before me, in the swirling darkness, lie the clustered rooftops of Moscow. They're black now, and crimsoned with fire. Clumps of ash, crisscrossed by searchlights, whirl above them in the night.

There is, of course, a colossal difference between the me of then and the me of now. Still, when I resurrect that distant image in my mind, I'm amazed. Where did that quiet child go, that shy and gentle dreamer? Where is he now?

The first step, it seems to me, was my arrest. In 1942 I received a summons to appear for work at the aviation factory. I glanced at it and threw it away without a second's thought. The negligence, it turned out, was criminal. At the time there was a well-known law regarding a general and obligatory labor conscription. Any breach of it was severely punished.

A dreamer and a bookworm, what did I know of that? The world of my imagination was closer to me by far than the world of reality. Closer and more comprehensible and incomparably sweeter. I would invent colorful lands and people them with good, kind souls.

Real life turned out to be different. A month after my arrest I was brought to trial, sentenced to two years' imprisonment, and dispatched to the local Moscow prison camp.

DEPRIVED OF THE SKY

My first concentration camp was strange and frightening—not just because it was the first, either. I was never to run up against anything like it again.

The fact was that the camp, as such, didn't exist. It was a peculiar kind of prison set up in a foundry in the Krasnaya Presna section of Moscow. Having refused to work at one factory, I now found myself, under guard, at another, worse by far. An irony of fate, you might say, or perhaps only the odd sense of humor of the secret police.

The prisoners lived here deprived of the right to take walks or breathe fresh air. Instead of the sky, a smoked stone canopy hung over our heads, cutting us off from the world outside. One of the spacious factory shops had been re-equipped and transformed into a living quarters. A dining hall had been placed in a somewhat smaller shop and farther on, at the end of the hall, the main casting shop thundered and roared. There proceeded, in the asphyxiating heat, in the carbon stench and dust, the desperate work of boiling metal, casting mines into molds, and forming the upper casings for shells.

The work was heavy and exhausting. It took me a long time to get used to it. All the same, little by little, I managed. In the long run, a prisoner adjusts to everything. Getting used to the people, though, took a lot more doing.

The group in our cell included, along with the "politicals" and common criminals (people basically like myself), quite a few thieves. They lived apart, in the corner farthest from the entrance. Beside them lived the youths: homeless children, street rabble, and apprentice thieves.

These young "shoots" gave me a mocking and unfriendly reception. In their eyes I was a crank, a *fraier,* a "stuffed deer" (a term used in their circle for members of the intelligentsia). And if the adult thieves treated "deer" like me with a certain measure of indifference, the young behaved with cruelty and transparent arrogance.

Two boys ruled the rabble and gave it its tone. One of them, nicknamed the Kid, was tall, gaunt, and, apparently, very strong. The other, Snuffles, looked like his complete opposite: short and fidgety with filthy skin and a harelip. His movements were affected, his speech lisping and unclear. When he did speak, a sticky froth would foam at the corners of his mouth. He was to be my main enemy here.

I had barely appeared in the cell when he called me over, looked me up and down, and smirked. Then, making a face, he added with a lisp: "What you in for?"

"Nothing . . . an *ukaz.*"

"I know." He was quiet. "So, you feeling scared?"

"No," I said. "Why should I?"

"Right," he sniggered. "People here are the same as on the outside. Better even, maybe. They're suffering for the truth. Besides, you don't look like the kind that scares easy, right?"

"Right," I agreed.

"Just a happy kid, right?"

"Uh-huh . . ."

"Well, seeing you're so happy, let's play!"

I wasn't feeling much like playing, but how could I refuse such a simple little request, especially after the compliments. He suggested leapfrog and, reluctantly, I agreed.

"Bend over," he said and with a laugh he ran up and jumped right on top of me.

Startled and enraged, I tried to throw him off, but no luck. Snuffles was hanging on with a vengeance.

"C'mon," he ordered, kicking me painfully in the side. "Get moving!"

What could I do, trembling and seeing nothing around me but laughing, jeering faces. Much later I learned how to handle someone who's jumped you from behind. It's a terrible, sometimes even fatal trick; you grab the attacker by the legs, flip him over on his back, and crush him with the entire weight of your body. I would learn a lot of things later on. At the moment, though, I was helpless, confused, and shamefully weak.

"Giddap!" Snuffles insisted, spewing spit.

There was a hysterical, threatening tone to his voice, and I carried him, dragging myself from one end of the cell to the other. Again and again.

Finally, when they left me alone, I staggered back and collapsed on my bunk and lay there for a long time, suffocating with despair and injured pride. Even now, almost thirty years later, all I have to do is recall that incident and my hands begin to tremble involuntarily with helpless rage.

Dostoyevsky once said, "A man would have to be shamelessly vain to write about himself without embarrassment." Maybe. All I know is that I write without shame about myself. I write to re-create the past as accurately as I can—to recapture all the circumstances that first led me to the thought of violence, murder, and revenge. That sweet thought wasn't born full-blown. A whole succession of similar events preceded it.

Snuffles' last dirty trick had to do with bread. I've already mentioned that our camp was unique. Even in the way they fed us. The staple of our diet was buckwheat, from which they prepared kasha and soups. We could have as much of it in the dining room as we wanted, and still we starved, tormentingly, fiercely, incessantly. It was uncleaned, unpolished, and absolutely indigestible.

The prisoners had to subsist chiefly on bread and boiling water. We'd get our daily five-hundred-gram bread ration in two parts: three hundred grams in the morning, two hundred at dinnertime. Like many of the others, I'd carry off my evening portion with me and eat it in the cell on my bunk.

On one such occasion Snuffles crept up on me from behind and knocked the ration from my hands. It fell and rolled along the spit-covered, cement floor. As I squatted and reached for it he struck me one sharp blow across the fingers with the metal heel of his boot.

"Hey," he said with a chuckle, "I like this game. Try again. . . . What're you waiting for?"

I was sitting on the floor, still recovering from the shock and the pain. Then, with a moan, I got up and flung myself at my enemy. I lunged at him with my undamaged left hand, aiming straight at his face, at those cloudy eyes and that vile, slobbering mouth.

I didn't get him, though. The Kid grabbed me by the shoulder and yanked me back. The next thing I knew I was reeling from a blinding blow. God knows what might have happened next if the older convicts hadn't intervened. From the thieves' corner a tall, dark-haired man in a quilted jacket and striped sailor's shirt came toward us. "What's the racket all about?" he asked.

"Nothing." Snuffles turned to him. "Just playing."

"Don't let it get out of hand," the thief said threateningly. "Understand?"

"I understand." Snuffles dropped his eyes.

"You better."

The man looked at me and at the bread by my feet. Turning to Snuffles, he added, "Don't you ever lay a hand on that

bread. Remember the law. And leave that kid alone." That's
how the evening ended.

The next day I found a small, narrow metal plate in the
foundry and secretly made it into a knife. Sharpening the
blade, I conjured up an image of Snuffles and saw the blade
sink into his trembling throat; I saw him wheeze; I saw him
choke in his own blood. . . .

I had every intention of settling with Snuffles that very
evening. But because of an air-raid alert, I didn't pull it off.
The sirens started up right after the retreat. As usual the
guards quickly locked all the doors, turned off the light, and
retreated to the safety of the bomb shelter. We remained in the
darkness under lock and key, in the fullest possible isolation.

Somewhere in the night the antiaircraft guns barked away.
Blazes crackled and explosions roared and echoed every
moment. Apparently the German bombers were headed our
way, straight toward Krasnaya Presna.

Suddenly a sharp whistle drilled through the sky right above
our heads. It drew nearer and nearer, filling the room with its
sound and splitting through our brains. You could almost feel
it physically.

"A demolition bomb," someone gasped. Instantly a heavy,
shattering blow rocked the room. The building trembled and
swayed, sprinkling a caustic dust down from the arches and
the sooty ceiling. Someone sobbed in the darkness. Someone
else went into hysterics by the door.

"The bastards, the bastards!" I heard a nasal cry. "They
locked the doors and ran. What if it was a direct hit? What if
they hit the factory dead center, what would happen to us?
We're in here like in a crypt. Walled in. Buried for sure, buried
before our time!"

It's Snuffles, I guessed, feeling a sudden and inexplicable
sense of triumph. So, you bastard, you're scared. You coward,
you're scared of dying!

Strange as it may seem, the bombing raid left me unperturbed. I was too busy thinking of revenge! The very thought
of it, apparently, inspired me, supported me, and set all my

other cares aside. I wasn't a child anymore. Without even noticing it, I had become a man fully used to cruelty.

MASTER YOURSELF

Three more days and nights passed. I waited out my time, patient and watchful as an animal. And then I got my chance.

At midnight, while the whole cell lay sleeping, I rose from my bunk and drew my knife out of its hiding place. Trying not to make a sound, I crouched and moved toward the thieves in the far corner.

I was right by the head of Snuffles' bed when panic suddenly gripped me. What was I doing? What would happen to me afterwards? An odd, feverish weariness took possession of me; my legs turned weak and soft as cotton wadding, the palms of my hands were bathed in sweat. And there, in the semidarkness of the prison cell, the figure of my father rose before me. Thickset, braced in his army belts, he moved slowly toward me and smiled, the little lenses of his pince-nez agleam. "The main thing," he said, smoothing out his mustache with the side of his hand, "is not to be afraid. It's one thing to use your cunning in a fight, but don't ever be a coward!"

I looked sideways in confusion at Snuffles. He was lying perfectly still, wheezing and gurgling in his sleep and smacking his wet lips. His head was tossed back and his thick, stringy neck was exposed and waiting for the blow—a blow I couldn't seem to deliver; it was beyond my strength.

"Father, Father," I called out in my confusion, "you said a fight. But this isn't a fight at all. Look for yourself: he's sleeping. He's helpless and unprotected."

"Then wake him up!"

"But . . ."

"Then everything will be decided. Master yourself. It's essential."

"Essential for what?"

"For becoming what you really are. Think about what's lying in store for you: a wretched fate, mockery, beatings—"

"So what?" I objected with sudden cunning. "You said so yourself. A beating won't kill you."

"No, but disgrace can. I know!"

"But not everybody—"

"Of course not." He shook his head sternly. "Only the best."

"What if I'm not one of them?"

"You are my son!"

"Still, raising a hand against another person . . ."

"I'm not talking about murder. Wake him up, make him look into your eyes. Let *him* be the one that's afraid."

"What if he doesn't scare?"

"Then what have you lost? There's nowhere left to go. It's already too late to step back. Risk it—play it to the end!"

With that, my father faded and dissolved without a trace. His image hadn't been with me for long, but it had come just in time. It was as if I had felt his support and acquired a sudden spiritual strength. No longer doubtful, I walked up to Snuffles and bent down over him.

Suddenly, though, the Kid, who was lying beside him, woke up and, yawning, raised himself on his elbow. He gave me a hazy look. Still not fully alert, barely able to tell waking from a dream, he moved his eyes and noticed the gleam of the narrow blade in my hand. His eyes instantly brightened, his face tensed, and, diving over Snuffles, he seized me by the collar of my shirt.

I knew that grip of his. I knew how dangerous those fingers were. Without a moment's delay, I slashed his hand with the knife. He shrieked, jerked back, and swore hoarsely.

It had been a good blow! A deep, slanting cut across his hand. A thick, dark stream of blood gushed onto the bunk and over Snuffles' head.

Howling and smearing the blood across his face, Snuffles leaped out of the bunk and, like a madman, threw himself against the doors.

A moment later the bolt thundered and a sleepy, gloomy guard appeared on the threshold. "What is it?" he asked.

"There," Snuffles babbled, shaking and poking a finger into the center of the cell. "Over there . . ."

"What do you mean, 'over there'? What're you talking about?"

"I don't know."

"You don't know?" the guard said slowly, studying his face. "Where's all the blood coming from, then? Tell me that. You prisoners start another one of your bloodbaths?"

"Of course not, Citizen Officer, what bloodbath?" Snuffles started to fidget. He was scared. "The blood's from my nose. Came out all by itself."

"Then why were you knocking?"

"I wanted to ask for medicine."

"What kind of medicine you expect this time of night?" the guard answered with a glower. "You gone crazy or something? Come on, wipe it up and get to sleep! Or I'll give you the kind of medicine you'll be remembering for the next ten years."

"Yes, sir, of course, sir." Snuffles hastened to comply. "Don't you worry about a thing, Citizen Officer. Everything's nice and in order here."

He was calming down now and trying his best to correct his blunder. But it was too late. The way the prisoners saw it, what he'd done was unforgivable. The only people who could seek protection from the guards were *fraiers* and bitches. Never thieves! After this, Snuffles was through. His career as a thief lay smashed against the rocks. The adult thieves started to ignore him, his young friends soon made him the butt of all their jokes.

Before too long the Kid moved to another bunk, making the break, once and for all, with his former friend. "Hey, you," the Kid said to me the next morning in the dining hall, "hey, Mr. Tough Guy, tell me, if I hadn't cut you off last night, would you have killed him?"

"Probably." I shrugged my shoulders.

"You would!" the Kid said good-humoredly. "I saw your mug. I know! Of course you would! And"—he screwed up his eyes—"maybe me along with him, huh?"

I was already getting a feeling for the style of this new world of mine, so I answered carelessly: "If I had to, sure."

"Good man!" The Kid started to laugh, slapping me on the back with a bandaged hand. "You're a real *chuma,** all right!" From that moment on I was stuck with the nickname of Chuma.

And so, in one blow—with one quick cut of the knife—I'd eliminated an enemy and, gaining a formal nickname, enhanced my prestige in the camp. My fate had taken a sudden turn for the better. Little by little, life brightened up and became easier to bear. It looked like my run of bad luck was finally at an end.

My impression couldn't have been farther from the truth.

TO THE THUNDER OF A SALUTE

One winter morning during a check I felt a sudden queasiness and fever, and an unpleasant dryness in my mouth. I had trouble breathing and a piercing, gnawing pain in my chest and back.

The doctor came. He quickly thumped my chest, put a thermometer in my armpit and, after one look at it, mournfully raised his brows. "I'm going to have to hospitalize him," he told the guard. "He's in bad shape. Very bad shape."

"What's wrong?" the guard asked doubtfully.

"Something with the lungs," the doctor replied, pressing his lips. "Pleurisy, probably. Unless I'm mistaken, of course."

The old pill-tosser wasn't mistaken. It turned out I actually did have a double exudating pleurisy, a lingering and nasty disease. And so I was dispatched to Butyrsky Central Prison Hospital.

My illness lasted for quite some time; the brutal conditions of my life in camp had begun to tell: the sudden changes in temperature (from the intense heat of the foundry to the damp

---

* From the Russian *chumovoy,* a prison term for an incorrigible tall-tale teller.

chill of the cell), the overtaxing work, the protracted malnutrition, and the over-all and desperate exhaustion. I'd barely come into contact with life and I was already a weary man. They cured my pleurisy by spring, but I was still hardly able to get up from my bed. I lay there, drawing slow and labored breaths, and staring at the bleached ceiling for hours at a time. It was riddled with damp spots of the most varied kinds; some of them reminded me of savage plants, others of gigantic insects. At times it would even seem that the insects were on the move, closing in like scavengers on my scent.

I would turn aside and look out the window into a smoky, gray, windy sky. Sometimes, in the evenings, victory salutes would explode in the heights. A brief volley of heavy artillery fire would thunder above the neighborhood. The darkness would part and turn rainbow hues. Thick, shimmering clusters of fire would scale the skies, hang there for a moment, and then fall back, extinguished in a gay, brightly colored rain.

Since the winter of '43 the salutes had been flaring with greater frequency and magnificence. The back of the war was being broken. The front was retreating toward the West.

Our infirmary cell had its own, mixed reactions to the news. There were quite a few soldiers among us, many of them captured while retreating from the German encirclement at the outbreak of the war. All were now serving time for treason, espionage, and collaboration with the enemy. Though unjustly sentenced and maligned—imprisoned, really, for nothing at all—they remained as patriotic as ever. They were sincerely overjoyed at the victories at the front and responded noisily and happily to the salutes.

There were some real traitors and turncoats among us— *politsai*, we called them—who reacted sadly and anxiously to the war news. Some of them stubbornly continued to believe in the might and indestructibility of the Third Reich. The reverses at the front were nothing more than temporary setbacks to them.

"Go ahead and brag," an old *politsai* with a gray, stubbly face said one evening. "It's just a lot of hot air."

"We know how to fight," a tall fellow replied, so pale he

looked almost blue. One of his hands was bound in a cast and rested in a wide gauze sling; with the other he grabbed hold of one of the bars on the window and stood there looking intently at the twinkling sky, bright with the varicolored bursts of salutes. "We can fight, all right, you can see that for yourself."

"Sure you can fight," the gray-haired man agreed, "but what good's it going to do you? It's all a shambles out there. No, boys, there's no comparing us with the Germans." His cheeks shook. "No comparison at all. They've got organization, discipline, power. Real power!"

"So how come they're running?" The fellow smiled. "How about that?"

"Easy," a husky, rolling bass boomed from the corner. "The German machine has smashed against the Russian shambles."

"Well," the *politsai* brushed it aside, "not for long. They'll be back. Just a little breather and before you know it they'll be back. They'll make up for it. Then we'll see what kind of song you heroes'll be singing!"

"Dry up," the fellow growled, walking slowly up to the graybeard. "Keep your trap shut, understand? One more word out of you and . . ."

"What're you so upset about?" The *politsai* was surprised. "You think you're any better than I am? We're all behind bars on the same charge, with the same sentence to pay."

And again, someone's derisive bass rumbled from the corner. "Yeah, equality for all! The fundamental law of socialism!"

Thieves usually didn't get involved in such political arguments. To them, the salutes had a special meaning. My bunkmate, an old pickpocket named Archangel, listened to the triumphant echo of the guns and put it this way: "Things are going good now on the outside. All them *fraiers* bustling around, having themselves a good time and swilling vodka. And when a *fraier*'s happy, let me tell you, work's a real pleasure. The poor jerk, he doesn't feel a thing at a time like that; he's blind as a bat, just asking to be taken. You hook him

by the vest and shake him down piece by piece. The second I
see me a decent fish I look him right in the eye. I study the
outside, see? If he's tight, he's in the bag! But if he's nervous or
angry, I got to be careful. He's got a nose like a dog on him
then. You got to use a special psychology for types like him.
That's what I don't like about the war; it gets everybody
nervous and depressed. What the hell. If God's good we'll live
to see peace and victory—and lots of happy days!"

I listened indifferently, as if from far away. I would lie in a
state of drowsiness for days at a time, without wanting to
speak or move or eat. Yet compared to what they were
handing out in the camp, the infirmary grub was fit for a king!
Dinner was three courses long. (I got the special high-calorie
diet for people who were especially ill.) The last course would
consist of a stewed fruit compote. That I'd drink; my neighbor
would put a quick end to the rest.

Archangel had a lot of diseases: chronic syphilis, rheuma-
tism, a prolapsed rectum, and something else I don't even
remember now. Apparently, though, the rich food didn't
disturb him in the least; he was unusually cheerful and chatty,
and hungry as a wolf. He'd make a habit of cleaning up my
dishes with dispatch. Once, though, he turned to me and said
sadly: "You're a godsend. Seconds on everything. What more
could you ask for these days. It's paradise! But I feel sorry for
you. The rate you're going, you won't last."

"Really?" I smiled weakly. "Why?"

"Why?" He got angry. "Why?! Take advantage of the
chance while you've got it. Feed yourself. Shake your antlers,
brother!"

"I don't want to," I said sleepily. "I don't want to hustle."

I turned aside and dozed off, covering my head with the
pillow.

The doctors' rounds woke me up. I saw people in white
robes bending over me; one of them, short and puffy, his face
as wrinkled as an old man's, looked somewhere off to the side
and asked: "He doesn't eat anything, you say?"

Archangel's voice answered instantly. "As God's my witness, Citizen Doctor. Just a little compote and a bit of tea on

the side and little parcels of stuff every now and then. Period. The poor kid's kicking the bucket right before my very eyes."

"I see you've been doing pretty well for yourself." The doctor laughed.

"I told you so myself," Archangel objected with hurt feelings. "I told you so myself!"

The doctor sat down at the head of my bed; he took my pulse and with a practiced gesture turned my eyelids inside out.

"Mmm, yes," he muttered, "we could have expected that long ago."

Then, moving off to the side, he had a prolonged discussion with his companion. Some muffled phrases flew my way. "Pellagra. Loss of vital energies. Subject to release."

When the rounds were finished, Archangel said: "They just dealt you a good card, pal. If they were talking about a release, it's a sure thing. They're going to set you free! As for me . . ."

He fell silent, raised his brows, and then added with a wry face: "I'll stay here and rot. Now, tell me, is that fair?"

Archangel was right, after all. I had been dealt a good card. It didn't take me long to realize that.

Within a week of our conversation, I was summoned to the doctors' commission. This time there were a lot of people to look me over and, once again, I heard that frightening and incomprehensible word—pellagra.

At the end of April I was informed that I was to be prematurely released from custody because of illness and my continued inability to work. I heard the news in the prison office. After reading my release order aloud, the duty officer gave me some papers to look over and sign. Once the formalities were over, an orderly appeared and led me downstairs to the quartermaster. There in the damp, gloomy basement he ordered me to undress at once. "Strip," he said. "No more State clothes for you."

I obediently removed my rough hospital underwear and pulled the slippers off my feet. Feeling the icy touch of the slippery tiles on my feet, I started shivering and asked with chattering teeth: "What about . . . my old clothes?"

"Stick around," he said, raking up the linen in his arms. "They'll give 'em back."

"How long do I have to wait?"

"Listen, buddy, that's not my problem. You know how many rags like yours we got heaped up here? Thousands! They still got to find them and check all the lists. It takes time."

"But it's cold."

"You'll live," the orderly said with a short little laugh. "A lot of other people spend half their lives waiting for something like this, and it never happens." And he turned to go, the heels of his shoes clicking along the tiles.

I was still speaking and moving as if half in a dream, not yet fully realizing what was happening. The cold brought me back to my senses. That's when I noticed I wasn't alone. Cowering and buckling his knees to his chin on a bench some distance away, a prisoner was sitting half-turned to me. He was as naked as I, with a closely cropped head and frail, protruding collar bones and translucent skin. Good God, I thought, they're arresting little kids, children almost!

A burning cigarette jutted from his mouth, and suddenly I had an overwhelming desire for a smoke. I hopped over to him on my freezing feet.

"Hey," I said, "can you spare me a cigarette?"

He let his eyes slip along me and took a drag, enveloping himself in smoke. Then, lowering his lashes, he said in a chilled, brittle tenor: "It's my last."

"Give me a drag, then."

"Ali right." The child nodded and, biting off a wet edge of the mouthpiece, he extended the butt to me.

He held it delicately, with the tips of his fingers, and I couldn't help noticing the shape of his hand. It was narrow and weak, almost lifeless.

"Go ahead," the child said, "take a drag. Unless you're squeamish, that is."

I clambered up beside him on the bench, crossed my legs Turkish fashion and sat there quietly for a while, lingering over the smoldering cigarette.

"They letting you go?" he wanted to know. "Or shipping you out?"

"Letting me go," I answered. "And you?"

"Same thing."

"They're sure taking their time about it. Can't find your things, right?"

"When it comes to letting you go"—he screwed up his eyes—"they've got all the time in the world."

And once again, with a sidelong glance, he asked quietly: "Illness?"

"Yes. Medical release. I got lucky."

"Me, too," he said sorrowfully. "Me, too."

"Doesn't take much to see that."

I ran my hand along his shaved head and his thin, bent, childlike neck.

"Where did they wear you out like that? There's nothing left."

"Nothing left," he repeated, and sobbed. His face contorted and thin strands of tears flowed down his sunken cheeks. "And it won't come back again. Ever! Ever!"

"Hey, hey," I said in embarrassment, "stop it. What are you, anyway? A little girl? You're going back into the open, you ought to be happy!"

He quieted down under my hand, and gently leaned his shoulder into me.

Suddenly the voice of the quartermaster boomed from behind a partition in the center of the room.

"Evdokima Anna! Front and center! Get your things!"

My companion trembled and straightened up. As soon as he got off the bench I realized he wasn't a boy at all. There was no mistaking it. But, my God, how little of a woman there was left in that dried-up body! Angular, fleshless, and dry, it filled me with pity. The girl apparently sensed my reaction. Covering herself with her arms she turned from me in embarrassment, dropped her eyes, and left quickly, almost at a run, for the bulky, smock-covered figure of the quartermaster looming by the partition.

A minute later he called me.

Deteriorated, crumpled, and smelling of mold and mice, my suit hung on me like on a peg. The shoulders sagged, the pants were baggy. Anna, in her bright little skirt and shawl, looked surprisingly well dressed and even a bit coquettish. That light orange kerchief brightened up her face and nicely matched the color of her eyes. Only now did I really notice them: they were large and brown, with hazy, golden twinkling sparks.

"Listen," I said, "I didn't realize at first. You're . . . good-looking!"

"I was once." She sighed. "I was in pretty good shape, all right. That's why I got burned."

"What article did they get you on?" I had even forgotten to ask.

"One of their favorites," she answered. "S.D.E. Ever hear of it?"

"No."

"You must be kidding."

"Honest, I don't know. What was the charge?"

"Prostitution," she said simply. "What else was I good for? Mama lost her ration cards in '42. We were starving. So I went out. With soldiers, with anyone who came along. That's when they hit me with the Socially Dangerous Element article."

"And here, in the hospital—"

"I know what you're thinking." She gave me a gloomy smile. "No, I don't have it. The doctors say I've got cavities in my lungs." Again her face softened and contorted pitifully. "It's worse than any kind of syphilis. I've got only one road left now and that leads straight to Vagankovsky Cemetery."

"Hey, lampwicks!" the quartermaster shouted hoarsely. "Break up the rally, you two, and beat it! Come on, get moving!"

I'd thought there'd be some new procedures to go through, some everlasting complications—but no, everything went surprisingly smoothly and perfunctorily. The silent porter checked the list and opened the steel, brass-studded gates. He let us past and slammed the doors with a heavy rumble behind us. Behind us! Behind our backs!

"Where are you headed?" I asked Anna as we walked away.

"Not far." She waved her hand. "Kalyaevsky Street."

"Can I walk with you?"

"No," she answered. "Later, maybe, if we're still alive." And then, staggering and raising her hands to her face: "Oy," she said, "it's like being drunk. All right, my dear, let's go as far as that corner."

We said good-bye and for a minute stood there on the corner without parting, just looking around, taking in the forgotten smells and colors on the street.

Unnoticed, the day had ended. Everything around us, from the outlines of the buildings to the silhouettes of the people running along the streets, had already softened and sunk into darkness. The lines had lost their sharpness, the colors had moistened and faded away. Or maybe it only seemed so because of our tears.

Anna was wracked with sobs. I stood beside her, supporting her by the elbow and feeling a salty, burning moisture gathering in my own eyes as well. To shake myself free of tears (I was still fool enough back then to feel ashamed of my weakness), I quickly tossed my head back to the sky.

At long last, after a year and a half of imprisonment, I could see the sky again, see it whole from end to end. It was broad and bright and laced with the smells of spring and an anguishing evening freshness. Streams of light blue poured from it, flooding the neighborhood. Suddenly the space took on a different color; it gleamed with fire and turned iridescent.

Above us, above all of Russia, a new victory salute now filled the air!

RETURN

It was late at night when I got back home. Toward evening the weather had worsened and a strong wind, stiff and smelling of melted snow, had struck me within two steps of the entrance, lashing me in the face and nearly knocking me off my feet.

After giving us back our things, the quartermaster had called Anna and me "lampwicks," a term they had back in prison for scrawny, burnt-out cases. It was the right word. There are any number of jokes on the subject in camp. Like this dialogue, for instance, between two prison lampwicks. "Hey," one of them says, "I really need some fresh air. What do you say we go see . . . the ladies?" "All right," the other one answers, "just as long as the wind ain't blowing."

No wonder I remembered the joke: I was one of them myself now. Stumbling and gripping the wall of the house for support, I made the last few meters of the trip with difficulty. I entered the familiar doorway and ran right into my mother.

When the first burst of emotions had subsided, she turned to me, wiped the tears off her cheeks and lashes, and said: "I was worried something had happened to you on the way. I was about to go looking for you."

"You mean you knew I was leaving?" I was dumfounded. "They don't let anybody know about that beforehand."

"I called there just this morning."

"You can call there? Can anybody do that?"

"I don't know about everybody." She smiled vaguely. "An acquaintance of mine set it up. From the Ministry. I wanted to find out how you were and see if I could bring you a little parcel with some Crimean Cahors wine. It's very good for you, you know. Very 'medicinal.' "

I never thought a great deal of my mother, but she did have one quality I must make note of here. All during my stay in prison, in every kind of weather, she had brought me parcels. Think of it: in hungry, impoverished wartime Moscow she'd found a way of getting me milk and fruits. And even some "medicinal" Cahors wine!

I remember, during the first few days after my arrest (I was in the custody of the regional militia then, waiting for my dispatch to prison), they had brought me a bundle of provisions: apples, sugar, sausage. Any parcel was cause for celebration in prison, especially for me. I hadn't expected anything at all! I had thrown myself at the little window (luckily it didn't have a barrier) and, pulling myself up by the bars, had quickly looked outside. The streets were snowbound and nearly deserted. A turbid, daybreak storm was howling overhead and through the stringy, freezing wisps of smoke and snow I'd seen the small figure of a woman moving off into the distance. She was dragging herself along, bending into the wind and stumbling through the snowdrifts. She stopped and turned around, shielding herself with her sleeve against the flying snow, and I recognized her at once! The bitter thought suddenly struck me—earlier, when I'd been free, she had never shown this concern for me, and had never wanted to take even one extra step my way. It must have taken a lot for her to remember her responsibilities and show a little kindness.

Now, talking with her in the entrance, I thought about what she'd done. How could I explain this capriciousness of hers? Was that what a woman was all about?

We stood by the entrance to the elevator. I touched the door and asked: "Is it working?"

"A working elevator?" she answered. "You act like you've just dropped out of the moon."

"The moon. Exactly," I muttered. Thieves believe that when a man dies he goes to the moon. Well, I'd been there and back.

"Let's go," she said. "You don't look well. You must lie down."

Following me up the stairs in the dirt-sprinkled darkness, she added: "There have been some changes in the apartment, so don't be surprised."

"What changes?"

"There's another family living with us now."

"How did that happen?" The news hurt.

"Well, my dear"—she shrugged her shoulders—"you weren't here, you know. The apartment was empty so they decided to 'condense' the living space."

"But you were here!"

"What could I do?" She brushed it aside. "You know how hard it is for me. I can't be everywhere at once—for two houses!"

"So, they condensed us," I said. "That's that. Is it a big family?"

"It's not small."

She stopped short and leaned against the handrails to catch her breath. "Some fellow with his mother, his wife, and a small daughter."

"Who is he?"

"I don't know. His name is Pyotr Yakovlevich Yagudas. A Ukrainian, apparently. And a swindler for sure! He walks around in a major's uniform and has nothing whatever to do with the army. A real swindler, mark my words! God knows what he does for a living."

"What's your guess?"

"Shady deals of some sort. But wait, you'll see for yourself."

They had "condensed" us, all right. Of our three rooms only one had been left to my disposal and that was loaded with furniture from all over the apartment: chairs, wardrobes, bookshelves. I was continually knocking over something. For quite a while the things kept interfering with my freedom of movement and barely giving me enough room to breathe.

Soon after I arrived my new neighbor suggested I sell the surplus. I agreed, and he quickly found buyers. Before I knew it, the room had been cleared out and made fit to live in again. The operation had another advantage—I'd done rather well by the sale and, for a while at least, didn't have to worry about money.

Yagudas demanded a five percent commission. "It's not much," as he put it, "I ought to ask for more, but we're neighbors! One's own people, after all. Anyway, my Party conscience wouldn't let me profit by the misery of others."

Portly, puffy-faced, with glossy jowls and a thin, almost lipless mouth, this neighbor of mine cut quite a figure. Every part of him exuded the kind of theatrical nobility most often associated with scoundrels and cardsharps on the stage. He moved with an exaggerated sense of self-importance and spoke slowly and weightily on any number of subjects, chief among them his own Party conscience.

What he did for a living was totally beyond me. Yagudas' affairs were secret, and his contacts and acquaintances of the most varied kinds imaginable. Quite often his guests would be military men, officers usually, as pompous and well fed as himself. "We are Communists!" you could hear him booming from behind the wall. "And don't you forget it! What distinguishes a Communist from a normal man? His Communist conscience, that's what! And what does that mean? It means that, for us, there is nothing more important than 'the Idea.' We are all warriors in its cause—soldiers of the Party! Some at the front, some in the rear, it's of little consequence where. Indeed, who can really say where the task is harder or the risk greater? At the front even an idiot can find glory, but for us, in the rear, heroism holds its tongue and goes unnoticed."

Civilians would come to the house as well—pushy and bright, with sharp and slippery eyes. Yagudas would hold brief and obscure conversations with them. Only rarely, through the muttering, would any of his ponderous words come clear: "What I said goes! A nominal price, you understand? And not a kopeck more. And don't try to play on my conscience."

Almost every tirade would end with the stereotyped phrase: "We are Communists!"

Who were they, I would wonder, turning in my bed. Who were these people? Speculators? Scoundrels? Or really Communists, Party members of a new breed?

At the time I was doing some hard thinking about a lot of things: about myself, about the world around me. The more closely I looked at the world, the more convinced I became that it was impure and unjust and totally unfit for the weak. The very same rules held sway here, the very same implacable laws as in the prison camp itself.

I had more than enough time to think. I was living alone then, without friends or acquaintances. Almost all of my relatives had been evacuated from Moscow. And, after visiting me regularly for a week and reassuring herself that I was well, my mother as usual disappeared.

I rested all alone in bed, regaining my strength; I pored over book after book, thought a great deal about what I had gone through, and wrote poems. I had hardly any contact with Yagudas' family, except for rare visits from his little nine-year-old daughter, Natasha.

"How come you're always lying there?" she would ask as she entered my room. "Are you sick?"

"Of course not," I'd say, closing the book and smiling. "Hardly at all now."

And another time: "Hey, are you—shady?"

"What do you mean, shady?" I didn't understand.

"You know, a shady person. That's what everybody says."

"Who's everybody?"

"Papa, Mama, Grandmother, everybody. They say you're shady. And—what's the word? Wait . . ."

She fell silent, blinking. Then, with an effort, she uttered: "A fel-on!"

"Really?" I screwed up my eyes. "What else do they say?"

"They talk about living space."

The door squeaked open and the trembling face of an old lady squeezed through the crack. "Natashka," she shouted, "you mean girl, fooling around in here and not giving people a moment's rest. You come right here! March! Akh, you're such a reprobate."

Late that night (I was already undressed and preparing for bed) a knock came at the door. It's Yagudas, I decided. He's probably come to explain himself. The little kid blabbed and now he's feeling bad about it.

It didn't turn out to be Yagudas, though. A mailman stood in the half-dark entrance. He took a thick white envelope out of his bag, extended it to me and said: "Sign for it."

"What is it?" I asked with surprise.

"A summons from the Military Registration and Enlistment Center."

THE DEVIL'S WORK

I was drafted into the army in July of '44 (I'd just turned eighteen) and assigned to the cavalry the instant I appeared at the offices of the Military Enlistment and Recruitment Center.

Apparently one of the members of the selection commission, a gray-mustached major in a Circassian coat laden with military decorations, had once known my father. He had served with him somewhere or other and attended his lectures at the Academy. Smiling and filtering the smoke from his cigarette through his mustache, he looked me over carefully and said: "A man of the Don by birth, I see. A real Cossack." He screwed up his eyes. "A little flea-bitten, I'll grant you. Not like your father, no indeed. But so what? You'll adapt; we've got the right kind of grub. The breeding's there and that's what counts!"

Thanks to him I was assigned to the Eighth Cossack Corps and left soon after in a noisy party of recruits. And so, still fresh from prison and shaky from my recent illness, I went straight into the ranks of the Red Cavalry. The major assumed that military service and a crack at some action had been my one and only dream. In fact, the only thing I'd ever really wanted, the only thing I'd ever longed and thirsted for, was a little peace and quiet.

There was no peace to be had. The same went for battle heroics, however. The front was leagues away by then, cutting across the west of Europe and bearing down somewhere near the German border. Our reserve unit continually found itself in the "second echelon," moving right behind the war. Far from seeing any real action, we were destined to a dismal garrison life in the remote little villages of Moldavia and Polesye, enlivened only by rare skirmishes with Nazi partisans, patrol duty, and endless precision drills.

The drills were always annoyingly the same. Every day from the dark of morning, before the trumpeters even signaled the dawn, to the dark of night, we'd toil through our duties on foot and on horse. Exhausting as they were for me, they did have their good points. As time went by, I learned the fundamentals of hand-to-hand combat and the proper use of a side arm.

Our squadron commander, Saraev the Kalmyk—"the Devil Himself," as we nicknamed him—once told me after our usual exercises: "Even though you're scum like the rest of them, you try. You can hack away like the devil himself! There's a rage inside you, and I commend it!"

The next time out, he showed me some cunning techniques with the saber and knife. The knife was a favorite weapon of his. He especially valued the ability to throw it, to "score" with it from a distance. Every time he'd run me through the proper moves, he'd paraphrase Suvorov's famous remark: "Bullets are fools, but blades are fine fellows!"

Saraev was a curious character: thickset, shortish, and bow-legged, he reminded me somehow of a spider, especially when he walked, swaying back and forth with his legs set firmly far apart. He had the personality to match, too: secretive, hot-tempered, and distinctly unfriendly. He hounded us mercilessly all through our training, finding fault with every trifle. Negligence was the one sin he could never forgive.

"Look how you're mounted!" he'd shout at one of us during our drill. "It's the devil himself! Don't curl in your toes, work with the legs, the legs! You're sitting like a dog on a fence. It's enough to make me sick." Then he'd ruthlessly wheel in the guilty detail.

"You're all scum," he'd conclude with a grimace. "If there's one thing in the whole world worth the bother, it's a horse. They have pure souls, free of sham and deceit. That's why I love them. A man is dung. You have to club a man and cherish a horse."

As a matter of fact, he did love horses, deeply and selflessly. One look at them and his brown leathery face would soften, the wrinkles would melt away, the eyes would moisten and turn warm.

I saw that look on Saraev a number of times by the horse lines. He'd be feeding his mouse-brown Turkmenian mount with bread, muttering and whispering—almost singing under his breath—into its trembling velvet ear.

That's how I remember the man the last time I ever saw him, the day our squadron was abruptly transferred on emergency alert to the neighboring region.

In a clatter of hoofs, making our saddles creak and kicking up hot dust, a hundred of us set off at a gallop. It was a cloudless, oppressively hot day, smelling of honey and ripe grasses. Thick blue dusty crops of oats lapped along the sides of the road.

I was riding in the front by the side of the column. From there I could see the thick, sweat-soaked back of the squadron commander and the glossy, foam-covered croup of his stallion. Saraev stopped at a fork in the road, turned his horse sharply, and raising his hand, shouted:

"Squa-a-a-dron, halt!"

The political commissar came up to him at a gallop. I heard their brief exchange.

"It's the heat," the Commander said. "We have to take a break. Let the horses cool off a little and have something to eat. Look at those oats! It'll be a real holiday for them."

"We'll be late if we do," the Commissar said doubtfully. "Our orders are to appear at fourteen hundred hours and it's now—" He pulled up the sleeve of his field shirt and took a quick look at his watch. "It's now just a little past one. And we still have at least fifteen kilometers to go."

"Relax." The Kalmyk brushed it aside. "We'll get there somehow. God knows what nonsense headquarters'll cook up next. It's the devil himself! You expect me to burn up the horses on account of that?"

We quickly dismounted, unbridled the horses, and left them in the field. Saraev stood quietly by the side of the road while they grazed, smoking and smiling and pursing his lips.

Our squadron arrived late. The section we were supposed to have joined had taken off long ago without waiting up for us. The following day Saraev himself disappeared. He was arrested and court-martialed for breach of duty. What happened to him after that I don't know. I never saw him again.

One more thing about the devil himself. The real one, that is, that I met up with in the virgin forests of Belovezhk.

It happened at night, toward autumn, in a small village in the woods that our cavalry patrol accidentally came upon. We galloped through the sleepy streets, past the fences and the darkened huts. My friend, the forelocked Asmolov, private first class, looked around and said with a sigh: "It's quiet. Just like back at home, on the farm. I used to go outside with a small accordion. . . . God, it was good! There wasn't a war to worry about back then, or army service."

He fidgeted a little in the saddle and then, pulling on the reins: "What I wouldn't do for a little home-brew right now."

Suddenly, we all wanted a drink. We combed through the village, knocking at windows, asking passers-by to sell us a bottle—just one little bottle. But there wasn't a drop of home-brew to be found. Finally an old man gave us the word. "There's nothing here, gentlemen. They took everything a long time ago. The Germans came and took, the bandits came and took. Even our own soldiers—them, too."

"That's impossible," I muttered in bewilderment. "Look, someone's got to have some. We're not going to argue over the price. Come on, old man, think!"

"I don't know, gentlemen. . . ."

The old man grabbed his beard, rumpled it thoughtfully, and raised his ragged eyebrows.

"Maybe the witch . . ."

"What witch?" Asmolov asked with surprise and a little smirk.

"There's one living here," the old man said. "Tells fortunes, makes potions."

"Where does she live?"

"Not far. Just beyond the ravine."

"Will you take us there?" I asked, smoothing the neck of my horse. "We'll all drink it together."

"No!" the old man shot back. "No, I'm afraid."

"What's there to be afraid of, you old fool?"

"A dragon flies to her in the night."

"A dragon?" someone behind me drawled in disbelief. "Hey, muzhik, what're you trying to pull? Knock it off." "Don't laugh," the old man answered sternly. "Don't laugh. Go there—you'll see." "All right," they said. "How do we get there?" "To the right," the old man said. "Turn at that lane, there'll be a deserted field full of weeds with a ravine right behind it. The witch's hut's on the other side. She's alone there. Don't get lost." "Well, what do you say, men?" I turned back to the platoon. (I was the oldest and took command.) "Do we go see the witch?" "What're we waiting for?" said Asmolov, straightening his reins. "For a shot of vodka I'd go straight to hell!"

It was late when we got there. The slanting, rosy strip of the sunset was smoldering far behind the crest of the ravine, making the "witch's" hut seem flat and black, like some illustration from a half-forgotten children's book.

In one of the windows a small orange fire glimmered. The hut was surrounded by a swarm of shaggy blue shadows that swirled in the bushes and streamed down to the gap, flooding it to the brim with a cold impenetrable darkness that smelled of decay. Advancing carefully along the rickety planked footways, the horses twitched their anxious ears and snorted as they nibbled at their reins.

"What a place," Asmolov muttered. "I don't like it, boys."

He pulled out his rifle and drew the bolt with a dry clank.

"What're you up to?" I turned to him. "Scared of the devil himself?"

"Just in case." He grinned. "Just in case."

We drew near the hut, dismounted, and looked inside the little window. There, in the semidarkness, something moved and rustled in a blaze of crimson reflections. Exactly what, though, we couldn't tell.

"Well, well," Asmolov said, "it's the devil's old lady, telling fortunes."

With a stroke from the butt of his carbine, he knocked at

the window frame. Inside, a dark face moved toward the glass, loomed for a second, and disappeared. Then the bolt on the door started to squeak. He went to the porch and saw the witch.

Hunchbacked and wrinkled, with a bent nose and a hand like a dried bird's claw clutching a branchy crutch, she looked like she'd come straight from the pages of an old fairy tale. She peered at us from beneath her brows and asked us with a wink: "Looking for vodka, soldier boys?"

"You got any?" Asmolov moved toward her.

"I've got some," she mumbled, "I've got everything. Vodka and onion and cucumbers. Wait a minute, I'll be right back."

She whisked behind the door and looked out again.

"Don't deceive me, though, I'm just an orphan."

"What're you talking about, old woman?" Asmolov said, tossing his rifle behind his back. He had already calmed down and was clearly having himself a good time. "We'll pay you fair and square, don't you worry about that. How much do you want?"

"Two rubles for half a liter."

"Sold." The bills rustled in his hand. "Give us a whole liter. And something to eat, too."

We found ourselves a comfortable spot on the edge of the ravine and drank. Night swirled all around, enveloping us in silence. It was good to lie there beneath the stars in the slippery, silky grass.

"Beats me what kind of witch she was," Asmolov said, munching on a cucumber. "It's all nonsense, anyway. Making a mint off people's ignorance. She makes a first-class vodka, though, I'll give her that. Real topnotch stuff!"

Suddenly he stopped, stood up and turned rigid. His jaw hung open and little cucumber seeds scattered from his mouth.

"Look, boys," he whispered. "There, over the hut. What is it?"

A glittering whirlwind of fire swept through the darkness, swirled and coiled above the roof of the hut, and, trembling into small particles, disappeared down the chimney. We were all silent for some time. Struck dumb, in fact. Then, with a stammer, I said, "You really think what they said about the dragon is true?"

There we were, at the end of a great war, in the middle of the twentieth century, looking at something like this. It seemed like a bad dream. The others felt the same. I wanted to wake up and shake myself free of delusions. We all began to move at once, talking loudly and animatedly. Responding to the voices, the horses grazing nearby started to neigh.

"Nonsense," Asmolov repeated, shaking a curly forelock. "An old lady's tricks."

"Then how in the hell did she pull it off?" exclaimed a gloomy youth called Sourpuss. "The fire didn't come out of the chimney, you know. It was the other way round. From the sky. I saw the whole thing."

"Who the hell knows?" Asmolov spread his hands in confusion.

"Exactly." I smiled.

"I'm going to check out that witch," Asmolov muttered, getting up and brushing the dirt off his field shirt, "and find out just what she's doing down there."

He set off for the hut at a waddle and then stopped in confusion. The Cossacks started to laugh. Asmolov ripped the carbine from his shoulder and fired at random, into the sky, right at a lilac star twinkling above the roof.

He fired and the star went out.

A greenish glow spread in the East. Dawn had come.

So much for my army life. I've said it already: no great deeds, no major events. The war barely touched me as it passed. The major events were still to come, in peacetime, after I'd been demobilized and returned to Moscow.

FLIGHT

I came back a strong, matured man, somewhat the rougher for wear. My mother took one look at me and threw up her hands.

"You're just like your father," she cried, "the same walk, the same look in your eyes. The only thing missing is the medals!"

"Just my bad luck," I joked.

"Quite the opposite," she said seriously. "The same thing might have happened to you that happened to Andrey. You know, don't you"—she started to cry—"they decorated him posthumously?" A bit later she added: "What're you planning to do now? Go to school? Get a job someplace?"

"Both," I said.

"Right," she approved. "It's really time to stand up on your own two feet! Dmitry Stakhevich Moor talks about you all the time, by the way. Go to him right away, he's a laureate of the Stalin Prize, a member of the governing board of the Writers' Union. A big man. He'll help you."

Thanks to my old teacher, I soon found work in the publicity department of the Stalin Automobile Factory (since renamed the Likhachev Factory), the largest of its kind in the capital. At the same time I began attending the Fine Arts Studio of the All-Union Central Council of Trade Unions, staffed, along with Moor, by such outstanding masters and teachers as Alyakrinsky, Ryazhsky, and Yuon. It was beginning to look like everything was going my way. After a multitude of misfortunes and ordeals, my life had finally begun to shape up.

The work was boring enough, but I didn't mind. I was working on colored advertising catalogues, and my studies were going well. At an exhibition of student works from the Illustrative-Poster Graphics Class, several of my prints were approved by the Artists' Soviet and received critical mention. The Board of Directors of the Trekhgornyi Textile Center purchased one of my watercolors of a victory salute (a field of bright fires against a blue background) for a handsome sum. And, before too long, a dress fabric based on my design went on sale.

At the same time I received my first publishing assignment —a rather important professional order for a series of illustrations to accompany the collected work of the famous folklorist and storyteller Afanasev.

"You're really coming along, old man," the young artist Aleksei Krainov said with a smile, respectfully and a little jealously. We were working together in the publicity department. "Half of Moscow is traipsing around in your cotton prints, orders are pouring in from everywhere. Lucky! Don't get too proud, though, or go around giving yourself airs."

As soon as I'd started work I'd made friends with him and with another graphic artist, thin and big-nosed David Gatlober. Our similar interests and creative schemes brought us together. There was a great deal in our pasts we also shared.

Like me, they had both felt the full weight of Stalinist repression. David had lost a brother in '39, and Aleksei, relatives on his mother's side. Both had been demobilized from the army just a short while before. As my seniors, they had seen some action and crossed with the troops through Europe, where they'd had a taste of another, freer way of life. Now, in our conversations, my new friends often recalled what they had seen, comparing it, often critically, with Soviet living conditions.

I hardly ever participated in those interchanges. I had something else on my mind. All of my thoughts and energies were devoted to my art, the only thing that really concerned me at the time. That and that alone! I had a weak grasp of economics, and politics I positively shunned as a dark and dismal business completely unworthy of the attention of a true artist.

I didn't manage to avoid it, though. Suddenly and ominously, politics invaded my world.

One morning I arrived at work to find Gatlober and Krainov gone. Their desks remained empty all day long and just before leaving that evening, one of the employees of the department whispered to me: "Looks like they've been arrested."

"How do you know that?" I was on my guard, whispering, too. "Did you see them?"

"Yes. They were here in the morning. Just five minutes before you got here. They'd just come in and said hello when they got called right back out."

"Where to?"

"To the office. The personnel inspector."

"Well"—I sighed with relief—"that's not so bad."

"You think so?"

"Sure. The only thing I don't get is why they're still there."

"But they're not," the girl said with a catch in her voice. "I saw a courier from the office. He told me. Apparently they were waiting for them. As soon as they got there, they were taken away. Under guard."

"But why?" I asked. "Why?"

"Who knows? For jabbering, they say. For seditious agitation. Like they belonged to some kind of underground organization or something. It's nonsense, of course. Still, I feel sorry for them. Such nice boys."

That night I had a hard time getting to sleep. Full of dark suspicions and premonitions, I paced up and down in my room, smoking one cigarette after another.

If they already suspected them of sedition, I was thinking, it's all over for them. And maybe for me, too. After all, I was their friend. As soon as the Chekists start looking into their acquaintances, they'll be coming after me.

My fears were well founded. The next day, while working on a new publicity sketch, I was called to the telephone. A soft, bearlike voice spoke right into my ear: "You free right now?"

"Not exactly," I answered. "Who's speaking?"

"The inspector of personnel."

I felt a sudden tightness in my chest. My heart stopped for a second and then started to pound. This is it, flashed through my mind. It's begun!

"I need to have a little talk with you," the inspector said. "We're reregistering passports, and there are a few points I want to clear up with yours." He fell silent, breathing heavily into the phone.

"All right," I replied, trying to speak as casually as possible. "When do you need me?"

"As soon as possible. What are you doing right now?"

"I'm finishing up a sketch."

"Sketch?" He was silent again, rustling papers. "Will it take long?"

"Twenty minutes, no more."

"Then come in twenty minutes." His voice had changed almost imperceptibly, growing slightly sterner and deeper. "Don't dawdle, though. I don't like to be kept waiting. Is that clear?"

"It's clear," I muttered, putting the phone back on the hook. "Crystal clear."

I lit a cigarette and looked around slowly, surveying the broad, brightly lit premises of the department. I knew I was seeing it for the last time and, in my thoughts, I bade it good-bye. I didn't have the luxury to linger, though. I had only twenty minutes at my disposal. Twenty minutes, one slim chance, just enough time to cross the factory, get outside, and dissolve in the crowd on the street.

Whistling lightheartedly and twirling my cigarette in my fingers, I made my way to the exit and slammed the door shut behind me. I looked around quickly. The corridor was quiet and empty. Carefully, stealthily, moving faster and faster all the time, I made my break for freedom.

I spent the night at the train station. I didn't dare go back home. Early the next morning, still without sleep, dirty, and tousled, I found a pay phone and rang my home number.

Yagudas answered. He sounded impatient and suspicious. "Where are you calling from?" he wanted to know.

"From my friends' place," I explained evasively. "I went walking yesterday and had a lot to drink. So I spent the night over at their place."

"Where's that?"

"What's the difference?" I said. "It doesn't matter. Something else does, though. Did anybody come to see me yesterday?"

"Yes," he answered softly and somewhat hesitantly.

"Who?"

"Some friend of yours."

"What did he call himself?"

"He didn't leave a name. He said he was your friend, that's all. He waited a while and then left. Promised to look in this morning. Says he has some important business to discuss with you. That's why I'm asking where you are." He waited expectantly and then said: "If your friend comes again, what'll I tell him?"

"Say hello to him for me," I said.

Yagudas was playing it close to the chest; he was clearly holding something back. The few friends I did have, he knew. This unknown "friend" of mine obviously belonged to another category. More likely than not, he came from Lubyanka, where, no doubt, the Chekists had "urgent business" with me. They were lying in wait for me now, and Yagudas was on their side. That's why he was trying so hard to find out where I was calling from.

I left the booth with a clear sense of imminent danger. They were after me, closing me in like an animal at bay. I'd have to make a break for it—it was my only chance. But how? And where? I had no papers (my passport was at the factory, in the personnel department) and almost no money. I marked time in the waiting room among the bustling crowds. At first glance, their mad rush here and there seemed mindless. Still, each of them had a special destination. Each of them was off on his own affairs, or to see relatives.

Relatives! I felt as if I'd suddenly awakened from a dream. Strange that the thought hadn't hit me before; after all, I had a relative, too, my father's older sister, Zinaida Andreevna Boldyreva. She was still living in Novocherkassk. She'd heard of me and would no doubt be glad to see me and take me in.

By nightfall I was already safely stashed away in a sleeping compartment on the Moscow-Rostov Express. All my money, down to the last kopeck, had gone for a ticket. The fact hardly bothered me, though. Two days and nights on the road, I decided, wasn't such a long time. I'd make ends meet, somehow, I'd go a little hungry, that wouldn't be so bad. The main thing was I'd get to Novocherkassk! There, at my aunt's, I'd fill up on the rich crops of the Don. Once upon a time she'd helped my parents; now she'd help me. She'd hide me, she'd look after me, she'd keep me safe from harm.

SEARCHING FOR FOOD

At dawn Novocherkassk swam out of the ashy darkness into view: wide, sprawled along the mountain slope, and gilded by the morning sun. Before I knew it I was walking down the streets of the former capital of the All-Mighty Forces of the Don.

I had only the barest idea of my aunt's address. The one thing I remembered was that her house was somewhere in the center of town on the same street as the private Belyaevsky residence. I also knew that the name of the street had been changed from Ratnaya to Red Army Street. The information was scanty, but for Novocherkassk it turned out to be more than enough.

The first old man I ran into (dressed in a faded Cossack service cap and wide trousers tucked into thick, knitted socks) eagerly explained how to get to the home of the Boldyrevs in great detail.

"It was a rich private residence once upon a time," he remarked, puffing at his curved pipe. "Now there's nothing left to look at." He screwed up his eyes and spat into the dust. "It's a dirty shame. Once there was one owner, now there are forty. Everybody's boss and there's nobody to send them all to hell."

As a matter of fact, the home did look slovenly and run-down. The facade was dirt-spattered and rusty with dampness, the main entrance was nailed up with boards. Linen had been hung out to dry on the curved grating of the yard. The women gathered here in a crowd to wrangle and gossip and scatter their sunflower seeds.

"Zinaida Boldyreva?" one of them drawled thoughtfully. "I haven't been here too long myself. Who is she?"

"She used to own the place," I said. "You mean you never heard of her?"

"Oh, the former owner!" she laughed. "Sure I know her. Andreevna. What do you want her for?"

"Business," I said drily.

"Well, then go upstairs."

"Where?" I asked, looking at the windows on the second floor.

"Right at the top," the woman explained. She broke into a laugh again, exposing her large, stained horse teeth. "Their mansion's in the garret, right under the roof!"

I went up a rickety, narrow staircase to the garret. I had trouble seeing the door in the semidarkness. I stumbled into it and suddenly caught the thick, inexpressibly sweet smell of fried potatoes. The aroma was intoxicating (it had been almost three days since I'd eaten, after all) and, entering the spacious, tidy room, I suddenly grew weak. I leaned against the side of the door and brushed the perspiration from my brow.

My head was spinning and I could feel the nausea rising in my throat. That's probably why at first I didn't notice the woman at the far end of the room. Short and gray-haired, in an old dark dress and shawl, she stood over a frying pan by the table.

"Hello," I said. "We finally meet. I'm Trifonov. Evgeny Andreevich's son."

"Evgeny's boy?"

She trembled, fumbled for the pince-nez on the table, and raised them to her eyes. "Which one are you? Andrey?"

"No," I answered, looking sideways at the pan and swallowing hard. "The other one."

She studied me for a moment. Then, narrowing her eyes and pursing her lips, she said guardedly: "Evgeny's boy. All right then, where were you living in Moscow?"

"Depends on when," I muttered.

"What do you mean 'when'?" She frowned. "I'm asking you, where did you live?"

"Different places," I replied, feeling uneasy and confused. I had expected a different kind of reception—certainly not an interrogation like this. "While my father was alive we almost always lived outside the city."

"Outside?"

"Yes, by Kratovo Station. That's along Kazansky Road. Then I moved to my mother's."

"And what's her address?"

I named the street and the number of the house. She was silent for a while and then, with a gesture exactly like my father's, she removed her pince-nez, breathed on them, and slowly wiped the lenses.

I waited for her to smile, to thaw, to invite me to have something to eat, to ask if I was hungry or not. She had something else in mind.

"Where are your papers?"

"Listen, Auntie," I said, "don't you believe me? Or are you afraid of something?"

"Of course not," she said. "That's not it. I want to have a look, that's all, just in case—"

"In case of what?" I interrupted her.

"A lot of things. They might suddenly come to check!"

"Well, if it comes to that, then I'll show you my papers. Or do you need to see them right now?"

"Yes," she said. "Yes. Right now."

I looked her straight in the eye and realized I had nothing left to hope for. She wouldn't take me in, she wouldn't save me, she wouldn't hide me. She was afraid! Afraid of everything. She was sick with terror. It had obviously been a long time since she'd believed in anything.

Without another word, I turned sharply, flung open the door, and went down the stairs, trailed by the intoxicating and tormenting fragrance of food.

Slowly, on cotton legs, I made my way to the train station. I killed time there hunting for cigarette butts on the platform and greedily drinking in the smoke. Then, attracted by a crowd of speculators boarding the Rostov electric train, I followed them and jumped on myself.

I didn't know where I was going or why. It was all the same

to me now. Desperate and homeless, I felt at a dead end. The situation was hopeless. I didn't have the passport to get a job; I had nowhere to live and nothing to live on. My only recourse now was to surrender to the police. And, who knows, if my recollections of camp and the prison hospital hadn't been so vivid, that's just what I might have done. But no, there was no way I could ever go back. Better to die, I was thinking as I stood on the crowded platform of the train, die beneath a fence, beneath a bush somewhere, just as long as it wasn't in jail, as long as I was free and on the outside.

That was, essentially, a thought of suicide, still undeveloped and unspoken, but a clear intention all the same. Strange as it may seem, the only thing that kept me from acting on it was hunger. I was just too hungry to die.

It was Saturday, a market day. The people I'd been traveling with (residents of Novocherkassk, mainly, and the surrounding large Cossack villages) were rushing to The Import, the central market of Rostov. All the conversations in the car dealt with produce and the price of goods. Eavesdropping on them, I decided to visit The Import myself. There would always be time to die; the main thing right now was to find something to eat!

I spent the better part of that day knocking around the market, waiting for the right opportunity, which, however, never materialized. The local dealers were hardened types, shrewd and sharp-eyed and well able to hustle anyone they wanted to.

I just didn't have the knack—I found that out soon enough—or the vaguest idea of what to do next. Weak and frustrated, I stopped to lean on a telegraph post. My lips were baked and cracking, my eyes were pinched with sweat. Dimly, I saw the edge of a wooden stall, a pile of boxes and sacks, and, beside them, the sweaty red face of an old woman selling fish fillets.

"Come and get 'em while they're hot!" she shouted in a monotone. "Catfish fillets. The real thing! Cooked in sunflower seed oil!"

The old lady was doing a great business. The pockets of her tattered jacket bulged with cash. One of them, apparently, had a hole and the money had been falling into the lining; her pocket positively sagged with the weight.

Someone from behind touched me lightly on the sleeve. I turned around and saw a rather skinny fellow with a snub nose, white eyebrows, and bangs.

"You grazing?" he asked with a wink. He'd clearly taken me for one of his own. "What do you say, want to do a little threshing?"

At the time I still had a pretty weak grasp of thieves' jargon. But that didn't keep me from catching the general drift of his words. Trying to look like an experienced thief, I said: "Sure I can thresh. Nice half-kopeck coins, just begging to be swiped."

"Want to team up?" the fellow said quickly.

My life as a thief had begun.

FIRST THEFT

One's first theft, like first love, is an unforgettable experience. No wonder that distant June day has been engraved so deeply in my mind. I remember it perfectly, in every detail. I remember how my new friend whispered in my ear: "Keep an eye out and distract them."

And how, in confusion, I'd replied: "How do you keep that bitch distracted?"

"Figure it out for yourself. Do a little arguing, pick away at something. Only get a move on, don't waste time!"

He looked like he was on springs, twitching and darting glances all around. He spoke in a quick and muffled voice: "It's an easy touch. We'll do it quick. Then we'll meet down by the shore, by the backwater, where the den hangs out. Ask anybody for Lenka the Farmer. They'll show you."

I nodded in agreement. Then, striding up to the old lady and playing a little with my brow, I asked her nonchalantly: "How much you selling them for, *mamasha?*"

"Ten rubles for two," she answered. "Hot, the real thing . . ."

"The real thing, huh?" I screwed up my eyes. "You talk a good game, but you deal in trash!"

Her face contorted, her brows lifted angrily, her eyes bulged. "What?" she asked, her hands on her hips. "Who's dealing rotten goods?"

She advanced on me, garbling her words.

"You saying *I* am? You? . . . Trash? . . . You? . . ."

While she raged, the boy with the bangs got to work. He stole up from behind and squatted down. A razor gleamed in his hand. The rest happened in a flash.

Delicately, with the tips of his fingers, he lifted the flap of the old lady's jacket and felt for the colored lining, heavy with cash. He drew it off slightly, measured it with his eye, and, with a smooth, decisive slash of the razor, cut it on the side.

A thick rain of crumpled ten-ruble notes fell right into the dust.

Another boy, dark-faced, with a checkered little cap cocked over his ear, appeared from out of nowhere. He squatted down next to the Farmer and helped him gather the scattered bills. Then they both darted behind the corner of the stall.

On his way out, the dark one turned around, gave me a conspiratorial wink, and pointed somewhere off into the distance toward a light blue shimmering strip of water.

The boys were calling me to the curve of the Don! Conciliatingly, I said: "Look, old lady, cool down, will you? I wasn't talking about you personally, just, you know, in general." With that I quickly stepped aside and plunged into the crowd.

A minute later, clear of the fish stalls, I heard a heart-rending howl. The lady had discovered her loss and was wailing for the whole town to hear.

I experienced no torments of conscience whatsoever. Quite the contrary. I was a hardened man, embittered at the whole world and everybody in it. I elbowed my way through the market and walked along the shore of the Don. I was headed for the thieves. My path lay clearly before me now. Fate itself had shown me the way.

My first steps along the path had been mere accidents, but from that moment on, no thought of changing my course ever entered my mind. The only thing that troubled me was my upcoming encounter with the "den," and the secret world of the thieves. What kind of reception would they give me?

I had no trouble finding them; they'd set up camp on a sandy spit of land washed by the dirty river waters, iridescent with black oil.

The den was "in session"—a peaceful enough scene from where I stood. Stretched out on the sand, the thieves were eating and drinking. Several of them had offered their tattooed stomachs and shoulders to the sun for a tan. Others sat in a circle playing cards to the crackle of strange, abrupt incantations: "I'm going for the kitty! Don't try to cover, four on the side and you're out!"

There were some women loitering around, women thieves, apparently, or prostitutes—maybe just friends of the thieves.

Suddenly a whitish head with tousled bangs popped out from behind an overturned wooden barge.

"Hey!" the Farmer shouted, whistling through his fingers. "What happened to you? Come on over and get your share!"

I drew near the boat, hunger clutching at my guts, my mouth filling with saliva. The boys were having a feast.

Tomatoes, sausage links, great, spongy hunks of bread were all heaped up on a piece of newspaper spread at their feet. A yellowish sea roach glistened nearby and an open bottle of vodka shimmered and gleamed in the sun.

"I was beginning to think they'd caught you," the Farmer said. "I look and you're gone. So, how're things over there? Normal?"

"Normal," I laughed, remembering the lady merchant, her distorted face, her quivering, piercing voice.

"Good," he said. "Relax. Want a drink?"

Without waiting for an answer, he snatched a bottle (he did

everything quickly!), splashed some vodka into a glass, and passed it to me with something to eat.

Silently, thankfully, I took the glass of vodka from his hand and drank. Then, like a beast of prey, I sank my teeth into a fragrant, crunchy crust of bread.

While I ate, the boys smoked in silence. Then, one of them (the fellow in the checkered cap) said, with a barely discernible accent: "Come on, friend, let's divvy up."

He fished around in his pocket and pulled out a crumpled wad of ten-ruble notes. He smoothed them out and put them in my hand.

"Take 'em! Nine red ones. Everybody equal, right?"

"Fine with me," I agreed and lapsed into silence, looking fiercely at the soiled little papers—my first spoils as a thief.

"It's peanuts, of course," the Farmer said, interpreting my silence in his own way, "but what the hell! You get what you go for. We'll give it another try this evening and everything'll be just fine. We got ourselves a r-i-i-ich market!"

He snapped his fingers and then, looking me right in the eye, asked: "Where'd you fly in from?"

"Moscow," I answered, tightening up inside. I was terrified of making the slightest mistake.

"Ever have to moor up anyplace?"

"Sure," I said. "Moor up," I knew, meant land in prison. I remembered the term from way back and had never forgotten it. "Sure I did. Big deal."

"Where?"

"Just about everywhere," I said, lazily sticking out my lower lip. "In Butyrsky, in the Krasnaya Presna."

"I hitched up once in Moscow myself," the dark one said in a guttural drawl. "Not at the Presna, though—in Taganka. Ever hear of it?"

"Yeah," I lied. "Who hasn't?"

"Well, put it there!"

He extended an open palm for a handshake and introduced himself: "Kinto." And waited for a response.

Just as I was about to shake his hand and quickly cook up a

nickname for myself, a slow, lisping, strangely familiar voice spoke from somewhere to the side. "Chuma, is it you?"
I lifted my head and saw Snuffles.

THE SON OF A TRAMP—THAT'S BEAUTIFUL!

My first reaction was one of confusion. This unexpected meeting with an old enemy promised no good. Disclosure—the one thing I'd dreaded from the beginning—now looked inevitable.

Twisting his wet lips into a smirk, Snuffles asked: "What're you doing here, Chuma?"

"You can see for yourself," I said. "Drinking."

"Well then, come along with me," he said, "and let's drink some more. You and I've got a lot to talk about. We're old acquaintances."

I got up slowly and stumbled after him through the burning sand. His tone puzzled me. I could feel the old arrogance there, but the words sounded soft, almost friendly. It was enough to put me on my guard. Something's fishy here, I thought feverishly.

When we'd strolled far enough away, he looked at me out of the corner of his eye and said: "So, you tied up with the gang, eh? Fell in love with the thieves' life, that it? Pretty funny!"

"So it goes." I shrugged my shoulders. "That's the card I got dealt. It's too late now to change the game."

"Doesn't it frighten you?" he wanted to know.

"What's there to be afraid of?" I answered lightheartedly.

"What do you mean? All sorts of things happen to a thief."

"Come off it," I brushed it aside. "You know I don't scare easy. You remember that night at Krasnaya Presna?"

A momentary shudder twisted his face. His eyes darkened and his features sharpened. His cleft lip trembled and rose, making him look like some kind of rodent. "Listen," he said tonelessly, "why dredge up the past?" He drew me aside and moved in close. "You want to make friends with me? You want me to help you?"

"What?" I stepped back in amazement. "Make friends?" I was expecting anything but that. It put me on my guard. "Are you—serious?"

"Sure," he answered. "We don't joke around here, buddy. If you want, I'll help you, put in a good word for you. So far, the thieves don't know a thing about you. But they could find out, you know. And then, well . . ."

He stopped for a moment and then, with a glitter in his eye, repeated, "So—you want me to?"

"Of course," I said. "Sure! Only, what's in it for you?"

"Simple," he said, forcing out the words. "Forget about that business at the Presna. Don't breathe a word of it. Nowhere and to no one. Understand?"

"I got it," I said.

Fate has some real surprises in store sometimes. Snuffles had concealed that old story about the guard from the boys. Now he was in my hands too. We were even.

There was something in my face he didn't like; my smile, probably. Lowering his voice, he said threateningly: "Remember, Chuma, if you start blabbing, it'll be bad news for you. You'll just be making trouble for yourself."

"The same goes for you," I answered at once. And then, with a sharp and vengeful thrust, I added: "Remember, Snuffles, so far the thieves don't know a thing. But they could find out, you know. And then, well . . ."

"All right." He frowned, sucking the air in sharply through his clenched teeth. "In the long run, we'd both burn. What good does that do you?"

"None," I admitted.

"Then let's make a deal."

"All right," I said.

Snuffles spat out his cigarette butt and wiped his mouth. Then, whispering and winking, he said: "Now for a real drink! Only not here with all the heat and dust. I'll tell you what"—he slapped me on the shoulder—"let's go to this place I know. I'll introduce you to some people. First, though, let's get your story straight. You come from a thief family. You grew up in a den, your mother is a prostitute, your dad's a tramp from the old days, the kind they used to call 'the grays,' okay?"

"Good God," I said, "you're a real crystal gazer! Almost everything tallies. My father really did wander around here once, and he *was* a 'gray.' "

"All the better." Snuffles winked. "The son of a tramp—that's beautiful! It's got a nice ring to it. Nobody here's going to stand in your way."

The thieves' hangout was down one of the more forsaken streets of the outlying district in the basement of a two-story corner building. It was cold and stuffy inside; a thick blue haze of tobacco rose in rings above our heads. A guitar twanged intermittently to the hoarse voice of a woman singing a convict's song:

> *"Don't stand on the ice, the ice'll fall through;*
> *Don't love a thief, he'll tumble, too,*
> *A thief'll tumble and land in jail*
> *And you won't like bringing parcels."*

Giggling and wiping his palms, Snuffles said: "The thieves are having themselves a hell of a time, all right!" He dragged me to a table where two men were sitting, a heavy, mustachioed older fellow in a cowboy shirt and a stoop-shouldered, lanky type with a long face and mournfully pursed lips.

"Greetings, Cossack," Snuffles said. "When did you get here?"

"This morning," the man in the cowboy shirt replied, "on the ten o'clock to Tiflis."

"Take care of business?"

"Not completely." He made a wry face. And then, nodding in my direction, he asked: "Who's he?"

"Just flew in," Snuffles hurried to explain. "Friend of mine. Real thief family, hundred percent."

And, leaning toward the Cossack, he said something softly. I didn't catch the words: the guitarist struck a new chord and a drawling gypsy melody wafted through the arches of the basement. It was the same husky, broken-hearted voice singing:

> *"Let's not, my darling, let's not, my dear,*
> *Oh, how the first time hurts!*
> *Right on the couch, with dirty feet,*
> *Mama will whip me for sure!"*

The flow of the melody was suddenly interrupted by dance rhythms. The low rumble of the guitar thickened and re-sounded as a new, male voice joined in the song:

> *"I will not, I can not,*
> *I just can't reach!"*

The guitar stopped for a second. A single string trembled almost beyond the reach of our ears and in that ringing silence the woman responded invitingly:

> *"You're lying; yes, you will;*
> *You're lying; yes, you can!*
> *I'll bend down and you'll be a man!"*

"Go to it, Margo!" they shouted from the corner. "Go to it, Queen!"

The strings began to strum impetuously to the thunder of the stamping heels. A disorderly dance had erupted in the corner. The crowd was having a good time and the room filled with a wild gaiety and passion.

Brushing his gray mustache out of the way, the Cossack put two fingers to his mouth and shattered the air with a highwayman's whistle.

His emaciated, stoop-shouldered companion (they hadn't nicknamed him the Straw for nothing) said reproachfully: "What's with you, my friend?" He moved aside, rubbing his ear. "You're not on the Georgian highway. You're in society now. Calm down!"

The Cossack wiped his fingers on his shirt and said with a moan: "But look at what that devil of a woman is doing! How can you hold yourself in?"

"The Queen can sing, all right," someone said over my shoulder, "but screeching about it won't do any good."

"I wouldn't say that," the Straw objected, "it has its charm. That's how they all do it in the West, you know."

"What're you talking about?" The Cossack screwed up his eyes. "Straw, you love to blabber!"

"Blabber?" the Straw said. "I'm speaking as a man of art." He lifted a finger. "As an old onanist and appreciator of Esenin."

While this conversation was going on, Snuffles disappeared for a second and quickly returned, loaded with bundles and bottles. He laid them all down on the table and pulled me by the sleeve.

"Sit down, Chuma. Let's drink. Cheers!"

When we'd all been served the first course, the Straw turned to me, twirled a glass in his fingers, and asked slowly: "What's your trade, little man?"

"Different things." I hesitated.

"Got a partner?"

"The Farmer and Kinto."

"Aha," he said approvingly. "Two fine boys. They're coming along nicely. They respect the rules. Well, little man, I wish you success."

That's when Margo came over to the table. A brunette with powerful breasts tightly laced into her blouse. She sat down beside me, crossed her legs, and knitted her fingers over her raised, uncovered knee.

"I'm tired, boys," she said, stretching her big body. "Two days without sleep."

"You're sure working a lot." Snuffles snickered.

"No secret about that," the Queen answered indifferently. "Business is good, and why not?"

Batting her eyelashes and surveying the table with a glance, she lightly touched me with her elbow. "Pour us a little vodka, curly."

I was fading fast. All the drinking, the exhaustion, and agitation of that mad day were finally beginning to tell. Leaning on the edge of the table, I lowered my head and slowly drifted off. For a while I could still hear the racket, the sound of dishes, the rumble of voices. At rare intervals indistinct sentences seemed to filter through the noise from far away:

"In Tiflis, boys. It's a rotten deal."

"As an old onanist and appreciator of Esenin, I . . ."

"What got you so hoarse, Margo, the booze? Or is it the clap?"

Then everything flowed together in a jumble and sank beneath a heavy shroud. The last thing I remembered was the sight of Margo's round, sun-tanned knee, rocking just an inch in front of my face.

So much for my debut in the high society of thieves!

They gave me a perfectly friendly reception (son of a tramp—that's beautiful!) and instantly enrolled me in the ranks of the *patsany*—their term for young people still short of a mastery of their profession or any real distinction.

Being a *patsan*, in essence, was about the same thing as being a member of the Communist Party Komsomol. The next step up wouldn't be so easy. For that, one would need considerable field experience, an unsullied reputation, and the recommendations of the adult thieves.

The procedure of "elevation to the law" differs little from admission to the Communist Party. As a rule, it happens at a general meeting. The *patsan* being presented to the society gives a brief account of his life, listing every possible exploit, offering each accomplishment up to the collective judgment. If the thieves agree on a judgment and that judgment is good, one of the authoritative thieves—one of the members of the Central Committee, so to speak—rises and adjourns the convocation with the ritualistic phrase: "Look on him, thieves, and look well! Remember, the sentence isn't subject to appeal. We're all responsible for him now!"

My turn would come later in the Caucasus, before the local train thieves of the town of Groznyi. Before becoming a legitimate criminal, though, I would have to do a good deal of knocking about in the south of the country. For the present, my main concern was the choice of a craft—what kind of a thief I would be.

THE LAWS OF THE TRADE

Although there's no end to the number of professions to choose from, they do fall into three main categories, more or less: pocket theft, apartment theft, and railroad theft. Safe-cracking and armed robbery can also be added to the list.

As I've already mentioned, I began with pocket theft. That's why I put it at the top of my list. Judging solely by the income it provides, the pocket craft is usually considered, by the unenlightened, to be a trifling and insignificant affair. And indeed, in any isolated case, the take isn't all that high, but in thieves' circles it's not the result that counts so much as the artistry involved. Picking pockets demands a special knack and a most rare refinement.

In my wanderings through the pleasure dens of Rostov, I came to know quite a few talented "screen men." The term comes from the fact that every pickpocket needs some kind of screen behind which he can slip into someone else's pocket. Without it, the job would be too risky, if not impossible. The pickpocket, after all, runs his business in the harsh light of day, right under people's noses.

Basically anything can serve as a defensive cover: a service cap, a handkerchief, a sheet of newspaper. Some, it's true, reject all the standard items, choosing to work "raw" by shielding one hand with the other. No matter what, though, everybody needs a screen!

The Goat, for example, a pickpocket from the southern city of Nakhichevan, availed himself of *The Communist* magazine. He even folded it so the masthead was visible. Decked out in a stern, semimilitary khaki tunic and square glasses (made of ordinary window glass), with a fresh copy of the magazine in his hand, the Goat cut a rather imposing figure in public. One look at him and you'd have thought you were dealing with a

Secretary of the Regional Committee of the Party. Generally, he plied his trade at night in stores and movie theaters. Those who worked the trolleys, buses, or subway, on the other hand, left for "work" early in the morning and then went out once again at the end of the day.

Among the train screenmen were three women who worked together: Mymra, Shushera, and Varka. Their style was distinguished by a certain originality and flair, for in this case it was Varka's abundant rear end that did service as the traditional screen. Marking a suitable sucker in the crush and press of the trolley (a solid citizen, as a rule, neither too young nor too old), Varka would steal up to him and start snuggling, rubbing up and down with her "equipment." "Working your rear," they called it. She would apply herself till her victim had weakened completely. Then Mymra and Shushera, both of them thin, wiry, and quick as mice, would ransack the pockets of the bemused passenger, thoroughly and with dispatch.

This asset of Varka's enjoyed a certain notoriety among the local thieves and was even the subject of several songs. Later on, her adornments were to serve her in a different and purely personal venture. But more of that later.

To the ranks of the illustrious pickpockets of the south one would have to add Leo the Kike, a true master. With a circus conjurer's ease and speed he could lift watches, unfasten gold cuff links, and open any lady's bag on the fly. All the same, he had bad days just like any other businessman. At moments like that Leo would turn to me sadly and say:

"Another zero. What're you going to do? Bastards wherever you turn. Ekh, if I could only get my hands on a fat little profiteer right now. Or a spy. Spies! God, how I idolize them. No matter how big or small." And, sucking lazily on his cigarette, he'd add: "You know what the trouble with our business is? You get burned so often. Either they're giving it to you in the neck or dragging you off to the cops. That's why I love spies. They make it so easy! They like the cops about as much as we do. They're so spooked they'll jump at a squeaky wheel. Scared, but loaded. Name me a spy that doesn't have money on him." He'd screw up his eyes and heave a deep sigh.

"Ideal clients. But where in the hell are you going to find them?"

He was joking, but there was some sense to it. Pickpockets, in fact, often ·o get "burned." They're constantly being beaten or dragged off to the police station. Those were the dues you had to pay. But I wasn't about to. Sizing it all up, I decided to find myself a quieter, more modest variety of thievery.

I chose the "locksmiths"—people dealing in apartment heists. Before too long I found myself a protector in the Cossack, the same heavy, flop-eared man I'd met at Queen Margo's establishment.

He was a reliable worker with a knack for spotting the right places to hit. In fact, he took on only those apartments he'd completely researched beforehand. He had a multitude of "gun layers" or informants, many of them small repairmen like plumbers, joiners, electricians, glaziers, who spent a lot of time in different homes and could evaluate the surroundings and learn the habits and daily schedules of their owners. Other reliable informants were doormen and cooks. The Cossack especially valued the children of the cooks, who suffered from feelings of inferiority and longed for more luxurious lives. He recruited one of them in my presence. The meeting took place in a restaurant. The Cossack had arranged a fancy dinner, with cognac, fruit, caviar, bubbly mineral water, and *shashlyk.*

The fellow in question, a narrow-shouldered, pimply young man with a massive Adam's apple and girlish curls, was dressed in an excessively long jacket and excessively narrow pants. He'd clearly altered the trousers himself, with clumsy, uneven stitches. He sat down at our table, said "Hello!" (in English), boldly splashed some cognac into a goblet, and hoisted it to the light for a closer look. He was already drunk—you could see that—drunk from the mere sight of the restaurant, from the gleam of the mirrors, the flowers, the place settings.

We got down to business. The poor little fop hated his mother's employers and despised his mother even more. He eagerly gave the Cossack all the information he needed. "Sunday's the best time of all," he announced. "The owners, damn them all, leave for their dacha. And sometimes Mom takes off in the evenings for the movies. To make sure everything goes smoothly, I'll drag her there myself. Don't worry. I'll take care of it. She won't get away from me."

He demanded an advance and got it at once.

The Cossack paid his informants liberally, as a rule. After all, he recouped his expenses with interest. He only worked when sure of success. Along with the regular plan of the apartment he received molds of all its locks.

There weren't many thieves who availed themselves of conveniences like that. Generally, most heists were "jumps," thefts performed at random, accidentally, or by inspiration. Under those circumstances, of course, any locked door would do. Still, you needed special instruments: a chisel, a collection of skeleton keys, and a "Thomas," the term for a small steel crowbar. The latter is ideally suited for break-ins. One end is sharpened (when necessary, it can replace a chisel), the other is bent back and split into a kind of nail puller, perfectly suited for tearing off "ear rings"—padlocks, that is—and door hinges.

A locksmith's tools are extremely heavy and cumbersome; it takes some skill to keep them hidden. The technique of a handsome old locksmith nicknamed the Grossmeister was quite unique. He'd hide his instruments in an empty folding chess board and march peacefully along without arousing the slightest suspicion.

Jumpers of this sort work primarily by day. There are night workers as well, but they have no use for the locksmith's equipment. Doors locked on the inside by bolt and chain are basically impregnable. No skeleton or master key is going to be of any help here.

As a rule, night jumpers enter through the window. Their main obstacle then is not a lock but the glass, which they cut with a diamond. Since a diamond screeches as it cuts, jumpers often prefer to break the glass in, sticking it to a piece of paper smeared in glue so that the splinters don't tinkle or scatter as they fall. Actually, any kind of sticky substance will do. I knew of one fellow, the Mug they called him, who used cherry preserves instead of glue. Every time he'd set off on "night duty," he'd bring along a little jar of preserves. The Mug never worked without sweets. He was an epicure. I can see him now: that low forehead overgrown with hair, those protruding ears, and those slack, slowly moving jaws, perpetually munching on one thing or another.

In spite of his menacing exterior and enormous physical strength, the Mug was an unusually obliging fellow of a quite sociable turn of mind. He resorted to his strength only in extreme emergencies, as if he were afraid of it himself. I recall one occasion when the two of us were going somewhere on a jam-packed local bus. I was suffocating and drenched in perspiration. Looking worriedly at me, the Mug asked: "You hot?"

"Suffocating," I answered. "There's nothing left to breathe."

"Don't worry," he said. "I'll fix it in a minute."

As soon as the bus drew to a stop, he gave a grunt and squeezed the crowd right out of the bus like so much toothpaste from a tube.

A woman beside me started to shriek and wail. The Mug turned around in confusion and said: "Oops. Overdid it again."

I was really sorry to see him arrested. Sheer stupidity did him in. Once again, he'd "overdone it." This time, that fatal lust of his for sweets was his undoing. After breaking into a large communal apartment one night, he sneaked into the kitchen, uncovered some halvah, and forgot about everything else. There he stood, a one-kilo tin in his hands, digging around and rumbling sweetly. A man appeared in the door of the kitchen: barefoot, disheveled, his eyes white with fear. He looked at the thief for a minute in silence and then, in a whisper, said: "Hands up!"

Why those words popped into his head, I'll never know. The man was unarmed. If he'd only said something else, things would have taken a much happier turn.

The Mug reacted instantly with a thoughtless, terrible blow.

Stepping toward the window, he let loose the halvah box and struck the man squarely in the forehead, killing him instantly.

The crash of the toppling body woke up the other tenants. The doorman's whistle shrilled outside the window and others answered the call. By the time the Mug worked his way down to the ground floor, they were waiting for him.

There are other kinds of burglars, "heavyweights" they call them, who deal not with apartments but with stores. It's high-risk work freighted with complications. Large stores, especially those selling furs and jewelry, have tight security and are under constant police surveillance.

The windows and doors are reinforced with gratings and wired with sophisticated burglar alarms. A formidable defense, but far from impregnable. I knew masters of the trade who could break through any wall known to man. One of them, an old Estonian nicknamed the Mason, simply used to chisel a perfect hole right through the brickwork and carry off everything in sight. Furs, though, were his true delight. During his career, he lifted a mountain of them.

His peculiar style had the police baffled. They hadn't the vaguest idea whom they were dealing with—an experienced, hardened professional or a dilettante. Every criminal tries to cover his tracks. The Mason, on the other hand, loved to leave them in full view. At the scene of every one of his crimes, right by the hole in the wall, the investigators would find all his tools, a few empty bottles of Riesling, and the paper in which he'd wrapped his food.

It was all intentional. By leaving his "handwriting" on the wall, the Mason was throwing a challenge into the face of the police. Each clue seemed to say: "All right, boys, come and get me, if you can!" Many of his colleagues criticized him for this. "Don't fool around with the cops," they'd tell him. And they were right. It wasn't too long before the police realized they weren't dealing with a novice—the man's touch was much too clean. They took up the challenge and set to work tracking him down.

Item one: The bottles of Riesling. Clear proof that the

criminal was not a Russian. What Russian would resort to a sour brew like that instead of vodka, especially in the wee hours of the night? Item two: The unchanging pattern of behavior. An indication the thief was probably an older man. Third: The imprint of the soles. These helped define his height. And fourth: The diameter of the holes. Always the same, they showed the width of his shoulders. Judging by the ashes he left behind, they also determined the thief smoked a pipe packed with Golden Fleece. The entire police machinery was set in motion, and before too long the Mason was behind bars.

Still, his arrest was based solely on circumstantial evidence. The main evidence necessary in a court of law was still missing. And he might well have gotten off if it hadn't been for his lover.

She'd been keeping his latest haul of furs at her place. Instead of handing the goods over to speculators and fences, the foolish woman decided to handle the merchandise herself. She was stingy, and couldn't bear the thought of splitting the take with profiteers. The authorities nabbed her trying to peddle the furs in the black market. And so the career of the famous heavyweight came ingloriously to an end.

Usually all such careers ended badly; sometimes even tragically. While in the Caucasus I made the acquaintance of three fellows specializing in jewelry stores. They worked swiftly, with precision, and even, I might add, with refinement. Their last job was especially interesting.

Through their informers the boys learned that a large shipment of gold articles and women's brooches studded with precious stones had just arrived at one of the local stores. They decided to take them.

It wouldn't be easy. The store was in a crowded area, right in the center of town, bordered by a post office on one side and a restaurant on the other. At dusk the police manned a special post there, so a night job was clearly out of the question. Armed robbery was a possibility, of course, but that would be too dangerous. The regional police office was right around the corner. So much for a daytime job, too.

Besides, our specialists (two young Armenians and a Mingrelian Jew) were cultured individuals with no love of crudeness and a pronounced distaste for any kind of ruckus.

And so they worked out an ingenious solution of their own.

Every day at noon, the jewelry store closed for lunch. The salesmen would lock the door, apply a wax seal to the latch, and take off for a cafe on the other side of the street. The burglar alarm was unattached during the day, but that hardly bothered the salespeople; they could always keep an eye on the store through the window and eat in peace.

One day a large truck pulled up in front of the cafe, totally blocking the view from the window. Apparently, it had broken down. Mumbling and cursing, the driver got down from the cabin and started tinkering around with the engine. He kept it up for exactly twenty minutes. When the motor coughed back to life and the truck drove off with a rumble and a clank, the street was once again open to view, affording the people in the cafe a clear vista of the store door, now bereft of lock and seal!

Twenty minutes had been more than enough for the burglars. Dressed like salesmen in blue smocks, they'd come out of the restaurant and opened the door with ease. Cleaning out the gold and the brooches, they had put them into simple shopping bags and carried them innocently back outside, loaded them on the truck and driven away scot free.

It was a huge take. The boys, however, never managed to enjoy it. The rest of their story is a bit obscure. The only thing known for certain is that their truck (a dump truck stolen from a construction site) was found days later on the outskirts of town by a fork in the road. Five kilometers away, at an abandoned dacha in the woods, the police discovered the bodies.

All of them, including the driver, had been shot point-blank. Who had killed them? And where had the loot gone? To this day it remains a mystery.

The idea that they did each other in while divvying up the spoils seems doubtful. They just weren't that kind. Besides, there were no signs of a struggle. The bodies lay across a table right next to a bottle of cognac and some half-emptied glasses.

Undoubtedly there had been someone else. Someone who'd appeared unexpectedly, made short work of them on the spot, and stolen off with the precious bags. Several thieves expressed the completely plausible idea that the only people who could have done it were the police. The ones who'd participated in the search in the first place. Three local Georgian Chekists had been the first to arrive at the dacha. Taking the haul from the boys and seeing how valuable it was, the Chekists had probably decided to keep it for themselves. To do that, of course, they'd have to liquidate the only other witnesses, the thieves.

It was an interesting theory. Maybe even correct. But who's to say? The criminal life is a dark enterprise; anything can happen to a burglar and usually does. After giving it some thought, I decided that this was one profession I'd gladly avoid. If the life of a pickpocket led to scandal and public abuse, the locksmith's trade ended far too often in blood.

THE CHOICE IS MADE

I was still full of doubts and indecision when I ran into the Straw. (This old "appreciator of Esenin" was a celebrated safe-cracker—known in the trade as a "bear hunter.") We got to talking and, partly in jest, I mentioned that I might want to become one of his students. He smiled in reply. Then, taking a sip of his beer, he said: "Be my guest, if you insist. Just remember, my little man, it's not an easy job. You have to study for a long time. I started out under Markelyche, may he rest in peace. Ever hear of him? What a strict old codger he was! A great master! For eight years this is how he held me." He clenched his bony fist with a crackle. "Eight years without letting me do a thing of my own! Train yourself, he'd say, learn to understand. I'm preparing you to be an engineer. And he was right. Cracking safes, my friend, is a far cry from horsing around at the market."

Gazing at my drawn and withered face, he added good-naturedly: "Mull it over, young man. If the business suits you, let me know. I could use a bright boy at my side."

No, it didn't suit me. Eight years of study was the equivalent of two courses at the institute. "Too long," I said heatedly. "Too much of a bustle. And for what? You spend all those years perfecting your craft and then, one day, bam!—you're busted and behind bars."

"Right," he drawled thoughtfully. "They don't go easy on safe-crackers. They give them the full sentence, as a rule. But what are you going to do? Right now we're having a beer, enjoying nature so to speak. Come tomorrow we could both be watching the sky through a big cage."

And, with a sigh, he quoted Esenin's lines:

> *"Rus fell silent in Mordovia and Chud,*
> *Silent but unafraid.*
> *And people walk her weary roads,*
> *People in shackles,*
> *All of them killers or thieves . . ."*

We were sitting in the shade of a little public garden by the train station. It was midday, a quiet hour. There were hardly any customers in the alehouse, just a few cripples and beggars working the area. They'd gathered in a gruesome gaggle behind a little table: twisted jaws, empty eye sockets, vanished noses, scab-covered cheeks and all—to play dice, drink, and swear.

"Now there's a risk-free trade for you," the Straw muttered, looking sideways at them.

"All they have to do is beg," I agreed.

"Beg, hell," the Straw objected, "they don't just ask for money, they take it! But they always get off easy in court. 'Invalids,' they say, 'your Honor, victims, heroes of the war.' "

Suddenly the cripples started to mutter and, with a rumble of their crutches, move to the exit. On their way out, one of them, a hunchback with a dark little old lady's face, stopped by our table and exchanged a few muffled sentences with the safe-cracker. I could barely make out the words, but the conversation had something to do with an office of some kind, and a room plan drawn by the beggar at the Straw's request.

"Drop by the General's widow's place on Bogatyanovskaya Street," the hunchback said on his way out. "It's all waiting for you there."

"Remember"—the Straw lifted a finger—"precision's the word."

"Don't worry," the hunchback said with a wink. For some reason he reminded me of the witch I'd seen when I was a cavalryman in the heart of the Polessky woods.

"He's a sinister type," I said, watching him leave.

"Him?" the Straw said. "No, he's a sweetheart. You should have seen his friend, though. Had all of Rostov scared silly last year, murdering everybody in sight. He'd nab drunks at night and strangle them with his bandages."

I asked the Straw to tell me the whole story in detail, but Snuffles interrupted the conversation. Tanned, windblown, and dusty, he'd come straight from the train. With his usual mix of giggles and jitters, he announced he'd arrived from Tashkent and was about to strike out for the Caucasus.

"The resort season's just starting for safe-crackers," he said. "A real bumper crop!"

He drained his beer and licked the foam from his lips. Then, fixing me with his beady little eyes, he said: "Listen, Chuma, what do you say we go, huh? It'll give you a chance to see how safe-crackers live. I've been meaning to spring the idea on you for a long time now. What's the market here got to offer you anyway? Crushing crowds, filth, a lot of noise. . . . It's a bore, old man! We got just the life for you: on wheels all the time. Breakfast in Tashkent and dinner in Baku!"

The life of the rails tempted me with its air of novelty and romance and, without a second's thought, I accepted Snuffles' proposal right on the spot. We shook hands and agreed on the exact date of our departure.

Snuffles called for the waiter and ordered more beer and big glasses of vodka for each of us. We clinked in a friendly toast and then, stretching and straightening the knot in his tie, the Straw said: "Come on, boys, let's go outside. I'm tired of this stinking place."

We spent the whole day and evening together, roaming through the town and hopping from tavern to tavern. Just as night was about to fall we set off for the General's widow's place on Bogatyanovskaya.

Every large city in the country has its thief district, its "pit," its refuge of vice. In Tiflis, for example, it's Avlabar; in Odessa, Peresyp and Moldavanka; in Kiev, Podol; in Moscow, Sokolniki and Marina Roshcha. The focus of the criminal world in Rostov, since time immemorial, has been the Nakhichevan suburb and particularly Bogatyanovskaya Street—a nesting place for prostitutes, swindlers, and profiteers. You'll find the underground exchange here, the black market. And that's just the beginning. This exotic lane has been celebrated in legend and song—not to mention quite a few four-liners as well. "They opened an alehouse on Bogatyanovskaya," one of the songs goes, "Where all the thieves gathered in throngs. Marusya, Rita, and Raya were there. Even Kostya, the Slob, came along."

Along with the alehouses a number of cozy little nooks, doss houses, secret haunts, and ditches are there to serve a thief's every need. "Ditches" are homes where fences and speculators run their business. Fences, incidentally, go by another, more poetic name, which seems to suit them better. They call them "Cains."

The ditch we visited belonged to a rather stately lady, the widow of a general who'd been a great war supplier during the Second World War. She'd inherited the home from him and owned all the rooms herself.

It was a comfortable little place, nestled in a lilac thicket at the end of a yard, surrounded by high fences. A wicket gate by the main entrance led out to the neighboring lanes, and we passed through it into the garden.

"Everything's been seen to," the Straw muttered, leading us to the house past the moist, fragrant bushes along the way, "with intelligence and, above all, taste."

He tore off a sprig of lilac, smelled it, and almost seemed to sob with emotion.

"A woman of class. You'll like her, boys. A born criminal! Well read and cultured to boot." The Straw sighed. "Ah, if only I weren't an onanist."

Indeed, the widow was as charming as he'd promised. A plump, mellow woman in a lace cap and a rustling silk dress, she received us cordially and treated us to an excellent home-made brandy. "If you're not in a hurry," she said with a smile, "do stay to dinner. We'll be having pancakes with sour cream and nice young ladies. . . ."

When dinner was over, I went outside and lighted a cigarette. After slowly touring the grounds I leaned against the wall and listened unthinking to the rustling of the night.

I was standing under a curtained little window open to the breeze. A greenish, murky light filtered through the blinds and softly spilled along the grass and bushes. Suddenly the lilac brightened: thick, grainy clusters stood out in sharp relief from the semidarkness. I raised my head and saw a male figure in the window. Someone had drawn the blinds aside and was watching me from above.

It was a bald old man with steel-frame glasses and sunken cheeks. Scratching his scanty beard, he observed me for a while in silence and then asked in a strained whisper: "Who are you? One of them? One of the high thieves, eh?"

"I'm one of them," I said.

It seemed like a strange question to me. As strange as the tone in which it had been asked. He didn't tally with the surroundings, with the character of the entire ditch.

"And who are you?"

"That doesn't matter," he said quickly. "That's of no significance whatsoever." Sitting down on the window sill, he added: "Got a smoke? If you don't mind, that is."

"Sure," I replied, passing him my pack of Belomors.

He quickly shook out a cigarette from the pack. He took a long time lighting up, though, breaking the matches with his trembling fingers. Finally he succeeded and took a hungry drag. Looking sharply into the thickets of the garden, into the wet, rustling darkness, he said, "I can't sleep. How can you around here anyway? There's always somebody walking, breathing, rustling. Listen! Do you hear it?"

His sharp-edged face, furrowed with wrinkles, twitched and twisted. I looked deep into his dilated eyes and couldn't find the barest trace of a thought—just naked fear and an agonized and feverish confusion.

"Listen, listen! There, to the left of the house. By the fence. Can't you hear it?"

"No," I said, "I can't. Who are you afraid of anyway?"

"Them," he answered.

"Them?"

"You mean you don't understand?" He screwed up his face and straightened his glasses.

"Nonsense," I replied. "It's safe here. Everything's been seen to with intelligence and taste."

"We might argue the taste part," he muttered, "but that's unimportant. And as for intelligence, well, they're short on that, too, believe me! There aren't any fools at work in those agencies, no sir, no fools. I knew a lot of clever Chekists. Even met Dzherzhinsky himself once."

He was beginning to make me feel a little uncomfortable. Suppressing a vague sense of confusion and irritation, I said: "Look, let's straighten something out. Who in the hell are you?"

"I don't know," he sighed, worrying his little beard. "That's something I can't figure out myself."

"Are you afraid of me?" I asked him.

"You?" He wiped his glasses, made a wry face, and lowered his brows. "No. Although I'm afraid of everybody right now. Myself included."

And, with a jerk, he stubbed out his butt, looked around the darkened garden, and slammed the window shut with a crash.

And so, without even knowing it, I'd met a new social phenomenon: the fallen Communist, seeking asylum from Beria's wrath in the criminal underground of Rostov.

The General's widow told us a thing or two about him. The fellow (an old Party member and friend of her late husband) had worked in the Donbassa Coal Trust as assistant to the director in the Political Division, a rather prestigious post. He'd done his duty diligently, a fact, however, that did little to protect him from disaster. As soon as he discovered that they had started a dossier on him and that arrest was probably soon to follow, rather than wait for the Chekists to come as so many others had done before him, he left his home, his family, and his work, and ran to save his life. What was he counting on? It's hard to say. There is no active political underground in any Soviet country, he knew that. He had no friends he could rely on, nor any savings. And he neither could nor wanted to steal. As a result, after wandering through the Northern Caucasus, he wound up penniless and threadbare at the Rostov freight station. That's where the thieves found him, emaciated, sick, and dying of hunger. He rested in bed for some time in one of the haunts of Nakhichevan and then moved over to the widow's.

"He's been living here ever since," said the General's widow, "hiding, afraid of everything, sitting perpetually under lock and key. A strange fellow. Sometimes I even think he's going mad."

"Isn't it expensive to hold on to a parasite like that?" Snuffles asked.

"It's no bother," she smiled, straightening her lace cloak. "He doesn't exactly eat me out of house and home. Besides, every once in a while they throw me some money, especially for him."

"Who does?" I was amazed.

"Your boys," she said. "Thieves. Who else?"

"But why?"

"They're not monsters, after all," she answered sensibly. "They feel sorry for him. They can see there's nowhere for the poor man to go. Besides"—she lingered over her cigarette—"if you think about it, just about everybody has someone in his family under repression, someone taken for political reasons. One person loses his parents, another his distant relatives.

When they look at him, they probably remember someone of their own."

"Well," I said, recalling some people of my own, "if that's the case, we're not heartless either!"

I got a few bank notes and tossed them on the table. The Straw came right over and counted out the money. With a smile, the old bear hunter said: "God, do I feel sorry for these political types. The authorities grind them into powder and all they can do about it is talk their heads off. Nothing wrong with that, of course, but every once in a while you need a little action."

"Right, right," Snuffles picked it up. "You got to act!" And with that he flatly refused to give his share. "The way I see it, that little assistant director of yours has a pretty good thing going," he said nasally. "He sits all by himself like a mouse in a pantry, with everything he needs. Why should I have to take care of him? In honor of what? I don't get my money off of trees. I got to put my freedom on the line for it. Every hour of the day. My own neck—this one here, I put it in a yoke. Let him get by on his own wits; let him give it a try."

"But what if he can't?" the widow objected. "He's a principled, pitiful man."

"Sure," Snuffles said, narrowing his eyes. "He can't steal, but he can sure as hell take money from thieves, is that it? His conscience lets him do that, huh? Look, he's made his own bed. Let him sleep in it."

Snuffles was getting nervous again, and all his sneering and sputtering were enough to make me sick. Still, I had to admit, he did have a point.

TRAINS OF THE TWENTIETH CENTURY

And so I became a train robber.

Like any criminal subculture, train-robbing has its different groups, chief among them those who work the local trains during rush hour. The main loot to be had there is luggage ("corners") and baskets ("squeakers"). When you think about it, the slang terms are quite expressive: a piece of luggage is indeed a compound of sharp corners and a basket squeaks.

There are many techniques for lifting the goods. One of the cleverest and most reliable is the so-called double shot. For this you need a special hollow framework covered on top with leatherette or hide. The second a passenger leaves his baggage on the floor and turns around, even for just a second, the thief is at his side. He covers the man's suitcase with his contraption and, slowly, without the slightest fuss, carries off the loot right before the eyes of the astounded mark.

Train heists are a special feature of life on the Russian road. There's an old story about the man from Odessa who, after years of traveling, returns to his hometown. Stepping off the train and setting his suitcases on the ground, he says in distress: "Everything's changed! I don't recognize Odessa." Suddenly he looks around and notices that all his things have disappeared. "There," he says, "now I recognize you, my Motherland!"

I have my reasons for talking about "life on the road." Russia, at heart, is a nomadic country. She lives on the trains, she finds shelter beneath their booming, homeless vaults. There she dozes and commits her crimes; there she prays and swears; there she searches for the truth, and sins, and steals. And all with passionate sincerity.

I first felt this distinctive Russian spirit during my wanderings. It was then that the images I was later to set down in verse began to grow and gleam in my soul:

The story of my life is incomplete without the train. The headlights, the platform's roar, are signs of a restless age. Fate has joined our fortunes to the bustle of the train. And like a beating heart, it keeps its endless watch. Along the stretches of open space, along the iron veins, the red freights flow like blood to feed the State. Along the jointed rails, the thundering metal rolls. And forging through the wet fog and the bitter chill, the trains of the twentieth century fly, Nomads, Windblown Shelters of the Age!

A train thief usually works at night. After getting a ticket and climbing aboard, he waits for the passengers to go to sleep. Then he cleans them out and sneaks away, disappearing from the sleeper at some small station in the middle of the night.

Tickets, of course, are far from obligatory. Every train thief has his own special set of master keys that will fit any passenger car from the outside. Still, rather than climb aboard, most train robbers prefer to travel under the car (in the "dog box") or above it, on the roof.

It's nice up on top: the wind whistling resiliently, swift lights twinkling overhead and whirling alongside, you get the feeling sometimes you're flying through a void, right in the middle of a starry sky.

Train roofs, however, are hardly meant for contemplation, especially if you're a freight car thief. The thieves often call these cars "German measles" because of their bright red color, but, considering the millions in valuables they carry, "gold mines" might be more appropriate. They're sealed and securely guarded, and the best way to get at them is in mid-course, when the whole train's going at full tilt.

After catching on to the roof of the car with steel hooks, these virtuoso thieves (always working in pairs, like mountain climbers, for greater protection) carefully lower themselves by a rope along the side, open the doors, grab the loot, and throw it outside, down a slope. Then they join it themselves, jumping out into the night, the whipping wind, and the deep, wailing darkness. That jump, that crucial and terrible decision to spring, is the real moment of truth in their work.

Freight robbers make a lot of money, but they don't usually live long enough to enjoy it. Then again, all the train professions are decidedly risky enterprises. At one time or another, every train thief must jump from the train to escape pursuit. One of my friends judged wrong on one of those occasions and slammed right into a telephone pole. I can still remember his face: the shattered jaws, the canceled eyes running out like liquid.

I remember another incident as well.

Snuffles and I were sitting on the roof of a car with another fellow called the Hoof. It was a clear and windy evening. Our train, the Moscow–Rostov Express, was nearing Voronezh. All around us, on both sides of the permanent way, the blue, dusk-swaddled steppes whirled by. Early, watery stars were gleaming overhead and, in the distance, on the horizon, the delicate, cloudy strip of the sunset was fading fast.

"God, how I love it, brothers," said the Hoof. "Just like this, on the roof . . . plenty of room, lots of fresh air to breathe."

He got up and looked around. Then he turned his back to the wind and started to light a cigarette.

I was lying on my back, cushioning my head on my arms. Suddenly, the latticed shadow of a viaduct flashed over me, darkening the milky fires. A quick, strangled shout cut through the air and drops of blood lashed my brows and cheeks. I raised myself on my elbows and looked for the Hoof. He was gone. Knocked down by the low span of the bridge. Where he'd been standing just a moment before, a smoldering cigarette now lay, herded along by the wind. About three meters away, a large, dark crimson blotch blanketed the roof of the car.

UNDER THE WHEELS

Snuffles turned out to be a good teacher. He was patient and attentive. And, little by little, I began to forget my enmity.

There really weren't any grounds for antagonism anymore. Our common secret had made us confederates and comrades-in-arms. Snuffles persistently proved that to me, not only in our work, but in our daily lives. He'd lend me money, take care of me, and continually assert our good relationship in front of the other thieves.

Incidentally, the Rostov road was swarming with thieves around that time. Joining Moscow and the area beyond the Caucasus, this route was, perhaps, one of the busiest in the south of the country. I spent the whole summer and the start of the fall there with Snuffles.

At the coming of the first frost, we chose ourselves a new route. Train thieves are true wanderers—which is why I loved them. They live like birds, spending the summer in the temperate zones of Central Russia, the Ukraine, and the Don, and heading in the late fall for the Caucasus and the shores of the Black Sea. Spring usually finds them in Central Asia, Turkmenia, and Uzbekistan, by the feet of the Khorosansky mountains, near the Afghanistan border. It's a healthful climate there; the apricots are already blooming while steam still floats above the gloomy snows of Russia. With the coming of summer the cycle is repeated. Right behind the flocks of cranes, the train robbers head north again, "for their native spheres."

That year an early and rainy fall came to the Don and the riffraff of the trains took off for the sunny town of Baku. Soon my friend and I headed that way, too. We didn't stay on the Baku route for long, though.

"It's too goddamn crowded and uncomfortable here," Snuffles said one day as we sat in an Asian *shashlyk* restaurant. "Let's strike out, old man, for Iran or Turkey! We'll go to Goradiz and Ordubad. We'll look in on the real thing, the real East, what do you say?"

I didn't object. Ever since I'd been a child, I'd longed to take a look at the real East.

The East, it turned out, was a dusty bore. A monotonous, endless, scorched-yellow plain stretched beyond the windows of the train. It had all looked a lot more imposing in the literature. In the pages of my childhood books the East had seemed mysterious and brilliantly bright. Here, by the borders of Iran in a region of ancient caravan paths, the only thing bright was the sun. Blinding and fierce, that damned blaze flooded the sands with an overwhelming, all-pervasive heat. There was nowhere to hide from it, and nothing left to breathe!

A hot, bitter wind beat at the windows, baking our faces and burying everything in the sleeping compartment in a crunching fall of sand. In search of some air to breathe,

Snuffles and I moved out to the platform of the train and then up on the roof. Soon, though, we had to leave that outpost as well: the metallic roofing of the wagon was like a frying pan.

It was then Snuffles remembered the dog box.

"It's got to be cooler under the wagon," he said. "Besides, tomorrow we get to Goradiz. There's a special-pass region there. They might want to check our papers. We'd better get out of the way beforehand. Who's going to look for us in the dog box?"

"Special-pass, eh?" I was amazed.

"Sure." He shrugged his shoulders. "The border's right nearby."

He poked his finger toward Iran: a yellow, malarial mirage, bordered by stunted willows and camel thorn. For the first time in my life I was looking at another country, and it was as barren as my own.

"If they were going to check us out here," I said sullenly, "why in the hell didn't you tell me before?"

He didn't answer. He growled something and, lowering his eyes, quickly began to light a cigarette.

We were at a deserted station just before nightfall, standing in the sand right by the side of the head car. Chewing at his cigarette, and narrowing his eyes from the smoke, Snuffles asked: "You ever traveled underneath the cars? You know what a dog box is?"

"No," I admitted. "Of course I've heard a lot about it. But I never had to—"

"Well, here's your chance."

"Okay with me," I said. "Only why didn't you warn me before?"

"Why, why, why," he said peevishly, brushing it aside. "How do I know why? I forgot, I didn't think. Why're you nagging? In the long run you'd have figured it out for yourself; if the train goes along the border—"

The whistle of the steam engine drowned him out. Snuffles jumped and looked quickly under the wagon. "Everything's okay," he said. "Follow me!"

And, with a wink, he whisked beneath the wheels.

A dog box is an ordinary storage box for the repair tools train crews may need on the road. Several cars have them: usually the head car, center car, and rear car. The box opens from the side nearest the platform. It's easy enough to enter, and makes for a comfortable ride. Experienced tramps, though, prefer to do without it, because it's too easy to be caught by a passing conductor, train worker, or, more likely, member of the railroad police, who make it a practice to look in there as often as possible at stops.

The kind of dog box Snuffles referred to is slightly different. Located underneath many of the cars, its purpose eludes me to this very day. It's an oblong metal box about six feet long and a foot and a half wide, open on one side. Whatever its application may be, it's perfectly suited for riding. It can accommodate one person in perfect comfort and two with some difficulty. Whenever two people do travel together, they have to lie sideways, tightly pressed into each other like tablespoons. If that's not bad enough, the person on the inside has to keep a tight grip on his comrade, to prevent him from falling. After all, the poor fellow's hanging half out of the box, right over the ground and the ringing rails!

Diving beneath the wagon, Snuffles fumbled for the metal box in the semidarkness, clambered into it, and stretched out his hand to me. His palm was sweaty and slippery and hard to hold. Maybe that's why I tried to grasp it so firmly.

"What's biting you?" he said jokingly. "You scared of something?"

"No," I answered, involuntarily relaxing my hold. "Me scared? No. Where'd you get that idea?"

Just then the train started to move, with a heavy, almost unwilling lurch. It twitched, awakened, and started to breathe. The levers, gleaming with black oil, trembled and champed. A brief tremor passed through the train.

I moved toward Snuffles and suddenly dropped, blinded by a blow. He had struck me brutally, with all his might. And then again. I fell, still holding tight to his hand.

Snuffles tore at my fingers, ripping and gnawing them.

Through the iron thunder and clang, I could hear the nasal, convulsive sputter of his voice:

"You think I dragged you out here so I could show you the East? You dumb *fraier!* I'm going to bury you and nobody'll ever know! Not a soul! It's a deserted road. Not a thief on it. And then I'll clear myself with the den. They think we're friends. Nobody'll ever catch on. I was your teacher, after all, your benefactor, your older partner! Well, I'll teach you now, you bastard! I've been waiting a long time for this. A long time. All summer."

He was choking on the words, tearing at my fingers, forcing me down to the ties, between the rails.

Almost flush against my cheek the wheel gleamed, smelling of dust and heated metal; it turned slowly, with a crunch. . . . Suddenly I remembered all about God. For the first time in my life I remembered Him for real and begged for mercy: "God," I cried out, "dear God, help me, save me, preserve me!"

Then (and I'll never know why) the train started to slow down. Once again the whistle sounded heartbreakingly in the distance. The buffers collided and clanked. The wheels flashed and stopped.

I'd been holding on to Snuffles with all my might, as numb as if I'd fallen into a strange kind of trance that spared me all sense of pain. Even if I'd fallen under the wheels and been crushed, I wouldn't have let go of that hand for anything in the world!

As soon as the car braked, I came to, set my legs against the tie and, with an almost superhuman effort, raised myself onto the dog box.

We were face to face now in the semidarkness. Snuffles opened his slobbery mouth in a convulsive scream.

I can't say I envied the position he was in right then: he was lying on his side, with one of his hands useless and my right hand clamping the other like a vise. I wasted no time taking advantage of the situation.

With my free left hand I grabbed Snuffles by the throat, jerked him to me, and started to squeeze. I could feel his throat beneath my fingers growing as soft and loose as jelly. And I kept on squeezing, putting all my rage and power into that one grip.

The train moved again, but I was safe now, lying right where my enemy had been just a moment before. Snuffles was caught beneath the wheels. The heavy, booming metal crushed him just as cleanly as it would have crushed me.

IN THE SANDS

I had one less enemy now, but my problems were far from over. I'd have to leave the train behind as quickly as possible. As soon as the Chekists found Snuffles' body (and that would happen soon enough) they'd start looking for me. After all, I'd been traveling with Snuffles a whole day and a night; we'd roamed the whole train together and a lot of people had seen us.

At midnight, during a brief watering stop for the train, I sneaked out from under the car, hid behind a sandhill in a ragged clump of bushes, and waited for the train to leave. Then I took off, leaving the rails far behind me.

I wandered aimlessly, toward the northeast, along the light blue sands and the wild, uncharted landscape of the night. I barely stopped to rest. By morning, I'd already put a lot of distance between me and the train tracks.

By the time the deserts brightened and the oppressive heat came up again, I had reached the ruins of a stone building (the remains of an ancient fortress, perhaps? the remnants of a mosque?). I staggered toward it, passed beneath the low arches, and lay down among the stones, dizzy with exhaustion and thirst. There was no water, but there was shade—a protection from the sun and shelter from strangers' eyes.

I stretched out blissfully in the shade and slowly reached for a cigarette. Before I could even light up I fell fast asleep.

I saw the train before me and the ringing rails. Once again I was lying with my cheek against the massive wheels and they turned with a crunch and blew dust in my face.

Once again I was praying and beseeching the skies for help. And the skies replied: "What do you want?"

And I answered: "Something to drink."

"Drink," the skies said. "Drink!"

"But where's the water?"

"Turn around!"

And I did and saw a dark, frothing stream before me. It broadened and swelled, flooding the sands and overflowing the rails. It washed my feet and as I scooped the dark moisture up in my palms I shuddered to find it so hot and sharp and sweet.

"It's blood," I shouted. "It's blood!" And woke up.

I rubbed my eyes and looked slowly around. And was amazed at how long I'd been sleeping. The day had long since died away. The thick dust had blanketed the old fortress and, in the west, through a break in the wall, a copper moon floated and swayed.

Well, I decided, I've got darkness on my side. I can go and look for water.

I had only to think it and beside me I heard a light, caressing splash. I got to my feet, listened intently, and then headed off in the direction of the sound.

There must be a stream somewhere nearby, I figured, licking my caked lips. I hadn't noticed it that morning, but that was easy to understand, after such a long journey. I'd drink my fill now!

I skirted a pile of sheet metal, hurriedly crossed some flagstones, and stopped short in confusion.

Before me, right by the gap, sat Snuffles. I could see him, glazed by the glow of the moon, down to the last detail. He was drinking straight from a bottle in his hand, sucking out the water with a gurgle and a smack of his lips.

He didn't seem the slightest bit surprised to see me. He gave me a wink and, extending the bottle, said: "Want some, old man? Go ahead, help yourself."

"No," I muttered. "No. Where did you come from? And why? You're dead!"

"Don't get so upset," Snuffles replied. "Take a drink. There's nothing I wouldn't give a friend, even water."

"But that isn't water," I objected, stepping back, "it's a dream! I'm dreaming you, you bastard!"

"What do you mean, dream?" He giggled and came toward me, crunching the sheet metal as he walked. "Real water—look!"

He turned the bottle upside down and a light blue stream trickled out into the sand. Several drops fell right on my hand and neck; I felt a fluid, tickling chill. My body contracted . . . and I woke up.

I was suffocating, in a sticky sweat, and lay there for some time, trying to piece my scattered sensations together. Apparently, the dream had ended. But the chill on my arm and neck remained—there was no denying that.

Interesting, I was thinking. How long have I been here already? Is it morning yet, or still evening?

I stirred and yawned and was about to get up when a cold, tickling stream suddenly flowed along my neck and ear.

I heard a soft, interrupted hiss. Something was rustling there, right by my neck. I squinted and saw a snake! I looked further and saw another. And another. And another. There was a whole community of them here, swarming all over the fortress, taking shelter in every nook and cranny.

I'm dreaming, I thought with horror. I'm dreaming. . . .

But I wasn't dreaming this time. Without knowing it, I had fallen into a den—a gloomy kingdom!—of snakes. For decades, maybe even centuries, they had multiplied here, living their quiet lives in freedom. Now I had disturbed them. They hissed and rustled back and forth. Apparently they were upset and looked at me from out of every fissure with the small, icy prickles of their eyes.

In some corner of my consciousness I realized that the main thing now was not to make any sudden movements. While I'd been lying there unawares, I'd stayed perfectly still. But how long could I keep it up?

Slowly, very slowly, I straightened out and began to slither. Several times I stopped and started, repeating the maneuver and, amazingly, the snakes didn't touch me. Maybe they took me for some strange breed of giant snake. In any event, I moved to the exit and after some two hours of wriggling and gliding along the rocks, finally reached my goal.

Once outside, it took me a while to catch my breath and pull myself together. Then I got up and looked around. Not too far away I noticed the brightly colored sloping roof of a nomad's tent. A whitish curl of smoke rose above it. There were people living there, and that meant there was water!

I approached the tent. Some noisy little kids were romping about in the sand. Chickens wandered back and forth and, laying his shaggy muzzle on his paws, a wolfhound, neutralized by the heat, dozed away. He raised himself as I approached, gave a few lazy yelps, and lay back down, baring his teeth and panting noisily. A second later a woman appeared from inside the tent—dark-haired and tall, draped in a long Asiatic dress that reached down to her ankles.

"Hello," I said.

She gave me a quick look and silently nodded her head. She had a tender face, soft and quite un-Asiatic. I wasn't looking at that, though: my eyes were on her hands. She was holding a pan of water!

I was struck dumb—completely incapable of tearing my eyes away from that gleaming, frothy moisture. I walked right up to her, ripped the pan out of her hands, and fell on it with a vengeance. One swallow and I stopped dead. The water was full of soap and stinking with some kind of alkaline solution. Apparently, the woman had been washing clothes in it.

I gagged and with a shudder of disgust threw the pan to the ground and started to swear long and hard.

In the very purest Russian she replied: "There's no point in swearing, my dear. I'm afraid you've only yourself to blame."

And, watching me spit and writhe, she added with a smile, "Don't worry, I was just washing the children's pants in it, nothing more."

She led me into the tent and treated me to a cold drink of fermented mare's milk. That's when I drank my fill.

By that evening, the two of us had switched to vodka. She took a bottle from a trunk and gave it a good shake. With a wrinkle of her brow, she explained: "You won't find any good vodka around here. This is from my husband's supplies. He keeps it for special occasions. If he ever found out about this he'd kill me."

"Where is he now?" I wanted to know.

"On a trip." She brushed it aside. "He left to see his brothers. They're splitting up their father's estate and making a mess of it."

"Will he be there long?"

"I don't know," she said, giving me a knowing look. "Don't worry, there's time. You can stay here three or four days without any trouble."

"Well," I said, lifting my glass, "let's drink to that!"

"All right," she agreed and, bringing her glass to her lips, she tipped it with a kind of desperate bravado.

That night we lay on the rug and, sated with each other, talked quietly. They called her Klava, and she told me the story of her life with the sudden and touching frankness characteristic of a woman in bed. It was simple, straight, and sad.

She was born and raised in the forests of Meshchersky, not far from Spas-Klepiky (one of Esenin's old haunts). There, in the woods, Klava spent her youth, and her recollections of those days were by far the very brightest of her life. She recounted all the little details of her country life, how they'd gone hunting for mushrooms, calling to each other in the groves. She recalled the rural revels, the fingers moving across the accordion keys, the squeaking of the swings. Then, abruptly, it had all come to an end. The war began and the front drew near. To save their lives, Klava and her parents left for the south and Azerbaijan. Soon after that her parents died.

She was alone now in those barren foreign lands, hungry and poor. She worked on construction sites; she dug the earth with a spade. There wasn't a ray of happiness in her life. Her only salvation at the time seemed to lie in marriage. So, when the old Kurd came along, she married him on the spot, without a second's hesitation. It was a loveless marriage, but that hardly stopped the children from coming, and quickly enough at that! She had three and it was already too late to change things.

"What do you mean?" I objected flippantly. "You could take off and leave him! What can that old Kurd do to you? This isn't Iran, you know."

"Could I?" She got up and looked sadly into my eyes. "And what about the children? They need a mother, you know. A mother! You dogs don't understand that. It doesn't mean a damned thing to you. There's only one thing you care about."

"Well, you could split the kids up if it ever came to that."

"Sure I could," she said slowly. "There's nothing you can't do if you put your mind to it. But women don't like to take off at random, you know, into the blue somewhere. If I ever found somebody to take me as I am, though, I'd leave in a second. Without a backward glance. And I'd be grateful to him forever. I'd wash his feet and drink the water."

Her voice suddenly broke and she began to sob. She buried her face in the carpeted pillow, while I caressed her warm and trembling back. There was nothing I could say.

What could I have said anyway? That I wasn't right for her? That I was a thief, a runaway, a hopeless tramp? That I'd killed a man and was hiding from the authorities? I kept quiet for a long time. And then I tried to say something. But she made me stop, running her palm along my cheek and smiling through her tears.

"Shh, you don't have to. . . . Be quiet. . . . Come on, maybe we'd better have another drink."

And so I spent the next three days enjoying the comfort of a woman's body. Then we parted. I never met Klava again, but she was often on my mind. After all my ordeals, she seemed like a kind of reward to me, a consolation.

A NEW PERIOD

After parting with Klava, I spent some time straying through the sands near the railroad. Then, one night at a small station, I caught a northbound express by the handrail and jumped aboard. As soon as the lights in the train windows had gone out, I slipped into a sleeping car with the help of a skeleton key.

The trip went off without a hitch and even included a few unexpected benefits. The conductress of the car (a redheaded, sprightly woman, no longer young but still willing) immediately took me under her wing and I rested in her compartment all the way to Baku.

A lot of my old friends were there, including Kinto, the fellow in the checkered cap I'd first met on my arrival in Rostov. He was here alone. His old partner, the Farmer, had been arrested the previous summer in a roundup. Kinto had been caught in the dragnet, too, but he'd managed to slip out somehow and flee. Now he was back in the Transcaucasus region plying his trade at the Baku "Green" market. He told me his story while we sat in the market snack room, a noisy basement of a place, mournfully sipping the sour local wine.

"Yeah," he sighed, "it's a rotten deal, all right. There's no boys left you can count on, brother." He shot me a sidelong glance and continued. "Anyway, I miss Rostov. That was one happy town! What've you got here? Nothing! I don't like Baku. My heart's not in it. If it weren't for my family, I'd have left long ago."

"Where do they live?" I wanted to know.

"Right here, on the outskirts of town," he said, "in Baladzhary. About twenty minutes away on the electric train."

"Family!" I muttered enviously. "What luck! You realize what that means, brother? To drop in and lighten your load any time you want to?"

He finished his wine, made a wry face, and wiped his palm across his lips. Then, leaving the glass behind, he said, "Want to come with me? I was planning on going there anyway.

Actually, I was supposed to drop in a week ago, but I couldn't make it. I forgot, sort of lost my head. And my folks are a touchy bunch, especially my old man."

"Who is he?" I asked. "What's he do for a living?"

"Come along and see for yourself," Kinto said, smiling slowly.

It was twilight when we got to Baladzhary. As soon as we arrived I dropped in at the train station food store and bought a bottle of good wine, a pack of cookies, and a big, glossy box of chocolates. After all, I figured, we were going to a home, to a real family—you've got to make a good impression.

Kinto took a skeptical view of the whole business. One look at the package in my hands and he raised his eyebrows. He wanted to say something apparently, but then decided against it. We still had a long walk ahead of us, down the sinuous, sleepy streets of the town. "Where's your house?" I was finally starting to get a little upset.

"Soon, soon," Kinto replied. "We don't have much farther to go. There, right behind that turn."

Around the corner the buildings suddenly came to an end. A wasteland stretched beyond; nothing but darkness and a cold wind, bearing the smells of wormwood and the smoke of bonfires. An unsteady finger of fire rose in the dark of the wilderness and somewhere, off in the distance, a horse began to neigh and a guitar delicately sounded. Suddenly the picture came clear.

"You're a gypsy?" I asked him in amazement.

"You got it," he said.

"I never would have guessed. . . ."

"What did you take me for?" He grinned.

"Some kind of Caucasus type, I guess." I shrugged my shoulders. "A Georgian, maybe. You got the name and the mug for it. It fits perfectly."

"Hmm." He nodded with satisfaction. "Good. All the better."

"I'm not the only one, either. That's what they all think."

"Let them keep on thinking it, too, my friend. And you keep quiet about it." Kinto turned to me and narrowed his eyes. "Agreed?"

"Sure," I said, "but why?"

"It's just that—" He was silent for a moment. "Well, there's not much percentage in being a gypsy. Especially among thieves. So why not save myself some jokes?"

"But," I objected, "as far as I know, gypsies are our kind of people. They're valued—"

"Valued, maybe"—Kinto raised a finger—"but not respected. Anyway, what's there to respect them for?"

"What do you mean?" I was confused. "Their roving spirit—"

"Oh, sure. But everything they do, the way they live and scheme and steal—all that is by their own special rules. And those rules . . ." Kinto made a wry face again and spat. "Well, why talk about it?"

We were already stepping into the campsite. The black slanted silhouette of a tent rose before us against the tossing flames of the campfire. Like a snarling little cloud a dog rolled under our feet, gave Kinto a sniff, and quieted down.

Throwing back the rag that covered the entrance, Kinto looked into the tent and shouted: "Hello, Father!"

"Hello," a deep, strong voice replied. "Come in!"

"I'm not alone, Father, I brought a friend."

"All the better."

A minute later I was sitting inside on a soft heap of rags. The gifts I'd brought went from hand to hand. I passed them to Kinto and he, in turn, gave them to an old lady in a flowery shawl. She opened the package, took out the bottle, and handed it over respectfully to the thickset, wrinkled gypsy with the shaved skull and the neatly trimmed beard.

"Let's drink, Father." Kinto winked.

"Let's," said the gypsy. "But not this . . ."

He turned the bottle over and gave it a shake. He knit his brows and looked at the writing on the label. With a smile and a flash of his steel teeth, he said: "Muscatel. That's for

women! Sweet slops—who needs them? No, we'll drink
something else."

And, turning to the old woman, he said something curtly
and gutturally in their own language. She immediately darted
into the far, dark corner of the tent and reappeared, holding a
bulky clay jug in her hands. Another gypsy woman just a little
younger crept out of the corner behind her, bringing bread,
sheep's milk cheese, and vegetables.

It was all laid in an instant on a mat at our feet. Kinto's
father took a glass and splashed something from the jug into
it. Then he carefully raised the glass on the back of his hand
and with a grand gesture passed it to me:

"To our honored guest, the first glass!"

I drank it and started to choke. The glass was full of the
very purest grape spirits.

"Well, what do you think?" The old gypsy laughed, grinning
and opening his eyes wide. "Pretty good poison, eh?"

We drank well into the night. A tremendous number of
people kept pressing into the tent. The tambourine clanged
drily, the women moaned, and someone's anguished tenor
sang broken-hearted, wild gypsy words to the strains of a
guitar.

Just before first light I staggered outside and stood there,
tossing my head back to the sky and thirstily inhaling the chill.
Then I collapsed and crawled under a wagon by the tent,
bedding down there in the grass.

For some reason, as I fell asleep I felt an unaccountable
anguish and depression. A reaction, perhaps, to the spree that
I'd just had? Maybe it was those gypsy wanderers' songs. Not
their words so much, but what lay hidden in their gloomy,
God-forsaken depths.

As gloomy and God-forsaken as my own fate, my entire,
good-for-nothing life! That was what had bred my depression.
I didn't know it then, but I was already poisoned by it, deeply
and forever. I didn't know that the fits of anguish would grow
with the years, that they would multiply and start to haunt me
everywhere. Even now, as I relate all this, the anguish lives

within me, stumbling through me like a drunken fool. And there's no escaping it, no salvation when it comes.

I woke up late in the morning, unglued my eyelids, and got up, wincing from a headache and overcoming the hangover and delirium with difficulty.

I had an unbearable desire to smoke. I reached into my pocket for my cigarette case, a gold case from my Rostov days, and felt nothing. I began to get upset. Could I have dropped it? But the other pocket was empty, too. And yet—I distinctly recalled this—there had been some money there; not a large amount, but more than enough to feel.

Suddenly, with mounting anger, I realized that I'd been robbed. Besides the money and the cigarette case, I'd had a watch—two of them, in fact—and a dagger. They were all gone. Someone had worked me over as I slept and picked me clean from head to toe. It was then I remembered Kinto's observation that gypsies live by their own special code.

Kinto's father looked out from behind the curtains of the tent. "Hey!" he shouted. "The night's over. Come on, let's have a drink!"

"Where's Kinto?" I asked gloomily.

"Off to see the girls," he answered. "Left last night."

"Where to, do you know?"

"To Baladzhary, to the station," the gypsy said. "He promised to be back in the morning. But we aren't going to wait for him. Come on, everything's ready. It'll get cold."

He dragged me out from under the wagon, took me into the tent, and sat me down beside him. And then, with the same courteous gesture as the night before, he raised a glass of spirits.

"To our dear guest . . ."

My first thought was to refuse. To refuse, raise a big stink, and demand some explanations. But he'd offered me the drink with the greatest cordiality. And everything about the gypsy, the protuberant eyes with the smooth play of colors, the big mouth, and those metal teeth that glittered when he smiled, radiated a sincere gaiety full of concern and simplicity. One look at him, and I softened.

The old man evidently had had nothing to do with the theft. Why spoil a good breakfast, then? I decided to wait until Kinto came back.

He didn't show up till that afternoon. After I'd called him aside and told him what had happened, his face turned gray and pinched and he wrathfully pressed his lips together.

"Who could have done that?" he strained out of the corner of his mouth. "Ay, the shame of it, the shame! The camp is crawling with scum, sure, but you're my friend, my guest, and everybody knows it! Although—" He hesitated and his eyes narrowed. "There is somebody that might not have known. You say you spent the night under the wagon?"

"Yes."

"Anybody give you any bedding? You know, a blanket, a pillow?"

"No, I don't remember. But then I didn't ask for any. I went outside for a breath of fresh air and collapsed."

"Aha," he muttered, "aha! Wait, I'll be right back."

Our conversation had taken place just outside the tent. Kinto rushed back inside and disappeared behind the flap. Suddenly the inside exploded in a burst of strident voices. A woman started to cry. Kinto barked back. Then a slow, heavy bass—the voice of the old gypsy, I was sure. He was saying something important and the entire tent fell silent for a moment.

The curtain was thrown back and Kinto reappeared. The old man came out immediately afterwards, holding a thin young woman by the hand, her face veiled to the brows by a brightly colored kerchief.

"Here she is, the scum!" Kinto said, blinking and chewing the dead butt of his cigarette. "My younger sister. Masha. She was on her way back from Baku yesterday around dawn, and she threshed you on the way. That's what I thought. It couldn't have been anybody else."

"But I didn't know, I didn't know," she wailed. "All I saw

was some drunk lying there by the wagon. How was I supposed to know?"

"Where are the things?" the old man demanded, his voice thick with rage.

"They're here, right here," the young girl said hurriedly, "all here. Father, let me go!"

She freed her hand and rubbed her wrist. Then she bent down and quickly lifted her long skirt, revealing another one right beneath it. Digging about in its pleats and folds, she took out the cigarette case and the watch. The gold she handed over to her father. Once again she raised the hem and from still another skirt withdrew the money, already neatly folded and wrapped in a little rag.

I couldn't have told you how many of those skirts she had on. While she was rummaging through them she got entangled in the pile and her kerchief slipped off her face. When she straightened back up, I gasped. Beauty like hers, as God is my witness, I'd never seen before.

She had enormous, smoky eyes, shaded by long lashes, a lengthened oval of a face, and a tender mouth with a slightly jutting lower lip. I stared at her and asked, bemused, "And where's my dagger? There, under the last one?"

"No, in the bushes." She pointed to the acacia thickets. "Over there."

"Get it!" the old man ordered.

We passed through the bushes into a small clearing. The young woman sat down by a pile of branches, dug around, and came up with the dagger. I stretched out my hand and she placed the knife in my palm. Our fingers touched and I could feel her trembling with fear.

What's she afraid of, the little fool? I wondered. Everything's over and done with.

Unfortunately, it wasn't.

"So-o-o," the old man drawled, turning to Masha. "Stand up."

And, scowling, he drew a heavy lash from behind his back.

"Father!" the girl cried pitifully, but it was too late. She lowered her eyes and hid her face in her hands, trembling in anticipation of the blow.

The old man walked up to her, took aim, and slowly drew back his arm. Suddenly I was shouting and rushing to intercept the lash.

"Stop! You mustn't!"

"What do you mean?" The old man was amazed. "She did wrong. She robbed a guest."

"To hell with that," I said, looking sideways at Masha and noticing her eyes widen with happiness and surprise. "I don't hold a grudge. Either about the money or the watch. I'd have given it all away gladly—"

"What you'd have given away is one thing," Kinto interrupted. "What she took is another. You understand?"

"I understand," I said. "I understand everything. But you have to understand, too. I can't let you do it."

"But she's guilty, isn't she?"

"Yes, of course," I had to agree.

"And we have a punishment for people like that," the old man spoke in a deep voice and drew the lash back for a blow. "We beat them hard and long. And it won't be for the first time, either. She's always done wrong and covered me in shame."

"Wait," I said, "wait."

"What is it you want?" The old man smiled into his beard.

"At least don't punish her now, on my account."

"Then punish her yourself!"

"All right," I said quickly, "I will."

I took the lash from the gypsy and, playing with it, said: "Go! I'll take care of it myself. Alone. The way I'm supposed to!"

When Kinto and the old man had gone, I turned to Masha and threw the lash away.

"Masha," I said, walking up to her with a smile on my face, "do you think I could lay a hand on someone like you?"

"You can't?" she asked, removing her hands from her face. "Or don't you want to?"

"I can't."

I'd have thought the words would make her happy, but—there's a woman for you—an arrogant, contemptuous smile slipped across her lips.

"Of course I *can* beat you," I said hastily.

"Then why don't you?"

"I don't know. My hand won't lift somehow—"

"And I almost thought you were a man!"

With that she turned aside and fixed her hair. Then, swaying her hips and catching the bushes with the hem of her skirt, she started to go.

"Just a second!" I roared at her. "Where do you think you're going?"

She neither answered nor turned around. She just walked away and disappeared into the shimmering foliage.

Suddenly I was enraged. I raised the lash from the ground, caught up with her in two leaps and, on the fly, slashed her violently across the back.

She trembled and instantly gave way, falling to her knees and throwing her hands above her head.

I raised my hand again and saw her eyes: they were filled with tears. "Forgive me," she whispered. "Enough. It's enough now. Forgive me!"

And she sank and stiffened, pressing to my knees.

GYPSY LIFE

I'd come to the gypsy camp quite by accident, without the slightest intention of staying, but I did stay, and all on account of Masha.

After that incident in the bushes she attached herself to me with a strange tenderness. The twisted lash had done its work. On the following day, at sunset, Kinto called me out of the tent with a mysterious look. He beckoned me to the steppe and there, on the edge of a ravine, I saw Masha. She was sitting quietly and thoughtfully.

"All right," said Kinto, "I've done what you asked me to, Masha. I've brought him. You can take care of the rest yourselves. I don't know anything and I want to know even less."

Kinto turned aside, walked off, and then stopped with a frown. "Look out, snake," he said, threatening Masha with his finger. "Look out. Even if you are my sister, my friends are a lot dearer to me, and don't you ever forget it!"

He stood there for a minute. Then, with a wave of his hand, he disappeared into the advancing darkness.

We were alone. It was quiet and chilly. Somewhere off in the grass a land rail was creaking and, from time to time, you could hear snatches of songs, the clanking of spurs, and the neighing of horses from the gypsy camp.

"Why does he talk to me like that?" Masha sighed. "Everybody curses and abuses me and nobody ever takes any pity."

She smiled and slowly shrugged her shoulders. Suddenly she knit her brows, gave a cry of pain, and said, "It's your work."

"Is it very painful?" I asked, full of repentance and pity.

"Feel for yourself," she said.

I carefully led my palm along her back (it was soft and pliant as a cat's) and beneath the thin fabric of her blouse, felt the large, swollen slant of a welt.

"Ay," Masha said, "how did you come up with a blow like that? Your hand is so small, like a child's. . . ."

She took my hand, placed it on her knee, and began to caress it. Lingering and looking through the fingers, she repeated: "Like a child's. Just like the rest of you. They say you're a thief. What kind? You're so tiny. I feel sorry for you. Come to me, my little one!"

"Listen," I said, "I don't get it. I stripped the bark off you, and you're the one who's feeling sorry?"

"I'm a woman," Masha replied.

It was said so simply and sincerely that I fell silent, as ignorant as before. Still, underneath it all, I could feel her unfathomable, bewitching rightness and her strength.

She was still talking, softly and melodically, mixing gypsy

words in with her Russian, but I wasn't listening anymore, or understanding a thing. I embraced her impetuously, and once again she trembled beneath my hand and moaned so softly I could barely hear.

"How sad," she whispered, "I can't lie down on my back. Well, we'll adjust. We have the whole night ahead of us."

And she pressed her whole body into me. Her mouth opened and I felt her breath and the chill of her teeth. And it was a while before we spoke again.

"The night is ours," I muttered, calming down now and drawing my breath with difficulty. "But what about later?"

"Later?" Masha made a wry face. She began to button up her blouse and straighten her rumpled hair.

"You mean this is the only night we have?"

"You want more?"

"Of course."

"Then we'll meet tomorrow, at the same time."

"It's not that," I said miserably. "I mean in general. For the future. Won't we be able to be—together?"

"So that's what you're talking about," she drawled, and fell silent, biting a blade of grass. "Ah, you really are a little child, aren't you? You've got a new toy and you can't let it go. There'll be trouble, I warn you. Didn't you hear what my brother called me? I may not be a snake, but, believe me, you won't be happy with me. What do you need it for?"

"I don't know," I said in confusion.

"Don't be in such a hurry. You mustn't."

Within a week, though, she had forgotten that conversation herself. We were lying together in the steppe, by the edge of the ravine. It was twilight and chilly and, up in the blue, the rising moon gleamed through its cloudy feathers. A reddish glow spread on the horizon and slipped along the waves of the feather grass that filtered the distant talk of men, the dull and frequent clatter of hoofs. The voices seemed to be drawing near. I stood up uneasily.

"They're coming this way," I said. "They'll see us."

"Lie down," she said peacefully. "No one will come."

"But they don't know—"

"They know," she said. "The whole camp knows. And for quite a while now. You think that's the sort of thing you can hide from people?"

"How do they feel about it?" I asked, lighting a cigarette. "What're they saying?"

"Different things. The young ones hate you, of course."

"Why?"

"On account of me, probably," she said simply. "You can understand that."

"I can understand. Well, what about the older ones? Your father, for instance."

"Tatu's keeping quiet, so far, and that's a good sign."

She took the cigarette from my hands, inhaled a few times, and with a sigh passed it back to me. "There's no place to go. All the same, you're my *rom* now. You know what that means? *Rom*—that's how we say husband." And, drawing right up to my face, she added slowly and ardently, "And I'm your *romni*. . . ."

And so my gypsy life began.

I stayed in the camp, quickly making myself at home. I learned how to dance pretty well and beat time for the *Chechetka* (a gypsy tap dance) and, like a regular *rom*, walked around in a painted Russian blouse and polished, squeaking leather boots.

The idyl soon ended, though, and I had to leave. It turned out I had more enemies than I'd realized. One night, along the road to the station, some young gypsies lay in wait for me (apparently the same ones Masha had been telling me about) and beat me to a pulp.

There were five of them; they circled and fenced me in a tight ring. Surrounded like that, I could neither break loose nor defend myself effectively. They fell on me with heavy sticks and whips. Not from the front, either, but from behind, striking me in the back and along my sides and ribs. Every time I'd get up from the ground to face the direction the blow had come from, I'd be knocked off my feet. Again and again

I'd rise and fall with a moan. Like a top, I whirled in the darkness, defenseless and deafened by rage and pain. Whitish faces loomed in front of me; I'd grab for them, but they were always beyond reach. And then I fell and didn't get up again. I didn't come to until the next day, in a tent.

The first person I saw was the old gypsy. Gloomy and scowling, he bent down to me and asked, "Who did it?"

"I don't know," I said. "I don't remember."

"Take a guess." The old man looked at me expectantly. He scratched his beard and pulled it to a point. "Who? Don't keep quiet about it."

"It was dark," I answered, "I couldn't make them out."

"All right," he said, with visible relief. "No evidence, no trial. Fine!"

Then, from out of nowhere, Masha was at my side. Wailing and sobbing, she sat down at the head of my bed and placed her soft, cool, tender hands on my face.

"I'm here, I'm here with you," she whispered, choking on her tears. "Don't be afraid, my darling. Don't be afraid of anything. I'm yours. Do you understand? I'm with you."

"That's something to be afraid of right there." Kinto suddenly spoke up. I didn't see him. I only caught the sound of his voice. And it was unusually severe. "Why are you like that? Why? You bring no joy, only hurt and pain. You see what they did to that boy? They broke his hand, they smashed his ribs. . . ."

"But how am I to blame?" Masha asked pitifully.

"Who the hell knows?"

"I'm here, I'm not with anyone else. . . ."

"But you make a lot of overtures."

"I don't do anything special. That's just the way it gets understood."

"Maybe," said Kinto, "but that doesn't make it any easier on him."

They continued to talk in their own language and in the entire interchange there was only one word I could understand: "Leave."

"Leave," Kinto repeated. "Things aren't any better here.

Someplace else, at least, you might be happy. Who knows, maybe you'll even get along together."

But we didn't. After resting a while in bed, I took Masha off with me to the North Caucasus, to Kuban, where we settled in a Cossack village. I had hoped to live in peace and quiet, free of adventures. The adventures, however, started immediately. Three days after our arrival in the village, Masha disappeared. When she came back days later, she was dusty, happy, and laden with a heavy bag across her shoulder. It turned out she'd gone from yard to yard, telling fortunes, living by begging, and asking for scraps.

I tried to convince her that there were better ways to live. I argued that I knew how to provide for a family. I might as well have been talking to a wall.

She kept on disappearing from home, once for a long time. She was a strange being, inscrutable, full of a kind of naïve depravity. Soon after that we parted, weary at last of each other and unable to come to terms.

STALIN POND

"Come on," said Kinto, "cheer up. Whatever happens is for the best!"

"Sure," I sighed. "I just can't help feeling sorry, that's all."

"Sorry for whom?" Kinto screwed up his eyes.

"For Masha. And myself. Maybe I was in too much of a hurry. Maybe I needed to wait and be more patient. Who knows, maybe, in the long run, things would have turned out better for us."

"Fat chance," said Kinto.

"Listen, old man, why do you hate her so much?"

"It's not that I don't love her." He stopped short. "But that's another story altogether."

"Still, she's your sister. Your flesh and blood."

"There's an old Caucasus proverb," Kinto said, "one that

makes a lot of sense. 'A beautiful wife is a husband's disgrace, a beautiful daughter is a father's disgrace.' Well, you could stretch it to 'A beautiful sister's a brother's disgrace.' "

"Don't exaggerate."

"I'm not," said Kinto. "Thanks to her, two gypsies went for each other's throats once. And that's when she was thirteen years old! Can you imagine? One of them was from another camp, the other was a good friend of mine. We grew up together. Things like that."

Kinto flattened the grass with his hand and got himself a cigarette. He struck a match.

"And don't forget what happened to you. Or doesn't a broken rib mean that much to you?"

"Enough," I answered quickly.

"So let's drop it." He took a drag. "Let's talk about something else. Khasan's coming this evening, the bastard. . . ."

We were on the outskirts of Groznyi, in an apple orchard by the shores of a marshy, duckweed-covered pond. The premises belonged to a local sanitarium for oil industry workers named, as the pond was, after Stalin. In fact, everything around here carried Stalin's name.

Stalin Pond enjoyed a certain popularity among the local thieves. Up to two hundred and more would crowd the shores of the pond, giving the sanitarium the look of a Scythian camp or a gathering of Zaparozhtsy Cossacks. The smoky bonfires lapped away at the dark, the wanderers' songs rang along the wind. Lying down in the grass by the green, glassy surface of the water, the thieves would retire from their labors for a doze and a drink, a little squeeze with the girls, and a game of cards.

The miners at the sanitarium looked down on all the activity with a mixture of bewilderment and despair. They almost never left the home. They preferred to leave the grounds completely to the thieves.

There was a kind of gentlemen's agreement between us and the administration of the sanitarium; as long as we didn't mess with the people resting there and left the sanitarium buildings alone, the board of directors wouldn't bother us. The same went for the police, even though they were perfectly aware of the situation.

We'd settle in at Stalin Pond for a happy, carefree time, usually devoted to playing cards. The games were big, the playing passionate, and the stakes high enough to attract every cardsharp and professional around. As a matter of fact, players would gather from every corner of the country. This was the thieves' casino, the Caucasus' own Monte Carlo. And the most successful player of all, the true king of the casino, was Khasan, the Crimean Tatar.

Short and fat, with a big, broad face, he had come to town about the same time as I. He'd already been living in Groznyi for a couple of months, visiting the pond every evening and invariably cleaning up the competition.

His game was stoss (or "shtoss," as the thieves call it, the classic Hussar game that was the undoing of Herman, Pushkin's hero in *The Queen of Spades*) and he played it like a virtuoso. When he shuffled and dealt, the cards seemed to come alive in his hands; they'd crackle and flutter, and as they fell each and every suit would settle obediently in its proper place.

During those two months, by the most cursory calculations, he'd ruined half our den and stockpiled goods and valuables worth more than a million and a half rubles.

Even Kinto had been fleeced. Three times he'd sat down across from the Tatar to do battle and three times he'd tasted defeat, leaving stripped to his shorts.

Now he dreamed of a new skirmish. "Maybe Lady Luck'll smile on me this time, eh?"

"Anything can happen," I said, "as long as the game's on the up and up. Listen, old man, Khasan's got something up his sleeve, I'm sure of it."

"You got any proof?" Kinto asked, keeping his voice down.

"No, just a hunch."

"What kind?"

"I've kept my eye out on him for a long time now and, I swear to God, he's got marked cards."

"But he's always sending messenger boys to the market for fresh decks," Kinto objected.

"That's the snag, all right," I admitted. "If only he used the same deck all the time. . . ."

"If, if," Kinto mimicked. "You're making it all up, that's what I say."

We were talking on a grassy knoll that sloped gently down to the pond. The day was slowly coming to an end. The cool, slanting rays of the sun were stitching through the leaves, the breeze was blowing, and the thieves were calling back and forth to each other in the cloudy thickets. Someone sang plaintively:

"Oy-yoi-yoi-yoi-yoi-yoi
I've no future and no peace,
Only the campfire's smoke above my head,
Only the black smoke and the wide world,
Wide world, wide world,
I've wandered all through it and what good has it done?"

Like clockwork Khasan arrived at sunset with his retinue of hangers-on and the four pretty, well-fed youths he used as messenger boys. It was said that the Tatar made use of their services by night as well as by day and that certainly looked like the truth. They'd obey his every wish swiftly and without complaint. While Khasan played, the boys would sit behind him, counting and piling up all the clothes he'd won, bringing him fruit and wine and heating up the tea on the bonfire. (Khasan was a bit of an aristocrat and loved his comforts.) Sometimes a disturbance would develop in the harem: the boys would start arguing and swearing in whispers. At such times, Khasan would simply turn his bulky body around and slowly, threateningly, deliver himself of one word:

"Hey!"

With that the youths would fall silent instantly and hold their breaths in fear and trembling.

After witnessing this one night, a thief said: "Hey, brothers, women can't hold a candle to those kids, I swear to God! If I ever get married, it's going to be to a pederast. That way I'll at least get someone faithful and devoted to live with."

As soon as they'd get to the pond, the boys would knuckle down to work. They'd build the fire, clean up the garbage from under the apple trees, and spread a brightly colored rug on the grass for Khasan to sit on.

He'd cross his legs and rest his elbows on his knees. Then, with a crackle, he'd open a sealed deck of cards and smile, gathering the wrinkles about his puffy, slanted eyes.

Then the game would begin.

I left for the train station to work and didn't get back to the pond till late that night.

The thieves were clustered about the campfire, buzzing with talk. The flickering tongues of light slipped along their faces and were reflected in the pond. From out of the crowd, Kinto came staggering to the edge of the water. There he stood, swearing his heart out in a rumble.

"What's up?" I shouted to him.

"Don't ask," he replied. And then, rumpling his hair and looking away from me: "Listen, Chuma, are you my friend?"

"Yes," I said. "What about it?"

"Then hear me out. . . . I blew it. I got wiped out. I wanted to win back some losses and I blew it all. Everything. Not just my stuff, either, but . . ."

"Mine, too?" I guessed.

"Yes, brother. Forgive me."

"What right did you have?" I said, getting angry.

"None, I know that. But there's nothing you can do about it now."

"The gold," I asked him hopefully. "You didn't touch the gold, did you?"

"Ah," Kinto sighed, turning his head away. "Ah, my dear friend . . ."

So that was it—he'd raided my stash (he was the only one to know about it), and that's what really got to me.

"What am I going to do with you now?" I hissed. "Well, what?"

"Whatever you want." He hung his head. "Forgive me."

"No," I said, "I can't forgive that. You and I are through, you hear me, you bastard?" I was choking on the words. "All right, we'll talk later. Right now I've got some business with Khasan!"

A minute later I was beside the Tatar. He was sitting, holding a cup in his palm, sipping tea.

"You want to play?" he asked, running his tenacious, appraising glance over me.

"Yes," I said.

"Well, then, come tomorrow."

"No," I said, "now!"

"It's late already. The game's finished."

I squatted down and looked him straight in the eye.

"Listen, Khasan, I've got a special score to settle with you. If you don't play with me right now . . ."

He reflected for a minute. He wiped his mouth and neck with a kerchief and, laying his cup aside, said: "What're your stakes?"

"Everything I've got," I said. "My jacket, my pants, my shoes. Everything goes, right down to the shorts!"

"All right." He nodded. "Three hands. Agreed?"

"Agreed," I said, breathing hoarsely and rapidly. "I agree to everything. Listen to me, Khasan, I'm going to beat you, I'm going to slaughter you!"

"And if you don't?" Khasan answered out of the corner of his mouth.

"Then my life is yours."

"Remember those words, thieves," Khasan said, looking around.

He passed me the deck.

"Deal!"

God, why did I ever get involved in that game? My plan was hopeless. Everything I did and said that evening couldn't have been more preposterous. I knew that, but I couldn't stop myself. I was completely mastered by my rage—so blinded, in fact, that I didn't even notice how and when the last hand ended.

Suddenly it was quiet. The people who'd thronged around us waited expectantly. Khasan's high, squeaky voice broke the silence.

"Your card loses. Pay up, please."

As everyone watched, I took off my jacket, drew my dagger, laid it down in the grass, and began to pull off my shoes.

Looking in the direction of the knife, Khasan suddenly said: "Let's have the feather, too!"

"Why?" I objected.

"What?" he said in amazement. "Don't tell me you forgot our agreement already?"

And, lifting his face and turning toward the crowd, he said with a grin, "Remind him, brothers, what were the conditions?"

Someone was kind enough to oblige. "The terms were clear. Everything, right down to the shorts."

"Precisely." The Tatar nodded and looked intently at me. "Did you hear?"

"I heard."

"Then pay up. In full! There's no mercy for you, understand?"

There was nothing I could do. I had to pay up. I tossed him my dagger and slowly undressed. Khasan scooped up my clothes and underwear and handed them over to his little boys. Then he got up and stretched.

"Well," he said, rolling his cigarette in his teeth, "that takes care of business. Now, brothers, who's for joining me in town for a little beer? I'm feeling pretty good. I think it's time for a little fun."

He spat out the butt and walked off in the darkness. The crowd slowly dispersed; some went with Khasan, others left for the train station.

Only a few people remained in the garden, gathered in a circle, quietly discussing something. I heard a burst of laughter and Kinto's voice calling from behind the trees:

"Hey, Chuma! How you feeling? Need some help?"

"Beat it!" I shot back in a rage. "I don't want to see any of you. You're all skunks, every last one of you! You aren't thieves, you're Khasan's lackeys, his stinking little bootlickers and slaves!"

I stood there swearing my head off, denouncing the thieves for all I was worth. I had the feeling I was saying something the boys would never forgive me for, but I kept on blathering anyway. Once the boys had had enough of it, they walked off, trailing their cigarette smoke in the distance and leaving me all alone.

"You're nuts," an old train robber named Botalo said as he left. "You don't want to make it any better. The hell with you. Go ahead, stay there and sit it out, like a monkey!"

As soon as his footsteps died out in the thickets, I calmed down. And started feeling miserable. I was sitting by the smoldering remains of the bonfire, resting my chin on my knees. The pungent smoke swirled around my face, but as the darkness thickened, it got colder and colder, sending shivers up and down my spine.

A cold, whitish mist, laden with the smell of mud and damp grasses, rose from the pond. Above the tossing leaves and the low tops of the trees the great icy stars twinkled away and the pockmarked moon rambled through the branches like a reddish smudge. Far off in the distance of the foothills, you could hear a slow, lonely wail. Something out there was pining in the night, a jackal probably, or a wolf. And looking up into the cold abyss of the sky, I suddenly started to wail, too, desperately, from the bottom of my breaking heart.

What could I do? I couldn't go back home looking like this (Kinto and I were living in the center of town with an Ossete acquaintance), and I was already getting uncomfortable sitting stark naked in the cold.

It's all so . . . stupid, I was thinking, trembling in a huddled mass. Everything I do is a bust. Not just this, but my whole life. What the hell was I trying to prove by challenging Khasan? I don't know the first thing about gambling.

There I was again, getting into another ridiculous mess and winding up in shit.

That's when I vowed never to touch another card again. Never! To commemorate the resolution, I decided to have an ace of clubs tattooed on my shoulder the first chance I got. That was the card the Tatar had used to crucify me.

A sharp rustle in the bush nearby brought me back to my senses. Someone was coming my way. I saw the murky figure of a woman darting in and out of the thickets. She stopped for a moment on the border between the light and the darkness and then walked to the bonfire. It was Queen Margo.

"I've come for you," she said simply. "Get up, let's go."

I got up joyfully—and then sat right back down, covering myself with my hands.

"How can I go?" I whispered. "Look for yourself."

"So I see." She laughed, throwing up her hands. "My poor boy, my little naked one. How in the hell did that happen to you?" She quickly took off her cloak and passed it to me. "Here, cover yourself."

A little while later as we walked along the dark streets of the suburb, I asked her about herself. "Where did you come from?"

"Rostov," she said.

"Been here long?"

"I got here yesterday." She paused and smoked her cigarette. "On business."

"How did you find out about me?"

"By chance. I dropped into the restaurant and some thieves were there, drinking, joking around, and talking about you. Soon as I heard, I came after you. I figured you must be catching your death of cold." Margo looked straight at me and added in a murmur, "What you need right now is a strong glass of tea with some spirits in it. That'll do the trick!"

"It sure wouldn't hurt," I said. "But where are you going to get anything to drink in the middle of the night?"

"Don't worry about that," Margo said gaily. "I can find anything."

"Where do you live, by the way?"

"Right here," she said, turning into the alley. "This is the place."

Later, wrapped up in a shaggy robe, I sat on the low,

upholstered ottoman, surrounded by a multitude of pillows. Margo's room was quiet, comfortable, and warm. Weakened by the tea and spirits I'd drunk, I lay back on the pillows, had myself a smoke, and feasted my eyes on her.

She was tidying up the table. When she finished she neatly shut the shade, tried the lock on the door, and with a sigh, started to undress.

She threw her arms back and unfastened the tight hooks of her collar. Her dress fell with a leisurely rustle to the floor and, stepping across it, she batted her eyelashes and said: "Well, am I pretty?"

She stood before me, tall, big-breasted, bathed in the trembling light of the lamp. The glow flowed along her shoulders, her lustrous skin, her resilient thighs. And, looking at them, I muttered as I rose:

"Beautiful . . ."

Like magic, all my sleepiness disappeared.

"Beautiful," I repeated. "What can I say? You are my Queen!"

"Well, come here, then," she said, "and let's crush the hell out of the bedbugs!"

KHASAN UNMASKED

I woke up the next morning drenched in a hot sweat, my head pounding with pain.

"It's the flu," Margo said, looking me over. "It caught up with you after all."

With that she straightened out my pillow and tucked me in. "Just lie there," she said, "and don't move. I'll go get some medicine."

She dressed quickly and left. In a short while she returned with a friend—a well-known Groznyi prostitute nicknamed Altyna.

A word or two about nicknames. In the criminal world, as everybody knows, proper names hardly ever exist. Once a man's arrived in thief society, he receives, as it were, a second christening based on his professional and personal qualities. I became Chuma, for example—a term in which my recklessness and quick temper played a role. There's always been a certain play of irony in the names traditionally given to prostitutes, too, like Mymra, Shushera, Altyna. Altyna, for instance, is the old Russian term for a three-kopeck coin. Thus, her name is also her price—and not a very high one at that.

Russian thieves don't hold prostitution in very high regard. Lady thieves, partners in work, businesswomen like Queen Margo herself are treated with much greater respect. She'd never have borne a royal title, in fact, if she'd been a common whore.

In the case of Margo's friend, the Groznyi girl, the nickname seemed totally inappropriate. Green-eyed, redheaded, with a soft face sprinkled with golden freckles that added to her good looks, Altyna was quite attractive.

I was lying in a semiconscious state, smoking a cigarette and lazily listening to the voices coming from the kitchen. Suddenly I was on my guard. Someone had mentioned Khasan's name.

"Hey, Margo!" I shouted. "What're you saying about Khasan?"

"Nothing much," she said, appearing in the doorway. "Just that Altyna had seen him a few times at the market, near the stalls."

"Near which stalls?" I wanted to know.

"The ones by the entrance."

"Where they sell playing cards?"

"Probably." Margo shrugged her shoulders. "I don't know."

"When did she see him?" I asked, getting up and stubbing out the smoldering butt. "Tell Altyna to come here."

"Why? What's up?"

"I don't know myself yet," I said, "but I've got a hunch. I've got to check it out first. Damn, why didn't I think of it before? Do you go to the market a lot?" I asked Altyna, who'd run in from the kitchen.

"All the time," she answered. And, twitching her little shoulder, she added, "I work the area, you know."

"And you see Khasan a lot?"

"Not every day." She gave it a thought. "But, yes, generally, as a rule."

"When did you see him for the first time?"

"Two months ago."

"Right there, by the stalls?"

"Yes," she said.

"What was he doing? Do you remember?"

"No," she muttered, knitting her brows, "he's not interested in women. And the feeling's mutual."

"Still," I asked, "try to remember. Who was he talking to?"

"A storekeeper. There's an Armenian working there, Sarkisian. A real old fox, shifty as hell. Looks like Khasan made friends with him. They've got some kind of deal going." She sighed and pursed her lips. "If I'd have known earlier, I'd have paid more attention."

"But what made you decide they had some kind of deal going?"

"What do you mean, decide?" she answered with surprise. "It was clear as day. I distinctly recall Khasan giving him some kind of package."

"Package?" I asked again quickly. "A big one?"

"No, not very. Just a paper package."

So! That was it! I'd guessed Khasan's secret. After arriving in Groznyi, he'd gone the rounds of all the market booths and bought up all the available cards. Then he'd marked them and returned them to the sellers. The dealers, of course, were in on it; that way they'd get double for each deck. Each time he'd organized his game, Khasan had sent his boys out to buy what looked like a perfectly new deck of cards.

I shared all my suspicions with the Queen.

"You may be right," she remarked with perfect good sense, "but you still need proof. If you ask me, the first thing to do is crack Sarkisian. If he corroborates . . ."

"We've got to lure him someplace," I muttered. "But how?"

"Luring him won't be any problem." Margo smiled. "My girls know how to do that." Turning to Altyna, she lightly slapped her tight thigh. "Easy as pie, isn't that right?"

"That's where the bread comes from." The girl laughed, reddening.

Margo chewed at her lip and said thoughtfully, "Make a deal with him for this evening. Meet him at eight and take him straight to the cellar near the train station. You know where."

And then, turning to me: "Who should we call?"

"Well, Kinto maybe," I said, "even though we're quits. Besides, it's just right for him. It was all on account of that Tatar that we split up in the first place."

"Good." Margo nodded, all business. "Who else?"

"You can call on Abrek, Botalo, Leo the Kike." I named a few of my friends. And then I cautioned her: "The main thing, though, is to keep it quiet. Remember, Khasan's crawling with lackeys. Half the thieves in town owe him something."

"But that just plays right into our hands," Margo protested. "That means they'll all be out to get him."

"In principle," I said. "But people have a way of thinking differently. Some would like revenge, sure, but others would toady right up to him. There's any number of bastards that'd tell him what's up. No, love, we'd better play it cagey."

Left alone, I spent a long time mulling over what had just happened. So, I'd been right after all! My hunch had paid off. All the legendary wins of the Tatar had been fakes. He'd tricked us and that, especially among thieves, was unforgivable. Closing my eyes, I imagined the scene that would soon be played at Train Station Street. Among my friends, among those Margo was sure to find, there was a certain Abrek. I'd had my reasons for thinking of him. Dry, dark, covered with scars, the fellow worked the surrounding mountains as a bandit and was well known for his brutality.

If Sarkisian ever fell into his hands, I was thinking, he'd crack like a nut. Falling into Abrek's clutches was a more terrifying prospect than falling into the hands of any member of the Cheka. For a second I even felt sorry for the merchant.

Without noticing it, I dozed off. A knock at the door suddenly roused me.

Consumed with curiosity, I quickly threw the lock—and shuddered. Khasan stood in the doorway! Not alone, either. His retinue crowded behind him. Screwing up his narrow, puffy eyes, he said from the threshold: "Greetings, Chuma. Get dressed!"

"What's this all about?" I asked in confusion.

"What?" He was surprised. "Don't tell me you forgot our agreement already? You threatened to destroy me. You threatened me in front of everybody. And then you said, 'If I lose, my life is yours.' That right?"

"Right," I muttered.

"Well, I've come for your soul."

And moving in on me, he added in a slow, quiet rasp: "Time for a new game, Chuma. We're going to play feathers. Plume to plume!"

He was speaking softly, but behind the door, among his lackeys, a vague murmur rose, the barest whisper, the slightest rustle. At the sound of his words, my insides suddenly tightened.

Khasan had spoken the ritual phrase; he was challenging me to a duel! "Feather to feather"—"knife to knife."

In principle, a thieves' duel differs little from the more conventional kind. Surrounded by a multitude of seconds, the antagonists face off with sidearms (knives, in this case). And, just as in the traditional confrontation, there are unalterable rules and prohibitions in effect.

One of them is that no quarter be given to either side. A fight between thieves is a fight to the death. That's the main difference between a thieves' duel and an ordinary one. That, and the fact that the seconds always support the victor to a man, swearing to shield and defend him before the authorities.

In the event of a police investigation (assuming they don't hide the body in time), the seconds serve as witnesses. The victor, whoever he may be, is declared to have been completely in the right; the guilt always lies on the side of the dead. It's always the loser, according to the general testimony of eyewitnesses, who was the true instigator of the fight; a bruiser, a violent man, it's always he who attacked first and was killed, killed accidentally, without malice aforethought and, of course, by his own knife.

Even though they're wise to what really went on and press for the truth, the police never get it. There's a special paragraph in the lawbooks dealing with the proper interpretation of "justified self-defense." The paragraph condones any defensive action up to and including homicide—if, of course, such action was justified and fully provoked. Naturally, in matters of this sort, a great deal depends upon the testimony of witnesses, and that's precisely why seconds are so important. The more of them, the better for the outcome.

Khasan had brought a whole gang of them with him. The excess, though, did little to delight me. Every last one of them was a henchman of his. I was in a tight spot.

"Get dressed!" Khasan repeated curtly. "Let's go."

"Where to?" I asked.

"Doesn't matter." He shrugged his fat shoulders. "How about the pond? It's nice and quiet there. Worse comes to worst, nobody'll be the wiser." And he gave me a piercing look. "Okay with you?"

"Why not?" I smiled, trying to talk as casually as possible. "It'll do. Wait just a minute."

I turned around, undoing the belt of my robe. Suddenly I remembered it was a woman's bathrobe and the only piece of clothing I had.

"Listen, Khasan," I said, "I'm ready to go wherever you want, but I'm stuck. You took all my clothes, and I haven't had much of a chance to get any new ones."

"You've got a point there," Khasan drawled. "Well, now what?" He knit his brows. "Since you can't go, let's do it here, long as your Margo isn't around. To tell you the truth, I can't stand to hear a woman cry."

Aha, I thought, so he doesn't know anything yet. The fact

that he came right now is just a coincidence. Not that it'll do me much good. The bastard's got the upper hand again! All the odds are in his favor.

"All right, Khasan," I said. "Let's cut the deck here. As long as the game's honest."

"What do you mean?" The Tatar gave me a broad smile. "Honesty's my motto."

"If that's the case," I said, "give me my dagger back. You remember it, don't you? You took it yesterday with my clothes."

"You mean that's the only one you've got?" he asked slowly.

"See for yourself." I spread my arms wide.

He was silent for a moment, mulling something over. Then he looked into the hall and waved his hand. "Come on in, boys!"

He started moving menacingly toward me. I leaped back involuntarily. Cooing and jutting out his lower lip contemptuously, he said: "Don't be so nervous."

He bent down and drew a knife out of the top of his boot. The dagger flashed an icy blue and disappeared. Khasan had tossed the knife and caught it on the fly. He did it again. And then he moved in, nestling the dagger in his half-folded hand, aiming the point at my stomach.

"Listen, this isn't by the rules," I said quickly (more quickly than I should have), feeling a wave of cold in my stomach and spine. "If we're going to play, let's do it fair and square. Where's my knife?"

"You mean this isn't yours?" The Tatar raised his brows.

"No."

"Forgive me, brother, but I was just about to give the little feather back to you."

He was having himself a good time. He stood with his squat legs spread wide, toying with the twinkling dagger. All around us, his army of lackeys crowded against the walls, filled up the room, and kept watchfully silent.

They were all waiting for the finish, and the upshot was as clear to them as it was to me. I'd been condemned and there was no way out. Everything depended on Khasan now, and he was in no hurry. He was too sure of himself for that. A born gambler, he'd always relied on his good fortune and it hadn't let him down yet.

Until now, that is. The door flew open with a crash, and I saw Kinto and Abrek standing on the threshold. Margo was right behind them, holding a pale and weeping Altyna up by the shoulders.

"Well, well, well," said Kinto, letting out a prolonged whistle. "What have we here? Why, it's Khasan! In person. How convenient, we were just about to go looking for you."

"What do you want from me?" Khasan asked.

"Can't you guess?" Kinto screwed up his eyes.

Slowly, he circled the room. Then he drove one of Khasan's little boys away from a chair and sat down; moving his knees apart and cushioning his chin on his hands, he continued:

"You can't guess? What's happened to you? You used to be so smart, so sharp; you knew everything! How to deceive thieves, how to mark cards . . ."

"What cards? What's this all about?" The Tatar was starting to lose his composure. His face got pinched and turned a dusty shade of gray. "I don't know what you're talking about."

"Sarkisian talked."

"Sarkisian?" Khasan whispered.

"Why, yes," said Kinto gently, almost tenderly. "Sarkisian. The one who works at the market? You've heard of him?"

"No," muttered Khasan, looking around him and moving quietly along the wall toward the center of the apartment.

"Well, he knew you. Even told us a thing or two. In detail. Just like at a confessional."

"I can't imagine what he could have told you." Khasan ran his tongue along his lips. "Anyway, where is he?"

"Alas," said Kinto, "he isn't anymore."

"What do you mean 'he isn't'?" I got into the conversation.

"Simple," Kinto muttered, "he isn't," and pointed over his shoulder at Abrek. "Your little buddy overdid it."

Abrek stood by the door, sucking on a butt that hung out of

the corner of his mouth, surveying the room from under his brows. There he stood, long, gaunt, and wiry, and beneath his heavy gaze, Khasan's little boys drew together, shuddering in fear.

"Abrek," I asked with a scowl, "what happened over there with you guys?"

"What's there to talk about?" Abrek shrugged his shoulders. "I made a mistake. He didn't want to crack at first, see, so . . . I got a little angry."

"A mistake!" Altyna suddenly spoke in a low, trembling voice. "You should have seen what that monster did to him!" She broke into sobs. "He tied him to a table and—"

"All right, quiet, calm down," Margo quickly leaned over her. "Quiet, my dear, be still."

"I'll be quiet," Altyna stammered, "I'll be quiet. . . ."

And, with that, she threw her head back and went into hysterics. "He trusted me and he came. His blood's on my hands!"

I flinched at those words. My worst fears had come true. Abrek had come on too strong. He was always overdoing it. Every affair he had anything to do with ended up in blood. Everybody knew that. I knew it; and so did Khasan.

Nobody noticed when or how the Tatar got to the window. Everybody's eyes had been glued to Altyna. Margo had been calming her down and giving her some pills to take; Kinto, swearing a mile a minute, had given her some water. I'd been busy too, so when the sound of breaking glass filled the room, we all turned to the window with surprise.

The frame had been torn off and left hanging by a hinge, the potted geranium had been thrown to the floor, and everything around it was littered with glittering glass, broken pieces of pottery, and red sprays of scattered flowers.

Khasan had disappeared. He'd taken advantage of the general commotion and jumped through the window free and clear. It hadn't taken much: Margo lived on the first floor.

"We let him get away," I shouted. "He slipped right through our fingers! What're we going to do now, brothers?"

"That was stupid, all right," Kinto muttered, going up to the window. He wiped away the fragments from the sill with his sleeve and touched the hanging frame.

"Stupid and careless. That's a hell of a way to do business. Ay-yai-yai. Well, all right."

He unbuttoned his jacket and pulled out a steel-blue Colt, glistening with oil, from his belt. He looked it over carefully, twirled the barrel, and like a cat leaped to the window sill.

"Where are you going to look for him?" Margo asked.

"I don't know." Kinto turned to face her. "What's the difference, anyway. He won't get far."

"Are you going to open fire right in the middle of the street? No, Kinto, that's not the way to do it!"

"Got any better ideas?" Kinto screwed up his eyes and squatted. "You're not going to let him go, are you? And how are you going to catch up to him later? And where?"

"Not at the pond, anyway," I said. "He won't show up at the den. He's not that stupid! He's only got one way out, now, and that's to leave Groznyi."

"True," Abrek's bass boomed from the doorway. (He'd been standing in the doorway, blocking the exit with his body.) "Khasan's no fool. But he's not going anywhere without his stash, either. A million and a half—that's nothing to laugh at! I'll stake my life on it, the first thing he does is get his hunk of gold. That's where we've got to look for him."

"But where's all the stuff hidden?" Kinto raised his eyebrows thoughtfully.

"We'll ask the kids." Abrek smiled. "They'll know."

As soon as he'd said that, a quiet panic spread among Khasan's boys. They'd gathered fearfully in a tight little cluster in the corner. Abrek gave them a long, hard look with his glassy eyes. Then he beckoned one of them with his finger.

"Come here, my little dove. Do you know who I am?"

"Yes," the boy answered readily. He moved close to Abrek and suddenly seemed to draw back, as if from a sudden blast of cold.

"Did you hear what we were talking about?" asked Abrek. "Yes."

"Can you show us Khasan's apartment?"

"I can! But which one do you want? He's got two of them."

"Both!" said Kinto. With a crunch of broken glass he leapt down from the window sill and slipped his revolver back under his jacket. "Both. And right away! There's not a second to lose."

Spitting out his cigarette butt, Abrek said: "Let's split up, then. I'll go with this one, you take one of the others."

"Right." Kinto nodded. He looked straight at the gang, gathered and whispering in the corner, and said imperiously: "All right, everybody, let's go! Show me where it is. You've got no choice. But understand this: if anybody tries anything funny, I'll lay him right out." With that he carelessly slapped the heavy, steel-blue Colt nestling by his stomach under his jacket.

DOUBTS

"What happened at the train station?" I asked Margo.

She sighed, looking sideways at Altyna, who lay face down on the couch, sedated and, by all indications, sound asleep. "You know this Abrek better than I do."

"I know him all right," I said. "He's a savage."

I remembered an incident in Tiflis—a monstrous event the local thieves of the Caucasus were still talking about. In one of the restaurants, at a dinner table, some thieves were having a conference. Abrek was among them. A certain Gogi, a local thief with a shady reputation, came up to the table. Some unpleasant rumors had been circulating about him. Word had it he'd been caught at a couple of dirty tricks he hadn't been able to explain away.

When Gogi got to the table the thieves dropped into a watchful silence. Then one of the more influential ones, an old Rostov housebreaker named the Demon, said, half under his breath, "Beat it, you bastard."

"Why?" Gogi stood up to him. "On what grounds?"

"Don't mess around with us," the thieves warned him. "You know what you did."

"I don't know anything," Gogi declared. "I didn't do anything wrong and I'm not going to answer for a lot of babbling other people do."

"That mean you're not going?"

"Right! And if I'm guilty of something, let's see the proof!"

That's when Abrek got out of his chair. He stood, walked right up to that miserable fellow, speared his eye with a fork, yanked it out, salted it a little, popped it in his mouth, chewed it, and washed it down with a glass of harsh Georgian wine.

"I can imagine what he did with Sarkisian!"

"Shredded his face with a knife," Margo said, nervously lighting a cigarette. "Made me sick to watch it."

"Where'd you put him afterwards?"

"In the basement boiler room. We had to throw him in the furnace so there wouldn't be any traces."

"Oh, God," I said, trembling, "God! What kind of a world are we living in? What's happened to me? Now the same thing's waiting for Khasan. What do I care if he's a cheat?"

"Pull yourself together!" Margo said sternly, stubbing out her cigarette against the table. "You should have thought of that before. It was all your plan, you know. You called the shots. Who are you going to blame for that?"

"Yes, yes, you're right."

Something snapped inside me like a string.

"I'm tired," I said in a thick, sleepy voice, "so tired! Margo . . . I don't know . . . I can't go on living like this."

"I understand," she replied, stroking my head with a surprising, almost maternal, tenderness and warmth. "I realize what you are now."

"What do you mean?"

"Don't fidget," she said, still stroking me and rustling my hair. "You're a man, of course, I learned that last night. Fine for bed, but still not ripe for business. There's a kind of flaw in you, just like there is in that other fool of mine, Altyna. It's your education that does you in, that need to be a good little person. People like you don't stand a chance in our world.

Goodness is like dung—they rub it in the ground for fertilizer. You're feeling sorry for Khasan. Well, he wouldn't have felt sorry for you, not one damn bit! He'd have been right, too, in his own way. He's an old swine, he knows what life is all about, and you still have to learn."

She lightly squeezed my fingers and scratched me with her nails.

"What an upbringing you need! Have to teach you everything—business *and* love."

"You just said I was fine when it came to loving."

"Yes"—she smiled—"you do have a talent, but not much training. You're still green and simpleminded. You don't understand the subtleties. Don't worry, though, I'll see to that. As long as you have the strength, the rest'll take care of itself."

Gradually, as we talked, I began to feel better. The wave of despair that had engulfed me fell away; breathing came easier and, after a while, I said: "Pour us some vodka, my dear!"

Margo nodded in agreement.

She quickly set the table and filled some small glasses. Then, holding hers high, she said, "Well, to your health!"

She screwed up her eyes inquisitively.

"How *are* you feeling, by the way? How's the flu?"

"You know," I said slowly, in amazement, "I think it's all gone."

And, indeed, it was. Apparently, the nervous shock I'd received that day had been the best medicine of all.

"What a day!" I sighed and tossed the vodka down. Outside the dark blue of evening was already thickening behind the broken windowpane. Somewhere off in the windy darkness the chase for Khasan was going on. New nightmares were in the making. As if in response to my thoughts, Altyna cried and moaned in her sleep.

She was lying with her arms spread wide apart, her breath labored and uneven. Her eyebrows were knitted and deep shadows gathered under her eyes. Two little wrinkles—two bitter little cracks—spread from the corners of her swollen mouth.

"Wake her up, Margo," I said. "Let her have a drink with us."

"She doesn't touch the stuff." Margo brushed it aside.

"Not at all?"

"Not a drop. She's a dope addict. She smokes opium, shoots it up sometimes. She's on it right now. I gave her a soporific, a triple dose. Let her get some rest and calm down."

"She's a good woman," I said, looking at her sleep. "Still young. I feel sorry for her."

"A woman!" Margo pursed her lips. "She was one once. The only thing left now is the name. And the appearance. A decoration, like in a theater. You understand what I'm saying?"

"Not really."

"They operated on her," Margo explained, lowering her voice, "and cut everything out."

"How did that happen to her?"

"Well, my little man, she was sick and didn't take care of herself. Thank God I found her in time. When I picked her up, I remember, she was lying in the dirt in a shed. Couldn't even walk, she was in such bad shape."

"Don't, don't!" Altyna suddenly muttered. She lapsed back into silence and then, in a quiet voice, added, "We'll meet in port."

"She must be remembering Leningrad." Margo looked back at her. "Her hometown. She came from a cultured family. Her father's a famous professor there."

Kinto reappeared just before dawn. He was dusty and exhausted. He sat down at the table, rolled a cigarette, and lit up.

"Can't stay for long," he said, "so listen to what happened. The Tatar got away. He gave us the slip!"

"You mean he didn't try to pick up his things?" I was amazed.

"Turns out he didn't have two places, but three. We found that one out later, by accident. The son of a bitch kept all the best stuff, the gold and the cash, by the train station, in a hut belonging to some crony of his."

"He had it all worked out right down to the last detail." Margo laughed. "Clever bastard!"

"You were in the hut, right?" I asked.

"What else?"

"When was it? What time?"

"Somewhere around ten."

"And he slipped out of here about two this afternoon." I looked at Margo. "Right?"

"I think so," she faltered, "I don't remember exactly."

"I remember," Kinto said. "When Abrek and I took off, it was a quarter past two. But what's that got to do with it?"

"During that time about six long-distance trains and a few locals pass through Groznyi. Now all we've got to do is make some inquiries."

"So that's what you're talking about." Kinto brushed it aside. "We checked that out already. He cast off on the four o'clock Rostov train. The boys saw him on the platform. Too bad they didn't know what was going on. But forget that. The main thing is, we've got his scent again!"

"Right," I said. "That's the main thing."

Involuntarily, out of some corner of my mind, I listened in amazement to myself. It was as if I'd become two people. In the morning I'd zealously exposed Khasan. By that evening I was already feeling sorry for him and lamenting the brutality of a thieves' world. Now, after learning that the Tatar had given us the slip, I was thirsting for vengeance again, helping the search, and hoping he'd be caught and punished. It's all so stupid, I was thinking, all this rushing around, contradicting myself. How many more changes am I going to go through before the night is out?

"I've just come from a meeting," Kinto said.

Margo got interested. "Well, tell us about it!"

"Everybody who ever owed Khasan anything was there. A hundred of them, no less. Botalo spoke. 'Finding Khasan's a matter of honor,' he said. 'It doesn't have anything to do with the money he took, it's a matter of principle. Acting like a bunch of *fraiers* the way we did—it's a disgrace! If we don't put that Tatar out of commission, we're going to be a laughingstock from Odessa to Vladivostok!' "

"Well said," I agreed. "Exactly!"

"By the way,"—Kinto glanced at me—"they all had a lot of nice things to say about you."

"He's a sharp little fellow." Margo patted me tenderly on the shoulder. "Talented. Only a little nuts."

"Stop it."

I brushed her hand away and then, scowling and smiling at the same time, said: "Anyway, it's just the other way around. Fact is, I'm a fool."

"Stop putting it on," Kinto said. "If it wasn't for you, Khasan wouldn't have been exposed in the first place. Everybody knows that."

"And if it hadn't been for you," I replied, "Khasan would have spilled my guts on the floor."

"That mean we're even?" Kinto said slowly.

"Looks that way to me."

Kinto got up and gave me his hand.

"Let's forget what happened, old man. Don't bear a grudge. Let's part friends, okay?"

"Okay," I said, pressing his dry, hard palm. "But why part?"

"I'm off."

"After Khasan?"

"Yes, we've got a whole brigade drawn up. The train's leaving in forty minutes."

Filling up the glasses, Margo said: "A toast." And she winked. "To success!"

We clinked our glasses in a spirit of friendship. Then Kinto turned toward the door. As I watched him leave, I got a sudden attack of anxiety.

"Wait!" I shouted. "You can't go without me!"

"But you're sick," he muttered in confusion, turning around in the doorway and fingering his cap. "Margo said so yesterday morning."

"That's right," she chimed in, pulling me by the sleeve. "And just where do you think you're going dressed like that? Take a look at yourself. You haven't even got any pants!"

"So what?" I brushed it aside. "We'll find pants somewhere, won't we, Kinto?"

He shrugged his shoulders. I walked toward him, staggered, and clutched for the back of a chair. The room suddenly darkened and started to spin. Objects swam around me. A reddish cloud slipped along the edges of my consciousness and for an instant clouded my vision. And through that crimson haze, Margo's voice seemed to call from far away. "Look . . . you can feel it yourself. . . ."

"I'm not sick," I whispered hoarsely, "I'm drunk. I got over the flu a long time ago. I just drank too much. It'll pass."

"But you've got a fever," Margo said. And I felt the cool touch of her hand on my cheek. "You're burning all over. Lie down, my dear, lie down."

"Where's Kinto?" I asked, objecting weakly.

"He left already," she answered, putting me back into bed. "He left. Now, go to sleep."

THE QUEEN AND HER FRIENDS

The incident at Stalin Pond had taken its toll. I fell ill and stayed in bed with a raging fever for two weeks. It was time well spent, though. I got to know a little bit about Margo and her many affairs.

As it turned out, Margo wasn't just head of the local Rostov den. She belonged to a solid corporation of underground establishments embracing almost all the cities of the Northern Caucasus. And that wasn't all. Margo had a finger in a number of other, very lucrative enterprises, including the resale of stolen and forged documents. It was this last activity that had brought her to Groznyi in the first place. Groznyi, ex-capital of the ex-republic of Chechen-Ingush.

I think I'd better add a word or two of explanation. The

events I'm relating took place in 1946, soon after the republic in question had been liquidated at the express orders of Stalin himself.

As in the days of the Babylonian captivity, people moved along the mountain roads laden with goods, their straggling cattle mooing, their children crying through the night. The only difference was that the armed guards were dressed in the uniform of the Red Army and over them an awesome red Soviet flag fluttered, a flag representing the government of the people and, as word had it, the most righteous power on the face of the earth.

The guards drove the people to the railroad, then into freight cars, and sent them off beyond the Urals for resettlement in Central Asia and Siberia. The operation was conducted with remarkable dispatch. In fact, they cleaned out the territory of the republic in no time at all.

Quickly, perhaps, but not completely. Not all the inhabitants of the hilly country were subject to exile—only those whose passports declared them to be of pure Ingush or Chechen stock. Besides, a number of them had hidden during the roundup and others had given the convoys the slip, quietly returning to their hometowns. Whatever their route of escape, they were all now in need of new papers.

It was a simple case of supply and demand. A black market instantly developed to provide the population with documents of every kind: passports, references, birth certificates, and identification cards.

Swindlers, counterfeiters, and scoundrels from every corner of the Soviet Union converged on Groznyi and the surrounding towns. Specialists from Leningrad and Odessa, though, were decidedly in the majority, and it was with the Odessa contingent that Queen Margo had her main contacts. Margo was seventeen years older than I, and still remembered the classic Odessa of Mishka the Jap, Semka Rabinowitz, and Sonka Golden-Hand, a world of contrabandists, of portside thieves, of daring muggers and the dashing knights of Moldavanka.

Her old friends would often come to call—the frail and nimble Mark, for instance, with his carefully trimmed mustaches and his almost lipless mouth. He was constantly giggling and rubbing his palms in short, nervous movements.

As soon as he'd sit down he'd fold one spindly leg under him and twist the other like a corkscrew around the leg of the table. Contorted like that, he'd wipe his palms and launch into lengthy conversations with Margo. They'd grown up together in the same house on the shores of the Black Sea and he'd often recall their early years with a kind of elegiac sadness.

"Your late mother, Margo," he'd say, sighing and fidgeting on the chair, "was a wise woman. We won't ever see her likes again. I don't recall the year exactly—let's see, '28 it was, yes, '28, when I received my first honorarium for the affair with the merchandise invoices, she said, 'Mark, it gladdens this old heart of mine to see you young people. Little by little you're making a name for yourselves. It seems like only yesterday you and Margo were fighting over a little pot and running snot-nosed through the streets. Now, look at you, a thief already, a man of merit and distinction. And my little Margo, she's well established, too. I can see the underwear she walks around in—enough to make the Italian consul's wife green with envy. And if anyone says otherwise, let him roast in hell. You youngsters have made me happy and now I can die in peace.'"

The Novitsky brothers, well-known engravers and specialists in printing seals, were frequent visitors, too. They were a happy bunch. One of them, Arkady, played well on the guitar. The other, his older brother Yakov, was fond of delivering toasts that were intricate, involved, and rarely to the point.

"Once upon a time, a flock of birds was on the wing," he'd begin, raising his glass over the table and unharnessing his thick lips. "After a long flight it settled on the sea and then continued on its way. One small bird, though, a wily thing, an egoist in short, decided to sneak away and graze upon the grass. 'Let the others toil and labor,' she thought as she settled down on a bush, 'I like it right here!' It was a *fraier*'s thought she never had the chance to finish. For suddenly some wolves fell on her and ate her in a trice. And more power to them! Why? Because you should never, never leave the flock. You should always hold on to your own and cleave to the flock. It's the law of the dialectic! So, I drink now to our Margo, may she live to be *two* hundred. To our Queen, who knows the laws and respects them. When things were smelling sweet here in the Caucasus, she remembered her Odessa and instantly sent for us! Once, long ago, we'd helped *her*. You remember, Arkasha, that little certificate we forged for the regional court? When Margo's defense counsel produced it, the prosecutor had a stroke. Lost the power of speech he did and, as far as I know, still hasn't got it back. We came to Margo's rescue and now she's come to ours. And that's beautiful! How else are we going to stick together?"

I remember an amusing chat I once had with the Novitskys. I'd been sleeping, I recall, and was awakened by a heated conversation. As far as I could tell, the brothers were discussing the passport policy and the internal politics of the state. I listened for a while and then chipped in:

"Explain something to me, will you? Not so long ago the republic here was in a kind of state of siege. MVD troops everywhere. Now the place is full of Cheka people. Right?"

"Right," the brothers agreed.

"Then how come they haven't made a move to clamp down on us? Why are they leaving us alone? How do you make sense out of that?"

"Simple," Arkady said. "The militia's not the only agency in charge of law and order around here. The military commandant's got a say, and he doesn't give a damn about thieves. The Ingushi are what he's after. Political enemies, not us."

"The Ingushi? What do they know about politics?"

"Not much maybe, but the MVD does."

"What are they after them for?"

"God knows," Yakov muttered, scratching his shaggy red beard. "That's not the point, though. The Communist Party has the same system we do—guilty until proven innocent. If they accuse you of something, you damn well better be able to justify yourself, or you're an enemy, pure and simple."

"Stalin's got a saying," Arkady chimed in. "Goes something like this: 'If we enforced our laws the way thieves do theirs, we'd have reached Communism a long time ago.'"

"Come off it, Arkady, you're lying," Margo said.

"The hell I am!" Arkady answered seriously. "Go dig around in his books, you'll find it."

"What did you do, dig around in there yourself?"

"Me? No. But Kostya the Count did. He told me about it and you're not going to doubt Kostya, are you?"

"Well, if it was Kostya . . ." Margo shrugged her round shoulders.

"Well, if it was the Count," Yakov replied like a distant echo.

Arkady took his guitar off the floor and lazily strummed a chord. As it faded, he said with a laugh: "You know, if you think about it, who's Stalin anyway? A big thief, just like the rest of us."

"Like us?" Yakov was offended. "I beg your pardon! You're talking about thieves, cultured people. And, judging from everything I've heard, he's a common Avlabar thug."

"If he was," I broke in, "I'd call him to a meeting and tell him a thing or two. That's what I'd do. No, boys, don't go around insulting decent, self-respecting thieves. He may look the part, but, take my word for it, he's not one of us!"

"He's a bitch, pure and simple," Queen Margo said slowly and distinctly from the corner.

Kostya the Count, incidentally, was a tall, portly man with a sparkling pair of gold-rimmed pince-nez perched on the gristly bridge of his nose. He was bald as an egg, with a mouthful of gold teeth that flashed as he smiled. The son of a Galician tailor, he posed as a Polish aristocrat and pulled it off brilliantly. Polished, scented, and always perfectly dressed, Kostya created an imposing impression wherever he went.

A masterful student of the legendary Rabinowitz, he was also one of the last exponents of a dying breed of conmen and swindlers. It was a sheer delight to listen to him talk to Margo, recalling the names of old friends, acquaintances, and teach-

ers. Smoking a cigarette in a long amber holder and sipping a
sour wine (he had no use for vodka and drank only the driest
of wines), he'd expounded in his slightly affected, nasal voice:
"Ah, my dearest, how time flies! It's a dreadful thought, I'll
grant you, but there's hardly a soul left from the old days. And
what people they were, my God! What a gathering that was on
Deribasovskaya and Lanzherona and—where was it now?—
that place where we first met?"

"You must be thinking of the den on Pushkinskaya Street,"
Margo would prompt him, "opposite the tobacco factory.
Lyubka the Flea was still with me back then. They slaughtered
her later in port, poor dear."

"Yes, yes, that's it. On Pushkinskaya. Sema, Sonechka,
Kolya the Greek—what men of refinement! There were
others, of course; the Jap, for instance. To be perfectly frank,
though, I didn't like Misha—too coarse. It's the intellect I
value, my dear, brilliance and wit. All gone, now. But, back
then, ah. . . . You hardly saw the real Odessa, by the way. It
had already begun to degenerate by the time you arrived. Still,
what people there were even then! Your protectress, Golden
Hand, was an absolute charm, a woman of great wisdom. Till
she hit the bottle, that is. But that's another matter. What can
you expect of a woman in her cups?"

"That's exactly what she said to Semka," Margo laughed,
"the night she threw up on his coat. 'Monsieur Rabinowitz,'
she said . . ."

"Yes, yes, I remember. The main thing, though, is that the
last of the aristocrats are dying off. Back in '32, by the way, on
the White Sea Canal, in the Voitinsky Sector, I ran into my
old teacher. God, what they'd turned that man into! He was a
complete wreck, thin, broken, his eyes watering, his hands
atremble. Those famous hands of Syoma's. Hands of a genius!
After something like that, how can you keep on going?"

The Count fell silent for a moment, languidly sipping his
wine. Then he continued in a drier tone of voice: "Still, you
have to try. And so, my precious, to business!"

Margo's business here was quite simple. She was the
swindlers' main supplier of documents cornered from the local

pickpockets. Every Saturday, like clockwork, a handsome older woman would come to call with a shopping bag full of the weekly catch of the screen men.

Several thief groups worked for Margo, not only in Groznyi, but in Mokhachkala and Ordzhonikidze as well. Each of them would send its merchandise in a separate parcel. Margo would take the bags and settle on the spot with the messenger. She'd pay the going price. (A new, clean passport was worth 300 rubles, a worn-out one only half the price. Union cards and every other kind of official paper would go at anywhere from 150 to 250 rubles.)

Then her friends would appear. Generally, as I've said already, they were Odessa people—although there were some notable exceptions.

One was a thin, swarthy, hook-nosed man. They called him Smoke-cured. He was an old friend of hers, too, but where and when they'd met was a mystery to me. One thing was sure: Smoke-cured was no man from Odessa! He couldn't stand idle chatter and had even less use for sentimental reminiscences. Silent and contained, he'd sit down at the table the minute he arrived and, whistling and screwing up his eyes, he'd dig through the documents and hold them up to the light. After taking the papers he wanted and stashing them in his brief case, he'd depart, leaving Margo a thick packet of money. He never bartered and would always settle generously, offering much more than any of the others.

Margo would ask him to stay a while and have a bit of vodka. Smoke-cured, as a rule, would be in too much of a hurry to accept. Once, though, he did, giving me my first real opportunity to get to know him a little better.

Casually, Smoke-cured started to recall Bucharest. It turned out he'd met Margo there as far back as 1942.

Aha, I thought, so that's what he is—a Rumanian! Of course!

But, just then, for no apparent reason, he started to curse the Rumanians. It's hard to explain, but of all Margo's friends, this gloomy fellow interested me the most.

I got out of bed (I was already well on the way to recovery

and had begun to walk) and sat down at the table. We started to talk, Smoke-cured and I, and I was amazed to learn that he'd been born in Novocherkassk.

"Then you must have heard about Denisov," I said.

"Denisov?" He raised his eyebrows. "He was some sort of general, wasn't he?"

"Commander-in-Chief of the White Army of the Don," I said. "Well, he was a relative of mine, on my mother's side."

"A relative?" he said in amazement. "How interesting. What happened to him? They kill the old man?"

"Not a chance. He got away. He's living abroad now, the same as almost all of my Novocherkassk relatives."

"Where?"

"In France. Paris, I think."

"Ah, Paris!" Margo sighed long and low. "Paris, city of my dreams. God, how I idolize France! What I wouldn't do for a little side trip there, just half a year, for a look at some real living."

And softly and sadly she sang:

> *"Naked girls are dancing there,*
> *The ladies all have sable wraps.*
> *Fops pay in gold just to impress*
> *And all the thieves wear evening dress."*

"Right," I muttered. "Just one little look. But how?"

"You have any leads on them?" Smoke-cured asked in a businesslike way.

"Till the war broke out my mother corresponded with somebody, I don't remember who, an aunt I think. And then—well, you know, the war started."

"Maybe nobody's left," Margo said.

"Unlikely." Smoke-cured laughed drily. "White Guardsmen know how to hang on to life. Besides, the Gestapo treated them with kid gloves."

"What difference does it make," I said. "It's too hard to get to France anyway. Hard, hell, it's impossible!"

"Nonsense," Smoke-cured replied. "Nothing's impossible."

He reflected for a moment in silence, tapping his fingers on the edge of the table. Then, screwing up his eyes, he said: "Do you really want to go abroad?"

"Of course," I said.

"You serious?"

"What about you?" I fired back. "Are you being serious with me?"

"You know I don't make a habit of joking around," he said slowly. He was about to add something else when Margo interrupted the conversation.

"Stop it right there!" she said. "For the love of God, don't go around mixing this poor boy up." She pressed me to her heavy breast. "Let's say you do go there. What'll you do then, eh? Open suitcases? You can't get rich at that. They don't think much of train thefts over there, and that's the only thing you know how to do!"

"That's not so," I answered in confusion. "That's not the only thing."

"What else?"

"Well, I don't know. I'll see when I get there."

"You'll end up seeing the same thing you see here: the blue sky through a big cage!"

"So what if I do?" I scratched the back of my neck. "You trying to frighten me with prison?"

"Listen, my dear, their prisons are different. And so is everything else. In the Russian underworld you have your own privileges as a thief. Here you're an aristocrat, there—there you're nothing but dirt beneath their feet, believe me! Who's going to need you there, you a foreigner, a new-come tramp. You don't know the first thing about their ways or their language."

"How do you like that?" Smoke-cured suddenly said. "You're in love with that boy." And, for the first time I could remember, he started to laugh. His eyes narrowed, his upper lip lifted, and little dry wrinkles coursed from the corners of his mouth through his dark, sunken cheeks.

"Admit it, you love him, don't you?"

"What are you talking about?" Margo got confused. "I've got maternal feelings, that's all."

"The most dangerous of all," Smoke-cured said with a yawn. He stole a glance at his watch. He scowled anxiously and got ready to leave.

"Listen," I said. "Where are you staying?"

"How can I tell you?" He hesitated. "I'm on the road all the time, my friend. I've got to be in North Ossetia for a few days, in Ordzhonikidze. From there I head to Rostov, and then it's the Ukraine. Afterwards, maybe, I'll drop by here again. Although"—Smoke-cured knit his brows and bit his lip—"I'm not too sure of that."

"But how can I find you?" I asked. "I still may need you."

"Need?" He looked at me intently, from beneath his brows. "You mean—in regard to Paris?"

"Well, let's suppose."

"If you've already decided," he drawled, "then fine. You know the city of Lvov?"

"I've heard of it," I said. "It's somewhere in the West Ukraine, isn't it?"

"Precisely." He nodded. "The westernmost Soviet city. So listen. I have friends there. Check with them. They'll see to everything you need. For the time being, this little note will do. . . ."

He quickly scribbled something on a sheet of paper. Then he got a thick white envelope from his briefcase, put the note in it, and carefully licked it shut.

"Here," he said. "Take it! I wish you luck."

"But where's the address?" I was surprised, turning the letter in my hand.

"We don't write down addresses, we memorize them," Smoke-cured said. "Learn that rule fast!"

"See?" Margo said. "You see what a fool he still is. . . ."

"It's nothing." He brushed it aside. "He'll wise up in time."

And holding me lightly by the wrist, he ordered: "Now listen carefully!"

He dictated an address to me, naming the street, the house, the man I was to ask for. Then he made me repeat it and, saying a quick good-bye, he left.

It took a long time to fall asleep that night. I thought about my Paris relatives and, closing my eyes, tried to imagine what they looked like. I'd hardly ever brought them to mind before—there'd never been any reason to. Everything related to the Belyaevskys and the Denisovs seemed far away to me, almost unreal. I tried to envision them, but I couldn't. The view was clouded by a shimmering mist speckled with the features of Paris. Paris the foreign, the mysterious, the alluring—what would she really be like? And what would I find there? Rest and deliverance from all my wanderings? Or was it all a mirage that would fade like so much mist in my hands?

AT THE CROSSROADS

In the morning Smoke-cured's letter was gone.

It had been lying under the mattress, at the head of my bed. I knew at once that Margo had taken it.

She was busying herself in the kitchen with the dishes. When I called her, she took her time coming.

"Why did you do it?" I asked sternly.

"Do what?" she said with a show of surprise. "What are you talking about?"

"The letter . . ."

"Why, what happened?"

"Out with it!" I said. "Start explaining. Well, I'm waiting!"

Suddenly, she seemed to go weak. She lowered herself into a chair and covered her face with her hands. After a long wait, she said slowly, "Do you really plan to use that note?"

"Why not?" I answered. "It's the first time in my life some kind of break has come my way, something with the smell of success on it."

"Are you sure it's success?"

"You're not?"

"No," she said.

"But why? You mean trouble getting across the border?"

"That, too." Margo nodded, making a wry face. "You don't really think—"

"What's there to think? Look," I objected, "it's a risky business, I know that. So what? You can't change that. Besides, I'm not going alone, they'll help me."

"Even so," she said quietly, "think about it. You're putting your fate in the hands of some people you don't even know."

"I assume they know what they're doing."

"They know their jobs, all right." Margo suddenly smiled. "You can bet on that!"

"Who are they, anyway?" I wanted to know. "Counterfeiters? Contrabandists?"

"Something like that," she said hesitantly. "Smoke-cured's got friends everywhere and they're all different. The old Turk's got his finger in a lot of pies."

"What do you mean 'Turk'?" I was surprised. "He's a Don Cossack from Novocherkassk."

"That's what he told *you.* He told *me* he was born in Constantinople. Anyway, that's not what matters. The main thing I'm trying to do is knock a little sense into that head of yours. Don't be in such a hurry. Don't go looking for trouble!"

"But listen," I began, "you can understand for yourself—"

"I understand," Margo interrupted me. "I understand, you silly fool. You're tired, you're looking for changes. But what if they turn out to be the kinds of changes you aren't going to like? Then it'll be too late."

"So? You want me to give it up?"

"Of course not, that's not the point," Margo answered with annoyance. And sadness. She seemed to be grieving over something.

"Wait a little longer, that's all," she said with difficulty. "Give yourself a little more time. Then if you can't stand it anymore, push off for Lvov. Nobody's going to stop you."

"Well," I said, after some painful reflection, "maybe you're right. Maybe there isn't any reason for rushing off. Still, about that letter . . ."

"Let me keep it for the time being," she said quickly. Like a little bird, she cocked her head to one side and turned her smoky eyes on me. "You're careless, you'll only lose it somewhere. And that's something you can't afford to do. Never, for any reason, God help you! Even thinking about it gives me the chills!"

And so the letter stayed with Margo. After giving it a little thought, I didn't ask for it again. Somewhere in the bottom of my soul I realized my friend had been right: for the time being, at least, there was no reason to rush.

The two of us soon left Groznyi. After a short stay in the Transcaucasus region, we left for Central Asia, lingering in Turkmenia and Uzbekistan, and then off to the Far East.

These trips were connected with my trade as a train thief. That wasn't the only reason, though. After deciding to leave Russia (exactly when didn't matter; it was the idea that mattered), after deciding sooner or later to go abroad, I found myself gripped by a strange kind of sentimentality. I traveled the Russian roads, consumed by that vague uneasiness, that aching sadness that usually afflicts us all on the eve of a parting with our native soil. A man seems to acquire a second sight at times like that, a special sensitivity, a feverish intensity and attention to detail. Everything that once seemed so empty and petty—the impoverished landscape, a sliver of moon in a roadside puddle, the squeaking of the floorboards in a hut—seemed infused with a deep and sudden significance.

I wanted to take it all inside me now, to remember and preserve it forever!

I was on the move through the East, rushing and grieving, lingering for long periods at a time by small, out-of-the-way train stations. And, wherever I went, Margo was right there with me.

A wise woman, she knew what was happening to me, and never left me anywhere alone. Still, consumed as she was with me, she never for a second neglected her own affairs. And she had them everywhere. In Ashkhabad and Bukhara she dealt in narcotics; in Vladivostok, it was some kind of shady currency operation.

This was a true businesswoman, with friends and associates

in every city we visited. All we had to do was arrive and instantly a safe lodging would be at our disposal. I confess that, in all my travels, I'd never had it so good before. In fact, my connection with Margo was a real help in understanding the full might and expanse of the criminal underworld.

In principle, the criminal world exists everywhere. Every society on earth is divided into two strata, an external, visible level and an illegal underground—the second being, so to speak, the mirror image of the first. Here, in the depths, you can find every major feature of life on "the surface," noblemen and plebes, transgressors and law abiders, each with their own social code.

Naturally, every underground is organized according to the traditions and mores of the country where it is found. And of all the underworlds, the one closest to the Russian (as far as I can judge) is the Italian Mafia.

Not that there aren't differences, and considerable ones at that, the main one being that the Russian criminal world, unlike its Italian counterpart, hasn't the slightest interest in the sociopolitical affairs of the country at large. It lives its own, hidden life. The "legitimate" world bears the same relationship to a Russian thief as a henhouse to a fox. The problems of the henhouse are of no interest to the fox. His only concern is to penetrate it, satisfy his appetite, and get the hell out in time. The Italian Mafia, as far as I can tell, feels perfectly at home in the henhouse, where it not only eats its fill, but determines the pecking order of the birds themselves.

The Russian criminal world has existed since time immemorial. During the reign of Peter the Great, according to official estimates, there were more than thirty thousand thieves on the outskirts of Moscow alone. Nor was Moscow the only city to be so honored. On that subject there are any number of folk sayings. "In the city of Orel and Kromy," one of them goes, "you'll find the best thieves, but Elets City is the father of them all." The country, in short, was teeming with thieves. But they lived apart, running separate, isolated gangs. A solid, powerful organization didn't really develop until the end of the last century.

The organization went through an accelerated period of growth right after the Revolution, during the years of the New Economic Policy. By the start of the Second World War, it already embraced the full extent of the State or, to put it differently, one-sixth of the land mass of the entire planet. By the end of the war, as I've already mentioned, a split was occurring in thief society: a period of dissolution, much like the Time of Troubles, leading to the most brutal infighting. Little by little, the Russian Mafia (I'll still avail myself of the term) began to break down and fall into decay.

I came upon it just as the dissolution was beginning to show. Externally, the organization was still strong. While the disintegration proceeded in the prison camps and torture chambers, things on the outside still seemed relatively quiet. Life went on as usual, and one general code of ethics prevailed throughout the land, from the Bay of Finland to the shores of the Japan Sea.

It was there, by the Japan Sea, in a portside alehouse in Vladivostok, that I finally learned the full story of the affair with Khasan. An old friend and train thief, Botalo, told me all about it.

It turned out they hadn't managed to do Khasan in at once. He'd covered his tracks for quite some time. The thieves had finally caught up with him in Luisdorf, a suburb of Odessa. In the exchange of gunfire, however, he hadn't been the only one to fall. My friend Kinto had been hit as well. He was lying now in one of the dens of Odessa in severe pain, constantly calling my name. He missed me and desperately wanted to see me.

"He was too reckless," Botalo droned in distress. "We could have taken the Tatar from behind, from the shore, from behind the rocks. It would have been a cinch. That's what we were planning to do. But Kinto kept on pushing and ran right into it, the poor bastard. Now he's dying for it."

"They're taking care of him, though, aren't they?" I asked.

"Sure." He waved his hand.

"'What do the doctors say?"

"Different things." Botalo frowned. "It's a rotten deal, all right. Not much hope for him, they say."

I turned to Margo and our glances crossed. She looked at me and understood. She sighed lightly and lowered her lashes.

It was clear without words: the time had come to head back again. And there wasn't a second to lose!

THE HAND OF FATE

I was anxious all the way, afraid I might be too late. And I was. Kinto died a day before I got there.

Manka Kalyava—her name means "boot top," in Ukrainian—the proprietress of the den that took Kinto in after he'd been shot, brought out a small bundle from the back room.

"This is for you," she said, sobbing. "Kinto asked me special to give it to you."

There was something clanking and tumbling inside the package. I untied the rag and saw gold: the rings, brooches, medallions, and watches that Kinto had once stolen from my hiding place and lost to Khasan. We'd parted ways on account of that junk, and now my dear friend was paying back his debt.

My hands trembled, the bundle fell, the watches and rings rolled along the floor.

"Damned junk," I muttered, "what in the hell do I need it for?" I angrily crushed one of the medallions under my foot.

Manka, a heavy, old, mustachioed Georgian woman, fell wailing to the floor and grabbed me by the leg.

"Don't destroy it," she moaned, "it's worth money!"

"How much?" I asked.

"I can't tell you right off."

Groaning, she gathered up the pieces in her hand. Then she turned her colorless eyes to me.

"How could you do that? Fear the Lord, thief! For a little thing like that, if it was in one piece . . ."

"I'm not asking you about the medallion, I mean every-thing. How much would all of it bring?"

"You want to sell it?"

"The sooner the better," I said.

"Well, I'll have to think it over and talk to a few folks." Manka straightened herself out and drew a strand of gray hair back from her brow. "There's gold and then there's gold, you know. Not to mention the extra costs. They're hot goods, after all. . . ."

"All right, all right," I said. "Think it over, do what you want. But in the meantime—"

I bunched my fingers and rubbed them right under her nose.

"How about a little advance?"

"How much?"

"Whatever you can stand."

We quickly came to terms and I received, by way of a deposit, a plump, crackling pile of ten-ruble bills. The next day I went on a spree and drank them all away.

My memories of this period are rather hazy. I was constantly drunk, staggering through the city with a raging pain in my soul, committing every outrage I could think of and surren-dering myself to dissolution. More than booze, I was taking morphine too. I'd been playing with narcotics for quite some time: hashish in the Caucasus and opium in Vladivostok and Central Asia. I'd even tried my hand at morphine and cocaine.

Cocaine was my favorite. Most people snort it, of course. Experienced drug users, though, prefer rubbing a little of it into their gums—a far more practical method. Entering the stomach mixed with saliva, the drug then has a more powerful and sustained effect.

I said I liked cocaine. That isn't quite true. The fact is I didn't like any narcotic enough to get addicted to it. The heavy debilitation and somnolence that follow a pipe or two of opium, the languor induced by morphine, and the sharp awakening brought by cocaine, all seemed too exhausting—and, frankly, rather boring—to me.

I've seen hundreds of addicts in Russia and thousands in the West and what I have to say may come as something of a surprise to them. To each his own, of course. But I love life in all its immediacy, in the flesh! To this day I see no real need to be continually turned on like that or, what's more likely, knocked silly, split in two, and submerged into a state of non-being. It was in such a state, in fact, that a good friend of mine, Kim the Korean, was hacked to death with an ax.

It happened near Iman, in a district by the sea. After sucking his 'fill of opium, Kim lay back on a straw mat to "swim" (a term thieves use for the floating sensation induced by narcotics). There he was, swimming and smiling. When he saw the ax raised over his head he didn't even tremble or question a thing. He took the blow without a murmur, in blissful submission. And that's the way I remember him: a cloven, open skull and a mouth frozen in a smile. A dead mouth along which green dung flies buzzed and crawled.

No, I can't say I like swimming that much. I don't want to be left weak and defenseless. So I resorted to narcotics only rarely, during times of desperate suffering, whenever my anguished soul thirsted for a moment's consolation. At times like that the very best prescription is a hearty swallow of spirits, a strong cigarette and, to top it off, several grains of cocaine taken on the tip of the finger and rubbed thoroughly into the gums. Wait a bit and watch the world turn from gray to pink.

Yes, I lived those days in a dream—an alcoholic delirium compounded by a narcotic haze. Dimly, as the murk slowly began to fade, I can recall a few, fragmentary, almost accidental scenes.

I see the catacombs of Odessa: a lulled, cavelike semidarkness, a noisy gathering, some girls, naked and dishevelled. One of them sits on the ground, resting my head on her knees. She murmurs something in a lazy drawl; whether it's singing or crying I can't really say. I don't remember her face—only the tattoos. The lower part of her belly is decorated with a large, oval inscription: "Welcome!" it says. And on one sleek thigh, another inscription: "Death to the cops, life everlasting to thieves!" On the other there's a heart pierced by an arrow and, beneath it, "I die in ecstasy!"

Another scene: a gypsy camp in the suburb of the city, by Near Mills. (These gypsies didn't live in tents, as was customary, but in barracks. "Wintering gypsies," they were called.) Sprawling on a dusty rug I smoke and talk with the gypsies about the Kopylyovs, Kinto's people. They know the family here. Not too long ago they were seen in Armavir with the old people and Masha. It turns out she had a son: a gray-eyed, bawling fellow named Mikhail.

"And the father?" I ask impatiently. "Who's the father?"

"Nobody knows," they tell me. "The fellow she lives with now took her when she was already pregnant."

"You mean she's married?"

"And how!"

"Living well?"

"Like hand in glove. Everybody should be so lucky."

"Who is he, anyway?"

"A guitar player from the band. He's performing at the Armavir Restaurant now. He feeds Masha, dresses her, spoils her silly. The lady got lucky, all right."

"How does he treat the kid?"

"You know what they say: 'Once you love somebody, the rest is easy.' He treats him well, like a father."

"And the little kid, he's really gray-eyed?"

"Saw him myself," answers an aged, dried-up gypsy woman, "gray-eyed with a touch of yellow. And a puny little face, thick-lipped, whining all the time."

It's mine, I realize all at once. Of course! And I feel the heavy beating of my heart. Mine! Mine! Mine!

Again I swill the vodka, wave like a rope, and stagger nearly senseless through the haunts and dens. Then, in a flash, like the blinding light of an explosion, the weeping, enraged, suddenly aged figure of Margo rises before me.

"What are you doing, scum?" she says in a trembling voice. "What are you doing? Listen to me. If you don't stop it, I'm going to leave you!"

I passed a month and a half like that until, finally, I came to.

It was, I recall, at dusk: a spring shower was drizzling, the dirt crunched beneath my shoes, and I was dragging myself back home. Tossing my head, I glanced up at our windows (we were renting an apartment on the fourth floor) and noticed they were dark.

She must be sleeping, I thought with tenderness and pity. She's pining, the poor thing. Good God, what I swine I am!

I quickly went up the stairs, unlocked the door, went in, and sobered up right there and then. Margo had made good on her threat. She was gone! The apartment was full of the traces of her hasty departure. Disorder reigned everywhere: handfuls of crumpled paper, fragments of string, rags of every kind were thrown all about. An unfinished bottle of vodka and an ashtray overflowing with butts stood on the dirty plastic tablecloth. And, beside them, a white envelope.

It was Smoke-cured's letter. I recognized it at once. Margo had given it back to me and the message was clear. "We're through," it was saying. "Now beat it!"

"What can I do?" I said aloud and, in the silence of the darkened rooms, the words sounded surprisingly hoarse and wild. What? Chase after Margo? But where? Where would I find her now? The whole country was at her disposal and if she was really determined to hide from me, I'd never stand a chance of getting her back.

Maybe I shouldn't even try, the thought suddenly struck me. Why bother? There's a certain logic to everything. I'd lost everything I ever loved. Now there was nothing left to hold me. Hadn't the time finally come to use the letter?

Only then did I notice the darkness had ended. Dawn was already breaking through the windows. Orange squares of light lay along the floor and the plastic tablecloth and the bottle on the table flashed a blinding white.

Without thinking, I reached for it (there was still enough there for one good drunk) and immediately drew back. To hell with it! It was high time to leave the mirage.

I met up with the old crowd at the first snackshop I went to for a little breakfast. They were pickpockets and trolleycar screen men mostly, who began work early in the morning and were fortifying themselves for the job ahead. Leo the Kike, long-faced, red-haired, and sprightly, waved to me from the other end of the room and called me over to his table.

"Sit down, Chuma," he said. "We've got something to talk about."

In between bites at a chicken wing, he said, "Listen, where the hell have you been? Two days already they've been looking for you. All over Odessa. Damn near walked their legs off."

"Who's looking?" I twitched. "Margo?"

"No, us."

"Where's Margo?"

"She left."

"Where to?"

"I don't know." He licked his fingers and moved the dish aside. "We dropped in at your place the day before yesterday. She was packing her stuff and rushing off to catch the train. We asked about you and did she give us a mouthful, oy-yoi! What happened with the two of you?" Leo screwed up his eyes. "You have a fight?"

"We had a fight," I confirmed dejectedly. "And it's all my fault. I let myself go, drinking, chasing after other women. . . ."

"No wonder we couldn't find you," Leo said reproachfully.

"What do you want from me?"

"You mean you don't know?" Leo laughed. "Oh, that's good, that's really good!"

"All right," I said. "Knock it off."

"There was a general meeting."

"So?"

"We talked about who to send to the International Conference. You know something about that?"

I knew a thing or two. I'd heard about it a long time ago, back in my Rostov days. The Straw, the Shepherd, and some of the older thieves used to talk a lot about the need for calling a conference. They'd even taken some steps at the time, sending off letters and discussing organizational details. None of it had seemed all that serious to me at the time, though. And now, with amazement, I learned that the conference was a very real event.

"The meeting went on for two days," Leo told me. "You can imagine all the gabbing for yourself. Anyway, they nominated ten delegates, and you and I are two of them."

"Why such an honor?" I smiled.

"Well, they chose me because I've got the languages," he explained. "German, Polish, a little English."

"And me?"

"You? Because, green as you are, you've got culture. You've read all the books. Besides, you even do a little writing. You'll know how to make a good impression on Europe. You won't fall flat on your face."

"Where's it all supposed to take place?"

"Lvov," said Leo, picking his teeth with a match.

"Lvov?" I couldn't believe my ears. "Leo, are you joking?"

"No." He shrugged his shoulders. "Why should I?"

So, I thought, it's the hand of fate! One way or the other, I'm headed for Lvov after all.

"There's only one thing I don't get," I said slowly. "Why Lvov, of all places?"

"Easy," Leo replied, and, almost word for word, he repeated the phrase Smoke-cured had once told me. "Lvov is the westernmost city in the Soviet Union—of all the major ones, anyway—and the most European. And get this, my friend, it's not far from the border. Forests and swamps everywhere, no problem walking right across the line."

"No problem, eh?" I had my doubts. "They keep our borders under lock and key, you know that."

"Sure I know," Leo said laughing. "You think you're the only one around here with an education? I enlighten myself too, every once in a while. I go to the movies. Not too long ago I saw a film—can't remember the title now—about border guards. Laid it all out on the line, they did. All the Chekists were wise and strong as steel. And all the crooks were idiots."

He grinned dreamily. "All of them, to a man, idiots and cowards. But loaded with cash. *Lots* of cash! . . . Ah, what I wouldn't do to get my hands on one spy over there, no matter how shabby. God, I love them! It's been a childhood dream of mine to meet up with a spy. Just one! Just to put the touch on him, just to pinch his udder. . . ."

When it came to spies, Leo couldn't stop talking. I knew his weakness. If I didn't interrupt him now, he could go on for hours.

"Wait! Hold it! I'm serious . . ."

"All right," Leo said. "Then none of that, brother, is any of our business. It's not us who decides, it's the den. The den knows what it's doing. And the one thing they want is for us to get the hell to Lvov on time."

THE THIEVES' CONFERENCE

The idea of calling an all-European Thieves' Conference had developed among the Russian thieves quite a long time ago—and for a very good reason.

It's no secret that criminal worlds exist in every country on the face of the earth. It hardly follows, though, that the habits of thieves are everywhere the same.

According to Russian law, a professional criminal hasn't the right to be in anyone's service or employ. Above all, he must have no contact whatsoever with the authorities. He can earn his living only with the aid of his specialty—his thief's trade. The principle involved is excellently expressed in the classic—almost biblical—formula: "A thief thieves, a *fraier* plows. To each his own!"

For Russians the formula had the force of law, both in the prison camps and on the outside. With one exception. While all "legitimate" activity was absolutely forbidden a thief on the outside, his brothers behind bars could work a *fraier*'s job as long as it was not within the boundaries of the camp itself, but outside, in the cold, far removed from the administration.

Going out on work detail to the taiga and the frost, digging the earth and cutting new roads through the forests, that was fine. Working in the camp itself, though, was another matter entirely! The convicts that did so were called "dummies," and with good cause. Once a person decided to latch himself on to a warm spot, he involuntarily started playing up to the authorities in every way possible. From there it was just a short step to betraying one's own kind (openly or on the sly) and cooperating actively with the Cheka.

During the postwar years, when prison camp conditions had become unbearable and the time of the great "bloodletting" had come, the criminals realized that they, too, would have to adjust somehow. After a good deal of doubt and dispute, they finally settled on several exceptions to the rules: thieves were to receive the right, in case of extreme need, to become team leaders and barbers. A team leader could always save and feed several friends at a time. Barbers have access to sharp-edged objects—razors and scissors—a distinct advantage during the period of intracamp bitch warfare. All the same, the exceptions were rarely made.

In Western Europe, it was quite a different story. Even in the truly thief countries of Poland and Italy, even in the Italian Mafia itself, no such prohibitions existed. A man there was fully capable of combining the incompatible: of being at one and the same time a bureaucrat and a safecracker, of working diligently in a store or cafe by day and fleecing apartments at night. The same principle prevailed in their prisons. Once behind bars, a thief could form an alliance with the screws without the slightest fear of reprisal. It was on precisely this point that the watershed was drawn.

It all began at the start of the forties, after Russia and the West had collided on the field of battle. World War Two had shaken up the entire continent. Borders disintegrated, the old order tumbled into rubble. There wasn't a thing—or an institution—on the face of the earth that hadn't been hopelessly muddled and confused. And for the first time, Russian prisoners got a taste of prison life abroad.

That may be a bit of an exaggeration. Several of the older

thieves, mostly from Odessa, had been in Europe even before the Revolution, to "practice their art," and had periodically fallen into foreign prisons. Still, these had been isolated cases. Now, though, a veritable torrent of thieves flowed into the occupied territory and from there, throughout all of Europe. In turn, during the years of the occupation, European thieves managed to visit the south of our own country. A considerable number of them ended up in Ukrainian prisons and when the front rolled back, they all fell into the hands of the MVD.

The convicts were continually changing hands, from the German police to the Soviet prison authorities and back again. Not that there was much of a difference. For whatever the distinctions between thieves, between the official "bureaucratic" departments there was absolutely no difference at all. The style of the German and the Soviet jailers was, in principle, one and the same.

After receiving and listing the convicts (a procedure that was identical everywhere), the authorities would divide the prisoners into convoys, Germans for the West, Russians for the East. That, essentially, was how the two worlds had met and mingled during the war.

The differences between the prisoners was discovered rather quickly. In the prison cells and camps of Russia the behavior of the foreigners was considered ambivalent and intolerable. It contradicted the general norm and moved the thieves of the Motherland to sharp protests.

Clearly some kind of general rule had to be hammered out and a unified decision reached on questions of ethics. And that, in short, was why the thieves had gathered in Lvov.

Along with the general problems of policy, though, I had some problems of my own. Somehow, I had to track down Smoke-cured's friend and hand him the letter.

As you might have guessed, I'd already opened the envelope and taken a look inside. Unfortunately, though, I was no wiser than before. Smoke-cured's message was written in Polish. A sharp muzhik, I thought, walking the streets of Lvov and looking for the address I'd memorized. A real conspirator. Well, let's see what kind of friends he's got.

The house turned out to be a wooden, two-story building in a little back alley, not far from a slaughterhouse on the outskirts of town. A tall fence surrounded the place. A shaggy, flop-eared dog clattered on a chain and met me with a nonstop bark that soon brought a woman rushing out of the door.

I introduced myself and handed her the letter. She turned it over and put it away without reading a line. Then, silently, she took me by the hand and led me into a half-lit, spacious room. It was the kitchen, as far as I could tell, with a stove in one corner and a set of shelves gleaming with copper kitchenware in the other. A long, rough-hewn oak table ran down the center of the room.

Apparently, people had just finished a meal in the room: there was still a smell of tobacco in the air, the floor was dirty and scuffed, and a pile of dirty dishes mounted on the edge of the table.

"One moment," the woman said and left.

I didn't have to wait for long. In fact I'd barely had time to light up and look around when I heard some heavy steps coming my way. The door flew open and a thickset man with droopy mustaches and a decorated Russian shirt came into the kitchen.

"Well," said the Ukrainian, giving my hand a firm shake, "let's get acquainted. Please sit down." He spoke a good, clear Russian, with a typical Moscow enunciation. "Would you like a little something to refresh yourself from your trip—a drink, perhaps, a bite to eat? No? Don't be shy."

He sat down on the bench, wiped his hands on his knees, and looked at me sharply from the corners of his eyes.

"So, you come from Smoke-cured. Judging by the letter, you saw him. Where, may I ask?"

"In the North Caucasus," I said. "Groznyi."

"Specifically?"

"In the apartment of a woman. You probably don't know her."

"Her name?"

"Margo."

"Ah, Margo," he drawled, smiling ever so slightly and touching his long, smoke-stained mustaches. "A charming woman . . ."

"You know her, too?" I asked, amazed for the hundredth time at the popularity of my Queen.

"I saw her once," he replied evasively. "A matter of necessity. . . . So then, the meeting took place in her apartment. But, surely, that was a long time ago. How much time has passed since then?"

"I don't remember." I was a bit confused. "Wait, let me think. I saw Smoke-cured somewhere around the end of September. It's April now, so that means half a year ago."

"Where were you all that time?"

"Different places," I muttered. "Tashkent, Bukhara. Then Vladivostok for a little while. But what does it matter? Surely my itinerary can't be that interesting to you?"

"No, no," he hastened to say, "not at all. We've all got our own jobs to do. It's just that I find your delay a little surprising. But that's neither here nor there."

And so we talked. I kept expecting the fellow to get down to business, show some interest in my plans, and discuss the details of the border crossing. The Ukrainian did nothing of the kind. The conversation was most general. We seemed to be going in spirals—capricious little circles and loops. As a result, we returned to Margo and agreed that she was a most unusual woman and fully worthy of her exalted nickname.

"When did you see her, by the way?" I asked.

"A long time ago," my interviewer said, "during the war."

With that he stood up in a businesslike way, thereby indicating that our conversation was at an end.

Once again the woman appeared who had led me into the house. Unbeautiful, her head covered with a gray kerchief, she quietly stood by the lintel, crossing her arms on her chest. Nodding her way, the Ukrainian said: "May I present Marya Tarasovna?"

I bowed. Marya Tarasovna continued to stand silent and impassive.

"She will show you to your room. You'll be living here for the time being. Remember, our rules are to be strictly kept!" He looked at me and screwed up his eyes. "Be on time for breakfast, lunch, and dinner—she'll tell you when. No running around the house. Start no conversations with anyone. If you need anything, ask the proprietor—me. Is that clear?"

"Yes," I said, taken aback by the authoritative, harsh tone of his voice. "Can I at least leave the premises?"

He smiled. "You may, of course. Only let Tarasovna or me know. That's the first thing. Secondly, if you are coming back at night, don't ever enter the house by the yard but from behind, through the kitchen garden. There's a little wicket gate there. They'll show you." And then, smoothing his mustache with his hand: "Well, that's everything, for now. We don't have too many rules, but they're strict. But then you don't look like the type that needs to be taught."

"How long will I have to stay here?" I asked, suddenly feeling a little uneasy. "My task—as you probably know—is to get across the border."

"I know," he said slowly, "I know. But there's a right time for everything. When it comes, we'll go into action. Till then we wait. There are reasons. Besides, haste is inadvisable. Cats do everything quickly—and they're born blind!"

After setting up in my new home, I rushed off to the Lvov slum section of Green Hill, where the thieves' conference was already in session.

It was proceeding noisily and—as is the case with most conferences—unproductively. The contradictions were too strong, the ideological divisions too sharp. Each of the sides was insisting on its own infallibility and refusing to compromise. The only healthy decision the thieves came to went something like this: "At home everybody's free to do what he wants, but on foreign soil, he has to abide by the prevailing laws."

In calling the conference, the Russian thieves had hoped for different results, but in the long run, they reconciled themselves to the formula.

I spoke before the conference only once myself—and without success. My interpreter, Leo the Kike, was drunk and muddled everything I said. At first I couldn't understand how my speech (composed in the highest seriousness with extensive quotations from the classics) could have been met with such peals of laughter. Later, though, I learned what had happened.

On the way to the train station restaurant for a dinner break, I asked Leo what he'd been jabbering about. Rocking back and forth and digging his feet into the dust, he replied with a smile: "I, uh, elucidated your thoughts. . . . You were talking about the meaning of the collective, right? About the fact that, without a den, without friends, every man is an orphan. Wasn't that it?"

"Well?"

"So I told them the joke about the orphan. You know the one I mean? See, they bring this homeless kid to the police station. 'You got a father?' they ask him. 'Nope,' he says, 'I'm an orphan. No family left at all.' 'What happened to your father?' 'Killed by a mob of muzhiks.' 'Well, what about your mother?' 'Dead from syphilis.' 'And your sister?' 'No sister either.' 'A brother, at least?' 'Sure, I got a brother, but he's no good to me. He's at the Medical Institute, in the laboratory.' 'What's he doing there? Working? Studying?' 'Oh, no, he's in a jar. He was born with two dicks, one of them right on his forehead. . . .' "

"You missed your calling, Leo," I said. "You should have been a master of ceremonies, not a pickpocket. Your talent's just going to waste."

CRYING AT NIGHT

Two days later Leo paid me an unexpected visit. He came in the morning, just as I was finishing my breakfast and the first sentence out of his mouth was: "Finally! My dream's come true! All my life I've been hoping and praying I'd meet a spy, one measly little spy, and this place is crawling with them!"

"Come off it." I frowned. "What spies?"

"You poor child," Leo said tenderly. "Didn't they ever tell you not to argue with your elders?"

"Some elder you are!"

"Well, I'm older anyway, and a little more mature. Besides, I've got some experience under my belt and—what do you call it?"—he snapped his fingers—"class consciousness! Yes, that's it—trust my class consciousness!"

"But where did you see them?"

"Right in the kitchen. And if you ask *me*, they're still sitting there right now."

"What're they doing?"

"Eating their scrambled eggs. Having a drink."

"Sure." I smiled. "Real suspicious behavior."

"Don't laugh, I'm not kidding." Leo started to get angry. "When I came into the kitchen someone was speaking in English, and as soon as he saw me he switched right back to Ukrainian. Besides"—he looked around at the door—"the mugs on those guys! One look at them and it's clear as day. Every last one of them's got Article Fifty-eight stamped clear across his brow like a brand."

He did a light, dancing step across the room and then said quietly: "How to get at them, though, that's the question. If I don't work at least one of them over, my name is mud. I'll never forgive myself as long as I live."

"Quiet," I said. "Don't even think about it. What do you want to do, undermine me?"

"What *are* you doing here, anyway?"

"I'm living here!"

"But why?" Leo raised his eyebrows. "Why here, of all places?"

"It just turned out that way," I muttered, walking to the door. "Look, let's get out of here. This isn't a good place to talk. I'll explain it to you later."

To be honest, I hadn't very much wanted to let Leo in on my plans—Leo the babbler. In fact, I was already feeling sorry I'd even given him my address in the first place. But it was too late for that. I'd have to tell him everything now.

He heard me out carefully.

"So that's what it's all about," he muttered. "Brother, you've really put your foot in it this time, haven't you?"

"What do you mean?" I asked, already guessing what he had to say.

"Don't you understand? Listen, my friend, these are all Bendera's boys." Bendera was the leader of the Ukrainian nationalist underground.

"How can you tell?"

"This is where they're all headquartered nowadays! This is their home turf!"

We were standing on the corner of an alley overgrown with nettles and burdocks, with a clear sight line to the house I was staying at. Boarded, gray, and surrounded by a tall fence, it seemed ominously silent to me now. Giving it an appraising look, I lit a cigarette and asked:

"Listen, Leo, you're not making this all up, are you?"

"It's an open secret," he replied. "Everybody's talking about it. But that's not the point. The problem is, they think you're one of them. You came from Smoke-cured and that's enough for them. No wonder the Proprietor hasn't tried pumping you for information, like where you've been and what you're up to. Did he say anything like, 'We've all got our own tasks to do?' "

"Our own *jobs*," I corrected him.

"There you are! Of course he thinks you're one of them! You have some special kind of assignment. . . ."

"You're probably right," I said despondently. Then, as a new thought dawned on me, I added: "But look, maybe that's to my advantage. After all, they've got to come through for one of their own, don't they?"

"True, they've got to," Leo said, making a wry face, "but it's a tricky situation. I'd never have risked it myself. They're shady types, tied up with politics and all. . . . What's an honest criminal like you doing messing around with them? You could get in so deep you couldn't get out again."

"Listen, I haven't gotten mixed up with them," I protested. "I don't plan to, either."

"But you already have," he said, shaking his head. Once again he looked at the house in the distance and added slowly: "Remember, if the authorities ever catch you with them, that's it for you. Kaput. Don't expect any mercy. You won't be dealing with the Criminal Investigation Department, but the MGB. And those guys have a lousy sense of humor."

I sighed. "Well, it's too late for that now. Besides, when you come right down to it, what's the difference whom I hang out with from here on in? Crossing the border's a political affair."

"That mean you've made up your mind?"

"Old man," I said, "there's no going back."

"You think it'll be better there?"

"I don't know. I'm not sure. Margo asked me the same thing. What could I tell her? I'll see when I get there."

"She was against it?"

"Right. As far as I could tell, she knew everything there was to know about it, but for some reason she just kept it to herself. Never did anything more than talk in riddles about it."

"She knew what was going on, huh?" Leo asked thoughtfully. "Maybe she did. I just remembered something that happened to her during the occupation in Odessa. Some German had been killed at her place. Killed, poisoned, I don't know which. Anyway, the cops rounded up everybody, including Margo. Nobody thought she was ever coming back, but half a year later, up she pops again, like nothing had ever happened. Business as usual. That was the first time Smoke-cured came on the scene."

"Did you meet him?" I was getting interested. "Did you ever run into him yourself?"

"Once, by accident, but I'd heard a lot about him. He was in with the Germans—that much was for sure."

"And now?"

"Now he's in with *them.*" Leo smiled and pursed his lips. "With your pretty little terrorists, and maybe somebody else besides. How can you figure these guys out anyway?"

"But listen," I said, "aren't they the ones you've always dreamed about? Why did you let Smoke-cured slip out of your hands?"

"No, my friend." Leo grinned. "For the likes of him I've got nothing but distance. I want a quiet spy, a meek spy, scared half out of his wits. Not that Turk, or Cossack, or whatever the hell he is."

"He's no beauty, that's for sure."

"You bet he isn't!"

"Well, you're going to be hard pressed to come up with anyone who is."

"Don't say it, don't say it." Leo dropped his eyes and pursed his lips again. "I think about that myself sometimes. But, listen, you can't live without a dream. You've got to have something to aspire to, you know!"

So, it was right out of crime and straight into politics. In search of a little peace and quiet, I'd landed in the heart of a terrorist underground.

And, to top it all off, they were fully prepared to use me in their affairs. Hardly a day went by without some report or rumor about an executed activist, a burned hut, a derailed train—the kind of sabotage they might soon be asking *me* to do. No wonder they were in no hurry to toss me across the border.

But even if they did, I'd still be at their mercy. Paris was a million miles away, and I had no idea how they'd get me there. Illegally, most likely, "along the chain," as they called it, but who knew where or when that chain might snap?

They'd let me into their organization on the basis of a letter from Smoke-cured. But just what had the letter said? How had he recommended me? What kinds of advice and instructions had he given them?

I'd been there two weeks already, consumed with anxiety and completely in the dark on what to do or how to do it. Should I keep on waiting? And if so, for how much longer? Wouldn't it be better to dump it all and beat a hasty retreat?

But, no, it was already too late for that. There wasn't a chance they'd let me out alive now. Any attempt on my part to leave would be interpreted as a betrayal.

And where could I run to here in Lvov? The entire area, all

of the western Ukraine in fact, was full of militant nationalists. They were even among the thieves. Smoke-cured and Margo had been connected with them, and they could hardly be the only ones.

Mulling it over, I set off to see the Proprietor. We'd spoken on a number of previous occasions and always with the same result: "You must wait," he'd say. "Everything in its own time. Haste is fine for catching fleas." Empty phrases signifying nothing. Well, no more, I thought. This time we really talk it out. I'll tell him who I am, where I come from, and what I'm after.

I was already at his door (he lived above me, on the second floor), my hand raised to knock, when I suddenly froze with doubt. What if it was all a lot simpler than I thought? Simpler, and more terrifying? What if the letter had already told them all about me and they were holding me for some special purpose of their own? They needed me—that must be it.

The Proprietor's room was full of people smoking and talking at the same time. The Proprietor had the floor. "Under the circumstances, it's our only choice," he was saying as I entered. The second he saw me he interrupted his remarks, walked up to me, and shook my hand.

"Hello, hello," he said quickly. "I can guess what you came for."

"Then maybe you can answer me just as fast."

"That's a little harder." He made a wry face. "Things have taken a bad turn, my little dove. There've been some complications."

"What kind?"

"You name it." He thoughtfully touched his mustaches. "Political and organizational. Look," he said, eying me from beneath his shaggy brows, "I'll come to you in the evening and we'll talk it all out. Right now, as you can see, I have some other things to tend to. You'll have to excuse me. Business."

"All right, fine," I answered, walking to the door. "Till this evening."

"Yes," he said. "Wait for me."

———

I had already dropped off to sleep by the time he came. He sat down with a sigh at the foot of the bed and said nothing for a while. You could see he was exhausted and overstrained: his face was dark and pinched and big, watery bags had gathered under his eyes.

Raising myself up on my elbow, I reached for some cigarettes. We both lighted up. Filtering the bluish smoke through his mustache, the Proprietor finally spoke:

"I didn't enlighten you earlier on our problems. Maybe I should have. In any event, I won't mince words with you any longer. Things are in terrible shape. The MGB's after us. You understand what that means?"

"I can guess." I smiled.

"We should have seen it coming a long time ago." He spoke in a depressed, rather muffled tone. "They've got troops quartered near the border and roundups going on all over the place. They've already raided a number of our secret centers."

"Does that mean the trip's off?" I was getting upset.

"Not exactly. We can still help you. But, under the circumstances, the best course for you, it seems to me, is a 'legal' one."

"What do you mean, 'legal'?" I stubbed out my cigarette. I was a little surprised.

"Don't be afraid," he said with a smile. "It's easy. Just relax and hear me out."

He placed his hand on my shoulder and continued.

"There's a special commission in Lvov for the return of expatriated Poles to their homeland. It's been in operation for a while and it's already sent a good number of them back. They're in session again. You understand what I'm getting at? If you were to drop into the general flow . . ."

"That 'flow' you're talking about wouldn't get me any farther than Poland. Then what?"

"The main thing is getting there," he said. "There won't be any complications after that. Poland's our country! You can get anywhere you want to from there."

"Look, that flow of yours has its problems, too. How am I going to open my mouth, for instance? I don't speak Polish."

"You won't have to speak," he shot right back. "Quite the contrary. All you'll have to do is keep your mouth shut."

He dug around in a side pocket of his jacket and pulled out a packet of papers.

"Look!" He laid some of the papers down on the blanket. "A certificate from the Commandant's Office, issued in the name of one Moses Filonovsky."

"Why Moses?" I asked.

"Because he's a Jew!" The Proprietor gave me a sidelong glance. He was clearly amused. "Got any objections?"

"Of course not," I said. "What difference does it make? If it's a Jew, then it's a Jew."

"Just what *I* thought." He nodded. "Let's move on."

"There's one thing I'm worried about," I interrupted him. "Is this document for real?"

"All our documents are legitimate. No hitch. We don't fool around with thieves' forgeries."

He smiled and bit the tip of his mustache. The dog! I thought. He knows exactly who I am! Damn spies, they all know it.

"But this Filonovsky," I began.

"Don't worry." He brushed it aside. "He won't give you any trouble."

"Still, he's around somewhere, isn't he?"

"Not anymore," he corrected me abruptly.

"I get it," I said.

"All right, then, let's not get off the track." He returned to the papers. "To supplement the certificate, here's another paper—the most important one you'll have. Don't forget!" He raised a finger. "It's vital. It's a finding from the Medical Commission, noting that Filonovsky, as a result of a concussion suffered at the front, is subject to nervous attacks and temporary loss of speech."

He extended the certificate to me: a crackling fresh document covered with signatures and stamps.

"Look here, now." He rustled the papers. "This is an affidavit and this is a service record. The whole dossier, okay? Believe me, they weren't easy to come by. We had to take a lot of people off their jobs to do it, and the way things are going nowadays, that's a risky business. We like to avoid that kind of thing, except under extraordinary circumstances."

And then, with a catch in his voice, he added softly: "And we may not even have this option left before too long. When you see Smoke-cured, tell him that!"

"Right," I answered.

I answered mechanically, without thinking. The meaning of the Proprietor's words hadn't sunk in at once, but when it finally did, I had a sudden, chilling attack of anxiety.

"When am I supposed to see Smoke-cured? And where?"

"In Peremyshl, most likely." The Proprietor shrugged his shoulders. "Where they dispatch all the repatriates. Why?" He suddenly screwed up his eyes. "You mean to say they didn't already tell you that?"

So that's it! I thought. They still think I'm one of them. No wonder he's been telling me so much.

"How can I put it," I muttered. "It's not that they didn't forewarn me, but, to tell you the truth, I thought it would happen someplace else. Anyway, it doesn't matter. Peremyshl it is. Only, where'll I look for him?"

"Don't worry about that," the Proprietor announced, getting up to go. "He'll find *you.*" And with his hand already on the knob, he added: "Till tomorrow. We still have a few things to discuss in the morning. In the meantime, though, take a close look at that paper work and, as the actors say, get into your part!"

The Proprietor left, wishing me a pleasant good night. The night ahead, though, was anything but tranquil.

What depressed me most was the prospect of a meeting with Smoke-cured. If he'd been a simple, honest crook or contrabandist, I might even have enjoyed seeing him. After all, I wouldn't be able to manage there at all without a guide. But that was the problem: he wasn't just a sharper, but a secret service agent. People like that have their own special interests to tend to. Things were looking dim for me. I was at Smoke-cured's mercy and what might happen after I crossed the border was anybody's guess.

I didn't have a second to lose. I had to run now—immediately—even before morning came. I got dressed in a hurry, swept up the Proprietor's documents from the bed, and put them under the pillow.

"So long, Moses Filonovsky!"

Then, cautiously, I looked out into the corridor. It was dark and quiet. Somewhere off in the distance I could hear a muffled sob, a woman's plaintive voice. It was, I realized, Tarasovna. She was crying, trying to muffle her tears. Why? God only knows. Somehow, though, her grief underscored my feeling of anxiety and my sense of disaster closing in on the house.

Trying not to make a sound, I stole past her tiny room, down the curving hallway, past the kitchen, and out through the door leading to the kitchen garden. I'd often used this exit and had no trouble orienting myself in the darkness. A minute later I was on the street, free, beneath the countless stars and the wavering mist round the moon.

I moved cautiously, without a sound. My old training was serving me well. I had some misgivings about the dogs; they knew me, but they still might start barking by mistake. Keeping to the shadows of the fences and skirting the open spots flooded by the light of the moon, I crossed the alleyway, stood on the corner, and turned back, trying to make out the features of the house I'd left behind. The only thing I could see was the sharp crest of the roof against the backdrop of the sky.

I stood there for quite some time, then turned to leave—and stopped dead in my tracks. Someone was breathing nearby, rustling and crunching on the broken bricks. And he wasn't alone. With every nerve of my body I could feel them right beside me, just a few steps away. Like me, they were hiding in the shadow of the fence.

At first I assumed it was a terrorist picket, a watchman of some kind, posted there by the Proprietor. But if that had been the case, I would surely have known about him. No, they were strangers, all right, and they were secretly preparing for something.

Could they be Chekists? The thought of it made my blood run cold. Just then I caught a hasty little whisper.

"How's it going over there?" one of them asked.

"All quiet," another whispered. "They must be sleeping."

"Maybe not," a third voice, low and hoarse, joined in with a little chuckle. "They're sitting there mum as mice in a hole. Doesn't matter. We'll catch them red-handed anyway."

They were silent. Then somebody said with a yawn: "I could do with a smoke."

A little flame flared up and, for a second, in the wavering light, I saw a face bent over the collar of an overcoat, and the little corner of a soldier's shoulder strap.

The low voice, with the clipped tones of an officer, now said: "Hey! Cut the light! You can see the alleyway from here, you fool! Stand behind the corner."

The match went out and the silhouette of a soldier walked off to one side and melted back into the darkness. The others disappeared as well, gathering behind the corner to continue their conversation in a whisper. I couldn't hear them anymore.

Slowly, I stepped away, keeping close to the fence and moving farther and farther back, toward the house.

I was listening to other voices now, voices inside me, rising from the bottom of my soul. The first one called me back to the house to warn the people there of the danger. The second shouted, "Run! Hide! Don't be an idiot! It's too late for the others, they're doomed already, but you can still save yourself. You're almost safe as it is, you got out of the trap in time. Why crawl back? Run, run, run!"

It was the voice of fear and it stifled me, drawing my strength away and throttling my will. There was a moment when I almost gave in. My hand was already on the wicket fence. I pushed and it opened a little. But just as I was about to plunge through the gate to safety, I remembered the woman, crying her timid tears into the night.

"So, they've caught up with us," the Proprietor mumbled, after hearing me out. "They work fast, the bastards." He'd been sleeping in his clothes. "They work fast, all righ.," he repeated, rubbing the sleep from his puffy face. "Well, they won't take us that easily."

Sticking his hand under the pillow, he pulled out a heavy pistol, drew the bolt, and slipped a bullet into the barrel.

"Have you got a weapon?" he asked me.

"No." I hesitated. "Never bothered to get one. Anyway, I'm more used to a knife."

"A knife, my little dove, is a toy. It's not going to do you much good in this situation."

He bent down to the night table by the head of his bed, rummaged around, and came up with a small nickel-plated German revolver with an inlaid pearl handle.

"Here! It doesn't look like much, I'll grant you, but don't let that fool you. By the way, have you got the documents with you?"

I shook my head. "I left them in my room."

"Where?"

"Under the pillow."

"Burn them. Burn them at once! No, wait, better let me take care of it."

He darted into the corridor and, suddenly, the house erupted in a panic. The hallways resounded with stamping feet and anxious voices calling back and forth. An acrid smell of smoke came from the neighboring room. They were burning something in a hurry.

Now's the time, I was thinking. Now's the time to go! I've done everything I can.

Just before dawn, clouds covered the sky and it grew so impenetrably dark that I was able to slip past the trap without getting caught. Holding my revolver at the ready (it already felt at home in my palm—firm, reliable, and tender), I worked my way into the yard next door, from there to a hayloft, then over a slanting fence into another yard. Farther ahead, I knew, lay the slaughterhouse grounds. From there it was just a short haul to the railroad station.

Easier said than done, though. Everywhere I turned I saw shadows, heard suspicious rustles and the clanging of metal.

What surprised me most was the complete absence of "chimers" (a term thieves use for chained dogs). Anywhere in the Russian provinces, even on the outskirts of Moscow, a gathering like this in the night would have been enough to raise a havoc of barking and yelping. Later, of course, I realized why. This wasn't a Russian town, but a Western one. Besides, it had been the site not long ago of a series of pitched battles. Almost all of the watchdogs had been killed or chased away, a situation decidedly to the advantage of the Cheka.

And to me. Slowly, painfully, I wormed my way through Lvov's maze of streets and stole along the outskirts, looking back at every turn, pressing myself in fear against the fences and the trees at every sound. At one point I almost collided with somebody in the dark. He passed me by, trailing a sour smell of shag and soldier's broadcloth.

It wasn't till I saw the outlines of the buildings at the train station that I drew my first calm breath. A dim green light was beginning to spread behind them. The low, murky sky began to lighten shade by shade. So, I thought, turning my eyes to the east, that's where I have to go now. I'd have to put the west behind me. There was no point anymore in looking back.

And, with that, I looked back.

It was an anxious and involuntary act. A sharp volley of gunfire had suddenly begun behind me, its echo magnified and multiplied by the deep silence reigning in the town.

Then an explosion. Its slow, heavy report rolled through the neighborhood, hiding the sounds of the gunfire. Little by little it began to diminish, and that's when I saw the fireball rise above the roofs of the houses I'd just left behind.

It climbed so high it seemed to singe the sky. The edges of the clouds reddened, and a flickering, gloomy light pierced their fluffy shroud.

The Bendera house was perishing in flames. I recalled the Proprietor's words: "They won't take us easily!" He'd been telling the truth. I found myself thinking that he and his helpers—whoever they were—had been honorable men. They'd known how to meet misfortune with dignity. They'd accepted their own extinction deliberately. Their courage was indisputable and to that, at least, I paid my deepest respects.

The gunfire, now light and remote, continued for some time, receding farther and farther behind the edge of the night until, finally, it died out entirely.

I stood there, straining every nerve, and looking at the west and the tossing edges of the fire. Then I turned my face to the dawn once again—and saw the very same glow in the east.

Over the station, above the thick orchards, the sun was rising, singeing the leaves, pouring its muddy crimson over the roofs, and rolling through the smoky, fiery haze. It seemed as if the entire planet were ablaze from one end to the other in a doomsday flame.

I didn't have time to ponder the subject, though. A crowd was coming my way from one side of the train station. A meeting with them would have been too risky, so, bending down, I plunged into a front garden, beneath a thick cover of acacias.

There in the overgrowth, waiting for the people to pass, I realized that it was time to get ready to appear in public. I beat the dust out of my jacket and buffed the shine back to my shoes. Hiding the pistol in the rear pocket of my pants, I went back out, whistling, to the road.

It was time to find my friends. They were settled nearby with the railroad prostitutes. I decided to pay my first call to the one putting up Leo the Kike. She was a short, plump, full-cheeked girl—called, not too surprisingly, the Bun.

"You know why I love my little Bun?" Leo once told me. "For her optimism! Feed and caress her, she laughs. Starve her, she still laughs. Beat the living daylights out of her, she laughs even harder."

This time, though, she met me with a long face.

"Get out!" she gasped from the doorway. Except for a blouse she was naked. "Get out while you can! You can't believe what's going on!"

"What's happening?"

"Searches, arrests, document checks wherever you go. Just tonight the bastards were here twice. Thank God, Leo hightailed already."

"When did he leave?"

"Yesterday afternoon. He got his things together and didn't even—" She suddenly flushed and her mouth contorted. "He didn't even say a tender word!"

Only now, standing in the threshold, did I realize how completely played out I was. I barely had an ounce of energy to spare. The strains of the night were beginning to tell—my anxieties, the casting about, the roaming. I had never known tension like this before. It was all I could do just to stand on my own two feet.

I didn't want to stay in Lvov a second longer. I left that day, traveling several stops in the dog box, under the train. And, wherever I went, at every stop and station, I saw army boots and horse hoofs, rumbling, clattering, trampling the cobblestones and dirtying the planking of the platforms. The railroads were teeming with Chekist patrols. It was too dangerous under the circumstances to travel farther. Taking advantage of a rainstorm, I stole away from the train and hid in the roadside rye, then went on by foot.

Basically the same thing was happening to me that had once happened at the Iranian border. I'm going in circles, I kept thinking, as I slogged mournfully through the mire and the puddles and the crops. Everything's going round and round.

Everything *was* repeating itself. Here I was again, rushing to leave the railroad as far behind me as I could. The only difference was that, back then, near Iran, I was faint from the heat and thirst, dreaming dusty dreams of just one drop of moisture. Now I pined for the sun!

A lilac cloud, dark as the night sky, hung over the plain, glittering and rumbling and releasing its rain without a letup, its icy streams lashing against my face and flattening the thick heads of rye. I was up to my waist in standing grain, barely able to move. There was nothing left to drive me but my fear.

Night fell almost unnoticed. Since morning a gray, streaming dusk had been swirling over the steppe. Gradually, it had darkened and thickened. Slowly, I began to notice that the lightning seemed to be getting brighter and more piercing. That's when I realized the day had already passed!

Suddenly a deathly white light flashed above me, splitting the overhanging cloud from top to bottom. For an instant I could see the surrounding area, the heavy waves of rye, glossy with moisture, a hillock, the silhouettes of huts. And, not far away, the slanting roof of a haystack. The vision flashed and disappeared, immediately followed by a violent peal of thunder. I dived for the haystack, dug myself a roomy hollow, and crawled in at once.

I dreamed strange dreams that night—dreams of the sea. I was swimming somewhere, choking back the water and drowning in the waves. And freezing, freezing desperately! No matter how I tried, I couldn't get warm.

I woke up soaking wet, shuddering with the chills. My clothing hadn't dried at all during the night. Everything around me was slippery and wet. As soon as I worked my way outside I realized what the problem was. I hadn't been sleeping in hay at all. (Come to think of it, where would I have found hay at that time of the year, at the beginning of May?) I'd spent the night in a pile of old potato tops dumped at the edge of an empty plowed field.

I've got to go to the village, I decided, looking at the hillside and the dim roofs in the mist. I'll ask them at one of the huts to let me in, to warm up a bit. There's nothing to be afraid of here in the sticks.

As I crossed the field, I was amazed at the silence that reigned in the village. I couldn't hear a cock's crow, the mooing of a cow, or the creaking of a well. What had happened? I was beginning to get unnerved. I scrambled up the slope and approached the outskirts of the village. Only then did I realize that many of the homes were destroyed, the yards cluttered and dust-covered, the only street pitted with shell holes. Everywhere I turned I could see traces of what had been an all-consuming fire.

Apparently some kind of front line had passed through here. I stood meditating on the tragedy that had been played out in this now quiet, bleak, and sinister spot. Suddenly, I heard something rustling behind me. I whipped out my pistol and spun around.

It was only a cat, peering out from behind a pile of charred boards. "Here, kitty-kitty," I called. It mewed in reply and, stretching its neck, came toward me with its tail on end.

What a strange walk it had. Uneven and tentative as if it were blind. The thought no sooner crossed my mind than I realized that the cat *was* blind. Drawing near, it lifted its head and two black holes gaped where once there had been eyes.

Shabby and covered with scabs, it rubbed up against me and mewed pitifully. The last survivor, I thought. But how was she going to feed herself? How could she live without the eyes to see? Wouldn't it be better to end her torment? Without even thinking, I raised my pistol, aimed—and lowered my hand.

She wasn't expecting a bullet from me, but a caress, or at least a little something to eat. To shoot her point-blank would have been a blasphemy.

As I left, I turned one last time to see her in the wavering streams of the fog. There she stood, still as a stone, tensely sniffing the breeze. Her voice as it flew to reach me reminded me of the distant weeping of a child.

And so I walked through the Ukraine, following the fresh tracks of the war. My path took me through deserted villages, past incinerated corpses and farms. After many ordeals, I landed in Konotop Prison and then in the detention camps of Kharkov and Cold Mountain. Soon after, I crossed the breadth of the country in an armed convoy, lingering a while at the deportation center at Vanin Bay. And then, boarded with the other convicts like so much cargo in the hold, I crossed the misty Sea of Okhotsk.

It was a tortuous route, but for all its twists and turns, one thing remained unchanged. Every minute, and with every weary step, I was moving steadily toward the east.

Part **|||**

"And with your hands behind your back

You walk a weary line, cursing your bondage."

—From a prison camp song

Our convoy reached the port of Nagayevo, in Magadan, late in the fall of 1947. Navigation was already at an end. Fierce storms were pelting the Sea of Okhotsk with sheets of snow. Low, scudding clouds whistled over the whitish, wind-pocked water, and at the neck of the harbor and by its rocky shores, a glittering jumble of ice was already massing and welding itself to the coast.

After the stinking hold of the ship, after the long days and nights of seasickness and claustrophobia, the salty, whipping wind acted like a narcotic on us. Stumbling, coughing, and huddling together against the cold, we descended the ship's ladder to shore to find ourselves at the deportation site, the infamous Central Quarantine Point (or Karpunka, as the inmates of Kolyma christened it).

If prison camps are hell itself, then you might call the deportation sites a kind of purgatory. People are detained here for a specified time for quarantining, sorting, and shuffling, before being dispatched to the local camp stations, or one of Dante's circles.

Some of the circles lie in mines deep in the bowels of the earth, some lie across the swamps and quicksand of the forest tundra, still others over mountains, or the remote corners of the taiga. There is no shortage of space. The system of the Kolyma camps, officially termed Dalstroi, occupies a territory roughly five times the size of France.

In the east of the country there are two major gold-bearing centers. One of them spreads across Krasnoyarsk region, the other is dead center in Dalstroi. It is from here, in Kolyma, that almost half the gold supply of the Russian Federation comes.

Besides gold, furs ("soft gold," as they call it), coal and mica, first-class wood, and precious minerals flow in to Russia. This hidden republic is rich, all right: rich, extensive, and terrifying.

"Kolyma, Kolyma, you're certainly blessed," goes one of the old prison camp songs. "Winter takes twelve months and summer the rest." The climate is unusually severe, the winters long and fierce. The polar night sets in at the end of September.

The day I first stepped onto the shores of Kolyma (it was four o'clock in the afternoon) the northern lights were already glowing over the docking point and the watchtowers of the camp. Shimmering, green strips of light spread and blazed in the heights, soaring and noiselessly disintegrating, illuminating the ground and the faces of the men with a dim, deathly light. Winter had already come to stay.

In the dead of winter the frost is so deep and so cold it takes your breath away. The air scorches your throat and the tops of your lungs. And the instant it leaves your mouth, the steam congeals and crumbles into dry, prickly sparks.

The frozen soil cracks like the arid bed of a desert salt marsh. Deep in the heart of the forest the trunks of the trees burst with a resonant boom. There's no sound more terrifying or more awesome in that white and windless silence.

The taiga is full of voices, each of them crying its terror and despair with a broken heart. The birds are silent then, the animals keep to their holes. Only men wander the distant woods and snowbound roads and work in the mines. Driven by the convoy, their black, baked mouths singed with the frost, the steam from their breaths sparkling and stinging, the polar flashes irradiating their faces with a greenish light, on they go, their hands folded behind them, cursing their captivity.

"Damn you, Kolyma, you marvelous planet," goes another popular prison camp song. "It drives you mad; there's no way out."

Lenin took up the song, too, as he lounged on his bunk in the quarantine barracks, preparing for sleep.

We were lying side by side. To the right of me was the Maiden, the young murderer with the face of an angel. To the left, an aged Siberian named the Wood Goblin. Lenin had built his nest a bit farther away, in the corner. Slant-eyed, with a bald, knobby skull, he pottered and sang, half under his breath:

> *"Farewell, my dear wife,*
> *Farewell, my dear children,*
> *You know that we drink*
> *This cup to the dregs . . ."*

"You know, brother, that song, it's about us." The Wood Goblin suddenly spoke up. (He'd been gone someplace all day and only just returned, taciturn and clearly depressed about something.) "You said it. We have to drink that bitter cup, right to the dregs. I can feel it in my heart."

"Stop bellyaching, for God's sake," Lenin said. "Who the hell do you think you are, anyway?"

"I'm not bellyaching," the Goblin replied. "It's the way I talk, that's all. . . . Still, what've we got to be that happy about? Dummies everywhere. I just ran into an old embezzler friend of mine I moored up with on Vladimir once. He told me a thing or two. . . ."

"Like what?" I asked.

"Well, you know . . ." The Goblin pressed his lips together and wiped his palm across his skull. "All sorts of things. About the bitches, for instance. Turns out they're all over the place here. Half of every camp point is bitches."

"You're crazy," Lenin twitched.

"Afraid not, brother," the Goblin said with a sigh, "that's the way it is. Bitches in Sasuman and Korkodon, too. And in Markovo and Anyuisk. And all along the main route. They've got their dens all over!"

He lit himself a smoke and started to cough.

"Mark my words, they've got bitches right here in Karpunka, too. Just the other day, he told me there was a real slaughter. Fifteen stiffs in one night!"

"Who did it?" the Maiden asked.

He'd been silent till then, lying with his eyes closed and seemingly asleep. Now he got up and leaned on his elbow.

"Who the hell knows?" The Goblin shrugged his shoulders. "I didn't check it out."

"What difference does it make," I said gloomily. "The point is, the thing's caught up with us, right in the middle of nowhere. We're in for it now."

"What do you expect, peace and quiet?" the Maiden asked. His fresh, rosy mouth smiled and his eyelashes fluttered, casting fluffy shadows on his cheeks.

"Don't you?" The Goblin cast him a sidelong glance.

"Me? No," the Maiden said carelessly. "What do I need it for? If peace and quiet was all I was looking for, I'd have gone in for a different line of work."

"Right." Lenin picked it up. "*Fraiers* have one fate, thieves another. Like it or not, we're at war here." He stared right at me and repeated his words. "At war! That's the law, and whoever doesn't understand it isn't one of us."

It's starting again, I thought. The bastard's out to trip me up again. When will he ever lay off?

Just then the Goblin started speaking, as if unwillingly, in my defense.

"At war—that's true, brothers." He screwed up his eyes. "But what's the good in that? And where do you get the notion thieves don't want peace and quiet? Everybody needs it, and nobody more than us!"

He poked his dark, knotty finger right at Lenin's chest.

"Look at you. How long have you been around? When was the first time you got caught?"

"A long time ago," Lenin said. "Back in '39."

"And where did you do time?"

"Taishet."

"Well, I've been drudging since 1930. With these hands I built the Belomor Canal. You understand? Kandalaksha, Medvezhegorsk, Segezh, I've been in all of them! And how many buddies never came back? Gives me the chills even to think about it. And I was in Taishet, too, a long time before you ever got there. In '33, when they were finishing the canal, they let us all go early. And then the quarantine started, and they slapped a new sentence on me. So what right have you got to talk? If there's ever been anybody who lived his life like he was at war, it's me. And what did I ever get for it? Nothing but punishment barracks, solitary cells, and hard labor zones! I've eaten shit all along the way, and now they're going to make me eat it again. . . .''

I'd never seen the Goblin so worked up before. He wasn't kidding, either. His fierce face, furrowed with deep wrinkles, turned blotchy with thick crimson spots.

"And if that's not enough, we've got the bitches to worry about now. There's no common ground there, it'll be a fight to the death. Either or. Either they make mincemeat out of us, or we hack them into cutlets. There's nothing in between."

"Right, right." Lenin took it up. "That's just what I've been talking about."

"Well, you're right. But, damn it, it's enough to turn your stomach! For youngsters like Chuma or the Maiden it's all new, but for me, I've had it up to here!"

Bending over the edge of the bunk, he spat and drew the side of his hand across his gristly Adam's apple.

"That's how fed up I am!"

"You're not thinking of tying up, of leaving us, are you?" Lenin said slowly.

"How can you tie up?" The Goblin brushed it aside. "How can you leave?" He dropped his head and seemed visibly to fade. "What can I do? Play around with locks, that's all. It's too late to learn anything new. I'm stuck with my craft. Forever. Whatever I've been, that's the way I'll stay. To the end. The only thing, though, is I'd like to do it in peace."

"Peace?" the Maiden asked. "Where are you going to find it? Not around here, old man. It stinks of blood. Only place you're going to find peace is in the hospital, the sanitary division, and the other world."

"Yes . . ." the Goblin drawled dreamily. "The sanitary division; just worm myself in there, fake some kind of illness. . . . What kind, though? The problem is, you've got to pull it off without a hitch."

"Well, if you're serious about it," Lenin spoke from his little corner, "pretend you're nuts. It's an old trick, but it works. If you can prove you're nuts, you're on your way out of here."

"But how? Ah, if I only knew . . ."

"What do you need to know?" The Maiden smiled. "It's a cinch. You said you've eaten shit all your life. So eat it *now!* For *real!* Start swilling the stuff and you're set. No one's going to doubt you then. It's a sure thing. Lots of vitamins in it, too."

"All right, cut it out!" The Goblin made a wry face. "Eat it yourself, if you like it that much."

Gradually we all settled down to our own thoughts—as heavy and dark as the windows of the barracks. The polar night spread beyond us. Out there, the cold, mysterious earth stretched for thousands of versts all around.

I had trouble falling asleep. Soon after I did, in the middle of the night, I was awoken by a heartrending shriek.

"Thieves! Quick! Come here!"

Half-awake, barely able to grasp what was going on, the thieves fell out of their bunks and rushed to a fellow standing by the door. He was leaning against the doorpost, a crimson seam slanting down his neck and cheek. His padded jacket was torn and drenched in blood. With a moan he touched the wound on his neck. He gazed at us with a glassy stare and, pointing a bloody hand at the doorway, said with a gasp, "Sleep, you bastards, keep warm—but out there, bitches are knifing thieves!" Then he slowly began to sink to the ground.

The thick darkness outside seemed almost palpable. The northern lights had long since faded. Stars now sowed the sky. Icy and distant, they seemed to underscore the darkness all around them.

Haltingly, I made my way. Not far from the entrance I spotted the figure of a man writhing on the ground. There were some other people there. As soon as they saw us coming in a noisy crowd, they huddled for a second and then scattered.

Without a second's thought, I rushed off in pursuit. Someone was pounding along behind me. Swearing, the Maiden drew up beside me, a steel blade glittering in his hand. Sly bastard, I remember thinking, he's already armed himself. And like a fool, I'm empty-handed!

"Where'd you get the feather?" I muttered enviously. "From the convoy?"

"Nope," he answered on the run, "I took it from the guy they pinned. They really did him in, the bastards. Nailed him in the neck and the side. And did you see the other one on the ground, by the barracks? Got him clean, looks like."

He caught his breath and gave me a push. "You see those two," he said, "on the left?" I did. "Well, come on, let's get them!"

I was running beside my friend, trying to imagine what I would do when the time came. He started to laugh. His upper lip raised rapaciously, baring his even teeth. Any minute now we'd be sure to catch up, and then what? The Maiden didn't have anything to worry about, he'd already managed to take care of himself. But I was unarmed. You can protect yourself from a knife, of course. There are any number of hand-to-hand techniques specifically designed for situations like that. Still, there's an old Don proverb that goes, "A Cossack without his dagger's like a woman with her skirts pulled up!"

The figures up ahead stopped and suddenly, from out of the dark, a new figure slipped in to join them. Then all three turned to face us. Realizing they wouldn't be able to give us the slip, the bitches had apparently decided to stop and make a stand.

There were only a few paces separating us now. Slowing down and contracting like a spring, I picked myself a figure on the outside. Suddenly someone grabbed me by the sleeve and pulled me to the side. It was the Goblin. Apparently, he'd been just behind all the time.

"Wait," he muttered hoarsely, "don't butt in. You've got to know what you're doing here."

"I know what I'm doing," I objected. "I learned this stuff in the army."

He didn't seem to hear me. He grabbed me by the sleeve again and threw me back and, jumping in front of me, stepped firmly toward the bitches.

"Come on, you bastards," the Maiden shouted. "Stand your ground. You won't get out of this alive!"

At that moment a light blue spotlight rolled above our heads, described a figure eight in the sky, and then dropped its blinding beam right down on us. I saw the faces of my enemies contorted with fear and loathing. The one on the outside I'd singled out for myself reminded me strikingly of Snuffles—the same stringy body and long neck, the same colorless, closely set owlish eyes peering into space.

He twitched, just like Snuffles, and muttered something, shading his eyes from the light. The spotlight beat down from the corner tower, followed a moment later by a burst of machine-gun fire.

An alarm rang through the zone. Outshining the stars, another light broke through the dark, coming from the other direction. It descended, leaned against the wall of the neighboring barracks, trembled, and slowly groped its way toward us.

"Run, brothers!" the Goblin shouted.

Instantly, the crowd scattered. The blinding, intersecting beams seemed to divide the people into two isolated camps: the bitches on one side and the thieves on the other.

We'd barely made it back to the barracks when the guards burst in, trailing the medics behind them. These night alarms were apparently nothing new to them. They gathered up the wounded and took them to the infirmary. We were ordered to shut up and go to sleep. "In case anybody's thinking of stepping outside," the head guard announced, a short Tatar in lieutenant's stripes, "the guards have orders to shoot to kill."

It took us a long time to calm down. The first thing we decided was to take turns from then on standing guard through the nights. We cast lots and, as ill luck would have it, my number came up first.

So passed my first night in Kolyma!

Settling down by the stove near the entrance, I lit up and spent the rest of the night looking into the fire, squinting from the smoke and meditating on my rotten luck. I hadn't had a decent break on anything yet. Everything I'd put my hand to had failed. I hadn't even gotten meat in my soup once. If that had been my usual run of luck in the past, what could I expect from the future?

JUDGMENT

I had my answer the very next day.

That morning, they drove us all off to a medical examination, a long, unpleasant, tedious affair. I didn't really recover from the activity of the night before until after lunch (no meat in my soup this time, either). I'd barely warmed up and drifted off into oblivion, in fact, when I felt someone pull me by the leg.

I leaned over the side of my bunk and saw an unfamiliar face with thick lips and high, freckled cheekbones staring at me.

"Get up, Chuma," the redhead said, "I've come for you."

"Who are you?"

"It's not important," he answered.

"What's it all about?"

"They sent me, that's all. I've been ordered to bring you. Get up!"

"Who sent you?" I asked, stretching and yawning, still dazed with sleep.

"The thieves."

"Why?"

"Come and find out for yourself."

"Where are they?"

"The next barracks over." He waved his hand impatiently. "The whole den's gathered specially for you."

Suddenly I was wide awake and on my guard. A legate from the den was standing before me. And the den—as everybody knew—was never summoned idly.

They were gathered in the darkest, most remote corner of the barracks. The first person I saw was Lenin. He was sitting solemnly on the bunk, his legs crossed like a Turk, resting his elbows on his knees.

"Greetings," he said, bending his knobby, swollen forehead. "Have yourself a seat, Chuma . . . Sit closer! We've been talking about you. . . ."

"What've you been saying?" I asked, sitting down and feeling a vague sense of discomfort. I didn't like the tone of his voice. And the silence that met me from the rest of the thieves was equally unsettling.

"So, what's it all about?" I repeated, looking over the gaggle of thieves.

"Oh, this and that. Maybe you can guess for yourself, eh?"

"No," I said, "I can't. And cut the dramatics. Give it to me straight!"

"All right, if that's the way you want it." He screwed up his face and smacked his lips. "Did you or didn't you ever serve in the army?"

That was the last thing I was expecting and, for an instant, I was dumfounded. How had he found out? the thought flashed through my mind. Who told him?

That's when the second thought came: I'm a dead man. Any thief who's been in the army is, by definition, a bitch. And there's a war going on with the bitches now. If I don't clear myself, they're not going to let me out of here alive. They'll knife me right where I stand. Whatever I do, I can't hesitate or admit to anything! I have to act as if I were under investigation. When it comes right down to it, nobody has any proof. There can't be. . . . Still, how did he find out?

"Well, Mr. Poet," Lenin said tenderly, almost caressingly, "cat got your tongue?"

That's when I heard the Maiden's silky voice: "Don't keep quiet, old man, speak up!"

"I'm not clamming up," I said slowly, letting my breath out through my teeth, "I simply find it repulsive to have to answer!"

And, breaking Lenin's stare, I challenged him: "Where did you get your facts?"

"From your own mouth," Lenin replied quickly. "You admitted it yourself."

"*I* did? Don't make me laugh. When?"

"Last night."

Lenin turned around. "Soso!" he called. Slowly, from out of the semidarkness, a swarthy southerner moved forward.

"Tell him, Soso," Lenin said politely. "Tell us all about it."

"Simple," Soso started to say in a guttural voice. "Last night, when we were chasing after the bitches, I was running right behind the Goblin—"

I heard the Maiden's lazy, ironic tenor:

"Right *behind,* eh? It figures."

Instantly a wave of laughter passed through the men on the bunks. I wasn't sure if the Maiden was playing into my hand or simply having fun. It wasn't easy to figure that fellow out. His little crack helped me, though; it instantly cleared the air and put the meeting on a more playful level. And for that, at least, I was grateful to him.

Soso, though, was out of his mind with indignation. "Listen to me, you! Don't you tease me!" He flew into a rage, waving his arms. "Don't you go making insinuations. 'From behind'!" He snorted and turned red. "I'm no runner, so what? Fighting's one thing and running's another."

"All right, all right." Lenin patted him on the shoulder. "Nobody's doubting you." Then, looking at the Maiden out of the corner of his eye: "Listen, you bastard, mind your own business." Turning back to the man from the Caucasus and placing his hand on his shoulder, he continued: "Don't be such a hothead. The man was joking and you—"

"What joke? Did you hear what he said?" Soso was still seething. "This is a serious conversation."

"Then go ahead," said Lenin. "So, there you were, beside him—"

"Absolutely!"

"And you heard everything?"

"I sure did."

"And you can repeat it now? For all of us?"

"Why not?" Soso shrugged his shoulders. "It was clear as a bell."

"Then go ahead," Lenin said quietly, insistently. "Tell the thieves what Chuma said yesterday. What did he say to the Goblin?"

"He was talking about the army. About all the tricks he learned there . . ."

They were all staring at me now, silently, expectantly. I could almost feel the weight of their looks physically.

"Oh, God," I said, trying to act as relaxed as possible, "what nonsense. Of course that's what I said!"

"Aha!" Lenin moved toward me. "Aha!"

"What do you mean, 'Aha!' " I said. "The question isn't what I said but how I said it."

"A-a-ah"—he brushed it aside—"that's got nothing to do with it—"

"Wrong," I objected. "It's got everything to do with it! I said I knew some army tricks, so what? Knowing them is one thing, being in the army is another. If we're going to start mixing the two things up, then . . . well, take you for instance!"

I turned directly to Soso and crooked my finger into his collar: "What are you, a Georgian?"

"Mingrelian," he answered in confusion. "Why?"

"You like *shashlyk?*"

"Sure I do."

"You know how they're made?"

"Yeah."

"Ever make them yourself?"

"You bet! Lots of times."

"Then maybe you're not a thief, but a cook," I said suspiciously.

"Wha-a-at?" Soso's jaw dropped and his eyes almost popped out of their sockets. "What did you say? You making insinuations again?"

They roared on the bunks. I spread my arms wide and said in a calm voice: "See for yourselves, men, we can all be accused of something. One of us knows one thing, somebody else another. What does it matter who knows what? And another thing: what's the point of wasting time like this? There are more important things to do. The bitches are roaming the zone, half the deportation's in their hands already."

"There's your reason!" Lenin said. "Half the deportation. That's why we've got to know who's with us and who isn't. And don't you twist it around!" He raised his finger and waved it in front of my face. "You're a real smooth talker. I know that. You know how to worm your way out of things—poet! Only that's not going to help you now. What happened in Rostov isn't going to happen in Kolyma!"

"What's that supposed to mean?" I asked, imitating the tone of the Caucasian. "What're you getting at?"

"Just this." He smiled. "Just this." And, frowning, he measured his words: "You say you weren't in the army?"

"No," I said firmly, "I wasn't."

"And you can prove it?"

"And you"—I screwed up my face—"can you prove the opposite?"

"Me? No." Lenin stopped short. "But there are people—"

"What kind? Like Soso, for instance? He isn't even Russian, there's no telling what he wouldn't dream up, given half the chance. Wherever he turns, he's seeing some kind of 'insinuation.' That's a laugh! Thieves"—I stopped for a second and looked around, my face a picture of bewilderment and indignation—"thieves, tell me, what's going on here? A den meeting or a Soviet court? Accusing innocent people without cause. That's the kind of trick they pull in court. I thought we were different, I thought we believed in justice and getting at the truth."

The den started to buzz. Someone growled from out of the semidarkness: "Stop this farce!"

And then another voice cut through the noise: "Where's the Goblin anyway? Let's get him in here. We'll ask *him* and that'll be that."

"Right." Soso took it up. "Let the Goblin say it himself. Where did he go?"

Frankly, I was more afraid of the Goblin than anyone else.

Soso wasn't a threat to me, I'd neutralized him without any trouble. The Goblin's disappearance had surprised me right from the start—surprised and delighted me. The thought of confronting him filled me with anxiety.

"I don't get it," said Lenin, scratching his bald spot and sounding a little perplexed. "The boys searched the whole zone, damn near ran their legs off. They're still looking for him now. He just dropped out of sight, nobody knows where."

"Maybe he left." The Maiden giggled. "Maybe he escaped?"

"How long are we going to sit here?" asked the man who'd called me to the trial in the first place.

"We'll wait a little while longer," Lenin said. "Maybe they'll find him. We've got the time."

"No, we don't," they objected.

"But the meeting isn't over," Lenin stated authoritatively. "Don't you know the rules? You can't let the matter drop. We've got to reach some kind of decision. They'll find the Goblin. He'll show."

The thieves waited for a long time. Some of them, out of sheer boredom, started playing cards. Someone else snored noisily. Then a song came from the corner:

> *"I've traded my suit and my squeaky wheels*
> *For a prisoner's peacoat . . ."*

It was one of my songs! And the thieves knew it. If they're singing it, I thought with relief, that means I have people on my side. Well, things are looking up. We'll overcome you yet, Lenin! We'll put up a good fight, Vladimir Ilyich! We'll knock heads and see whose breaks.

The door of the barracks flew open with a crash and a disheveled boy rushed in.

"Hey, we found him!" he panted from the threshold. "We found the Goblin!"

"Where is he?" Lenin started.

"In the sanitary division."

"What happened, is he sick?"

"Looks like it," the boy said, still trying to catch his breath. "Hard to tell, though, if he's faking or it's for real."

"What's he doing?"

"It's kind of weird." The small, sharp-nosed face of the fellow trembled and twisted in a grimace.

"What the hell is he doing there?"

"Eating shit."

With that the Maiden burst into a laugh.

"Is he really eating it?"

Nauseated, the errand boy nodded. "He's eating it, all right."

"How?"

"With his hands, straight out of the hospital john."

"Good show, old man!" the Maiden shouted. "So he took my advice after all. Ay! you dodger you, you old fox!"

He was in stitches now, holding his sides, groaning and choking on his own laughter. The others, though, seemed less amused. Someone spoke up impatiently, putting a quick end to the Maiden's glee.

"All right, dry up! Enough of the shit business! Come on, let's get back to the main point."

"Right." Lenin took it up.

"As for Chuma, there's nothing more to talk about. Without the Goblin there's nothing we can decide. Anyway, that's not the issue now."

"What is, then?" Lenin asked arrogantly.

"The fact that we're surrounded by bitches! Chuma was right. They're armed and we're empty-handed. That's bad news. We've got to do something. Somehow or other we've got to get our hands on some knives!"

With that the trial was at an end. The accusations leveled against me by Lenin and Soso went unproven. The key witness to the affair had quit the scene suddenly and, by all indications, for good.

For the second time now the old Siberian had saved my neck. It was strange how our fates had intertwined. The night before, he'd kept me from the bitches' knives. Now, by absenting himself, he'd kept me from the knives of the thieves.

For a long time afterwards I thought about the Goblin and his desperate decision to get out of the game. Everything has its limits, that clear, sharp line no one has the right to cross. . . . Now that I've put a little distance between myself and those events, I can see this disparity between means and ends clearly and calmly. At the time, though, on the bunk, surrounded by the den, I'd thought only of my own salvation. And the news that the errand boy had brought filled me with a burning joy. It shocked me, of course, and disturbed me, as it had all the others. But, regardless of that, my first feeling had been one of relief. I'd feared the Goblin then. If he'd turned up at the meeting, there's no telling what might have happened.

THE END OF LENIN

Here's the hard part now—the part of the story I'm still afraid to tell. Confessing to a personal weakness, come what may, is one thing. Admitting to something truly vile is another.

My enmity with Lenin had gone so far that the question of who would do in whom was unavoidable. If I didn't destroy him, then, sooner or later, he'd destroy me. He'd already tried and failed. Why should I wait for him to try again? After all, Lenin wasn't the type to settle for half-measures.

There's an old vagabond saying: "You die today, I'll wait till tomorrow." It was in that spirit that I decided to act. The easiest approach, of course, would have been to pick a fight with him, catch him on the point of my knife, and finish it all in one blow. This method was out of the question, however. Ideologically, we weren't enemies at all, but comrades-in-arms.

All conflicts among thieves are settled, as a rule, at general meetings. Under those circumstances, the best way to do an enemy in is not by force, but by guile. Close infighting is prohibited. Scheming, intriguing, and catching someone red-handed, though, are fully within the rules. I made full use of my rights with a clean conscience. Lenin had started it. Now it was my turn.

The events that followed played right into my hands. Soon after our clash Lenin was thrown into solitary. He'd argued with a guard during a morning check and received five days for his pains.

This event had unexpected consequences. Lenin was a drug addict, a fact to which, up to then, I'd paid little heed. There was nothing unusual about it; almost all of my friends and acquaintances, each in his own way, were attracted to drugs. But since getting hold of narcotics in prison was very difficult, if not impossible, all of them resorted to substitutes, usually any kind of medication with narcotic properties. The Maiden, for instance, used a cough medicine laced with codeine. Lenin subsisted on stomach drops containing opium.

When Lenin was in the barracks with us, he managed to finagle some drops by going regularly to the sanitary division and asking his friends there to help him out. Now, sitting in complete isolation, all his contacts were shut off.

A rumor soon spread through the zone that Lenin was in bad shape, thrashing around in hysterics and demanding to see a doctor in his cell.

Rumors of what was happening behind the cement walls of the prison cell usually reached the zone through a number of different routes: sometimes from people in the penal division itself who'd just served their time, sometimes from men on duty in the staff barracks. (Being in daily contact with the administration, lighting the stoves and washing the floors in the offices, these men were naturally well informed.) Among them a certain Kirei—a Crimean speculator of some renown in his earlier days—had earned the special trust of the convicts.

Kirei had accidentally overheard a conversation between

the prison boss (or "Godfather," as they called him) and one of the guards working the penal section, and immediately informed the rest of us about it.

Lenin's condition, of course, was no surprise. He was having withdrawal symptoms and there wasn't a single drug addict unfamiliar with them. Every passion has its price—it's a truth as old as the hills—and none more tormenting thar that of drug addiction. We all knew that. We also knew that getting a doctor into Lenin's cell was almost completely out of the question. Workers in the sanitary division were allowed to see the prisoners only in extreme emergencies. And even if a camp doctor had appeared in the cell to see Lenin, it was hardly likely he'd have helped him.

In principle all our tricks and ruses were well known to the administration. While the rules could sometimes be circumvented in the general zone, any attempt of that sort in the cells themselves was doomed to failure. It was a rare doctor (even though most of them were prisoners themselves) who would have risked his own neck in this way.

Among the doctors here there was only one person—a former medical student named Sema Reutsky—who might be counted on. Sema was a *fraier*, of course, but the kind of *fraier* thieves called "trained," or "a leper." Although he was a political type (they'd hauled him in on an Article 58, for jabbering), he was a man after our own hearts. A native of Odessa, he'd grown up among the tramps of the harbor in close contact with the gang and, ever since, had kept a certain spirit of adventure alive in his heart.

Lenin was counting on him now. The upshot, though, was different from what anyone might have expected. Three days after Lenin was locked up, Sema was transferred to the mine hospital at Sasuman. He left the deportation unexpectedly in the morning. And just before lunch that very day, the Godfather paid the prisoners in solitary a visit.

The Godfather spent quite a while in the cells, inspecting the quarters and talking to the prisoners. He was with Lenin, too (Kirei filled us in on that), and had discussed something with him. . . .

The substance of the conversation remained a mystery. The Godfather came unescorted to Lenin's cell. That was his usual practice, however, and a matter of no significance whatsoever. It was something else that intrigued the thieves.

Soon after the Godfather's visit Lenin calmed down significantly. His condition strangely improved and his attacks ceased, a fact that, naturally, led us to believe he'd finally gotten hold of his drops. That much was clear. But from whose hands? Certainly not from the cursed Godfather himself?

The assumption seemed incredible. But what other explanation could there be? And more: two days later our barracks was subjected to a sudden general search. The guards turned the place upside down and discovered the place (it was in a corner of the barracks, under the floor) where we hid all our weapons—our homemade knives and "pikes."

A word about weapons, by the way. Usually knives are made out of saws in prison, hacksaws especially. The web of one saw alone, for example, can yield three magnificent daggers. "Pike" is the term used for a metallic pointer about half a meter long, or for thick concrete-reinforcement rods sharpened at one end—an item in great abundance at any construction site. During the events described here, concrete warehouses were under construction near the Karpunka, and that's where we got most of our materials.

There are few weapons more terrible, or versatile, than a pike. Most often, as the name suggests, it's used for running a man through like a butterfly on a pin. A violent backhand blow from a rod like this can also crack a man's skull like a walnut.

I was more at home with a knife myself, and I approached the new weapon with some doubts at first. The Maiden recognized the value of the pikes at once. And when they took them away, he was more distressed and indignant about it than probably anyone else.

It was he, in fact, who first pointed the finger at Lenin for the search and seizure. "Who else is there?" he declared, sitting at night on the bunk, smoking and noisily sipping a steaming cup of black *chifir*. "He sold us down the river for a bottle of dope. It's as clear as two and two. What a bastard, calling for vigilance, looking everywhere for enemies, always questioning who stood for what. . . ."

"They're always the first to turn into bitches." Redhead, the old pickpocket, supported him. "I ought to know, brothers, I've been around a long time. There are plenty of cases like that."

I sat there next to the Redhead, smoking and sipping my *chifir,* not saying a word.

Chifir is an amazing drink, in wide use throughout the north of Asia. There's nothing quite like it. It's made out of regular "black" tea, but in a very special way. The recipe's simple enough: mix as much tea with as little water as you can. Generally, a hundred grams of tea for every liter of boiling water is a good measure. The method for preparing it differs, too. Rather than being drawn in boiling water, *chifir* is cooked much like a potato. And the result is a thick, astringent broth that sets the heart to quiver and the blood to a fever pitch. *Chifir* rings happily through your veins, clarifying your thoughts and awakening a rush of recollections. In the harsh conditions of the North, *chifir* is irreplaceable and far superior to any spirits. There's nothing more insidious than alcohol for keeping you safe from the cold. Every man of the North knows that. For, while alcohol stimulates you at first, it soon weakens you. *Chifir,* on the other hand, is far more reliable.

There are many *chifir* users among thieves, who usually drink it not with sugar, but with salt, relishing every swallow. Actually, a smoked fish is better, and if you can add a good, strong cigarette to that, you've got yourself a fine bouquet!

So there I sat on my bunk, slowly straining the thick, fragrant mixture through my teeth. I savored every swallow; I nibbled on the smoked fish, I smoked cigarettes that came straight from the cooks in the Special Personnel kitchen.

And I kept stubbornly quiet, even though I could have told the full story of how Lenin had managed to get his opium.

The fact was, he'd come by it honestly, without deceiving or betraying anyone. Before leaving, Sema Reutsky had managed

to slip into Lenin's cell with a bottle of medication, and I'd
been a witness to it all.

It had all been quite accidental. I'd been passing by the
hospital barracks when I suddenly remembered the Goblin
and decided to pay him a visit.

He was in an isolated ward at the end of the corridor. The
first thing I noticed when I got there was the odor—the
nauseating stench of shit acridly mixed with ammonia.
Holding my nose, I'd crossed the threshold and seen the
Goblin. He was sitting in the corner on the very edge of a
trestle bed. His dark face, deeply furrowed with wrinkles, was
bent, his wrists hung listlessly between his spread knees. I
called out his name—once, twice—but he didn't answer. He
didn't move. He gave me one look from beneath his beetle
brows and rolled up the whites of his eyes.

The room was in semidarkness. A whitish twilight oozed
through the barred window, but I couldn't see clearly—only
the general layout of the room, the figure of the Goblin
himself, his bent body, and his mute, baked, dark face. And
then there was the monstrous, overwhelming smell.

Convulsed and gagging, I staggered back out to the hallway,
quickly lit a cigarette, and moved toward the exit.

I ran right into Sema Reutsky by the door. He gave me one
look and asked, "What's with you, old man?"

"I've just been to see the Goblin," I gasped.

"Ah, the psycho." He smiled. "Couldn't take it, eh?"

"Couldn't help it," I answered. "How can he sit there,
putting up with it? It's enough to make you gag! Listen—" I
grabbed him by the sleeve. "Why?"

"What do you mean, 'Why?' " Sema shrugged his shoulders.
"You know what he's eating."

"I know." I nodded. "But still . . . What do they do, bring
it to him special?"

"It's just what the doctor ordered—literally. Soon as he saw
the Goblin, he decided he was faking it. So he ordered it on
purpose, the bastard. 'Let him eat it,' he says, 'I'll teach him to
play around with the likes of me. He likes shit, eh? Fine, he'll

get it regularly, three times a day. Then we'll see what kind of tune he starts singing.' "

Reutsky stopped for a moment, knitting his brows. Then, moving right up to me, he continued, lowering his voice, "There's only one thing I can't understand. Is he faking it, or is this Goblin of yours really sick?"

"Who the hell knows?" I evaded the question. Even though Sema was a good man, he was still a *fraier*. And revealing thieves' secrets to people like him was strictly forbidden. "You're the doctor, after all, you've got all the cards. . . . They'll appoint some kind of commission for him, won't they? They have to, don't they? What do you think?"

Sema waved his hand. "Of course, if this keeps up. The Chief said so himself. 'Either I break him, or I open a new field in psychiatry. Either way, it's all the same, the truth is sunk in shit. The more the Goblin eats it, the better.' That's exactly what he said! He's a bastard, but he knows his business, you can't take that away from him! And, worst of all, he's no fool."

"So," I repeated slowly, "the truth is sunk in shit. He's a philosopher, your boss, Semka."

"That's not all he's on to," Reutsky said mournfully. "They're shipping me out today on account of him."

Suddenly remembering he had only an hour and a half before setting off on the convoy, he started to rush. "I haven't got any time to spare and a lot left to do," he said, quickly bidding me good-bye. "I've got to go to the supply room and turn in some clothes. Then I've got to collect an old debt from the foreman. And still pop into the prison cell. There's a character there, one of your boys. He sent me a little note, asking for stomach drops. He was with me before. I knew him, sort of. Only I forgot his nickname." Sema screwed up his face, biting his lip. "Something to do with the Party. Stalin . . . Beria . . . no, wait, I've got it—Lenin!"

That's how it happened. I'd kept the truth from my comrades. I'd dissembled and saved my own skin. I'd betrayed a sworn enemy and brought his head to the block. The suspicion that now fell on Lenin was truly horrible.

Some of the thieves, it's true, still insisted the matter had to be looked into some more. "Don't be in such a hurry to decide," the doubters said. "Besides, you can't judge a man by default. Let Lenin get out of the cell, stand before the society, and speak for himself."

It was the voice of reason, but not everybody heard it. Most of the men were furious and eager for action. There were traces of the same kind of hysteria that had caught up the crowd of thieves at Vanin Bay, in the bathhouse during the deportation—an event that had unexpectedly ended in blood. This time was no different.

Back at Vanin Bay, the murder had at least happened in the open. Now everything was done in concealment, not only from the authorities but from the thieves themselves.

Lenin left his cell late in the evening. The den gave him a guarded, even gloomy reception, and he felt it at once. He tried to find out what the matter was, but no one would give him a straight answer. They were about to sound the retreat for the night and, since the gathering was expected to last a long time, the thieves decided to postpone the conversation till the following morning.

"All right, fine," Lenin growled, settling himself down on his old bunk. "We'll work it out tomorrow. Only remember this, brothers, the man who can get the better of me hasn't been born yet. And if he had, he wouldn't live three days."

Those were the last words he ever spoke.

The next morning, right before first call, Lenin's body was found in the lavatory, an oblong plywood stall right by the rear wall of the barracks. Judging by the signs, they'd jumped him in the dark and choked him to death with a towel.

Strangulation by towel is an old convict technique highly recommended for its cleanliness. It hardly leaves any marks on the victim's throat, with one inevitable exception: a light bruise or small abrasion at the back of the neck, where the towel is twisted tight.

Lenin bore the mark—a clear sign to the thieves that one of them had committed the crime. But who? The men were at a loss. Who could have been that desperate? Someone apparently had been interested in getting Lenin out of the way as quickly as possible, before the general meeting.

A COMPLICATED MATCH

A peculiar situation developed, almost unheard of in criminal society. The thieves were taking part in a murder investigation right along with the authorities. Of course, no one entered into close contact with the Godfather, but both sides were doing their best to get at the truth.

Nobody, however, succeeded.

Even though the Godfather never nailed the murderer, and finally dropped the whole affair, the thieves couldn't lay it to rest. And although their searches were equally fruitless, the case continued to keep them busy for a long time and serve as a subject for endless conversations and speculations.

The Maiden and I had a discussion about it once. It happened before nightfall, while we were sitting at a chess board, playing a very complicated match.

Almost everyone in the deportation had a passion for chess. Not because we were experts, either, far from it. The fact was that since chess, like dominoes, was not considered to be a game of chance, the authorities didn't forbid it or prosecute anyone for playing, so the camp mates—men with animal cunning!—often preferred it to a game of cards.

They played it, naturally, for profit. Like cards, every match was worth ten rubles and the competition at the chess board was as heated and fierce as at any game of *shtoss, ochko,* or *bura.*

No one here really knew how to play the game correctly; theory wasn't one of our strong points. But that hardly bothered us. We more than made up for it with other qualities: perseverance, inspiration, and a kind of instinctive skill.

One of the most gifted players was the Maiden. In the course of time he evolved a distinctive style, aggressive and characterized by an active movement of his rooks and sudden, powerful flank attacks.

I was an uneven player, constantly squandering my energies everywhere at once and often letting vital chances slip by. Sometimes, though, by sheer inspiration, I'd pull off some rather good moves, especially with my knights. Those little pieces, I confess, were my favorites.

So, there we sat by the humming stove, the Maiden and I, playing chess. I was ahead; I'd just made a successful move, taking one of his more valuable pieces with my knight and breaking into his offensive line.

"You dog," my partner muttered enviously. "You sure know how to move your knights."

"Of course," I replied, gnawing at the end of my cigarette. "Who'd know better than a Cossack like me?"

The Maiden bent over the board, lowering his chin to his palm. He sat there a while, rubbing his face with his hand. Then, with a sigh, he said, "Hmm, right. You'd think I'd have thought of all the moves. And it turns out the riskiest was this one, right here. Oh, hell! It's never where you expect it to be. Never. Not only in chess either. . . ."

"Right." I nodded. "That's the way the world turns."

Imperceptibly our talk moved to a discussion of recent events, and to Lenin's death. Carefully making his move on the board, the Maiden said, "Still, it's a miserable way to go—in the toilet."

"Nobody knows who did it, either." I took it up. "The doctor here put his finger on it, all right. Like he said, the truth is sunk in shit."

"Which doctor?" the Maiden asked distractedly, looking over the board.

"The head of the hospital."

"You know him?"

"Of course not. I just happened to drop into the hospital the other day for a little talk with one of the men there. You probably know him—"

Suddenly I stopped short, dropped my cigarette butt, and turned cold inside. I'd almost let the cat out of the bag! The last thing I wanted to do was mention Reutsky's name. If I attracted attention to him, I could suddenly find myself in a lot of hot water. He hadn't been transferred that far away: if they ever needed to, the thieves could easily make contact with him. Then I'd be exposed.

"Who's this you're talking about?" the Maiden wanted to know.

His eyes had been on the game; now, suddenly, he looked me right in the eye. I clambered under the table for the butt, got it, turned it in my fingers, and threw it away. And, lighting a fresh cigarette, said quickly: "Anyway, chances are you don't know him. He's just a chance acquaintance."

"Why were you in the hospital?"

"I wanted to see the Goblin."

"And what happened?"

"I saw him," I replied, wrapping myself up in smoke. "God, did I see him! Makes me sick to even think about it."

"Is he still eating it?"

"Three times a day, regular. He's gotten all black and charred."

"I bet," the Maiden laughed. "Doing a thing like that."

"How he sticks it out beats me." I spread my hands. "The smell alone is enough to break you."

"That's nothing," the Maiden drawled lazily. "He'll recover soon as he gets outside."

"And what if he doesn't? What if they don't let him go, then what? The way I see it, the doctor doesn't believe him. He feeds him shit three times a day on purpose, the son of a bitch. He's experimenting."

"He doesn't believe him?" The Maiden raised his eyebrows. "Ay-yai! That's bad news. Experiments like that can be the end of you."

"That's how it goes," I said. "Someone does Lenin in on the sly, nobody knows who, and this fool kills himself!"

My friend was still bent over the board, stretching his neck and eying me from beneath his fluffy lashes. I could tell something was troubling him.

"Nobody knows who killed Lenin, of course," he said slowly, "but it doesn't take much to figure out who it did the most good."

"Who?" I screwed up my eyes.

"You!"

"What?" I said, standing up.

"Yes," he repeated, "you!" And he carelessly waved his hand. "Don't worry, it's all right, we're alone, nobody's going to hear us. Just explain one thing to me and be honest about it."

"Well?" I leaned toward him, resting my fists on the edge of the table.

The Maiden hesitated for a second, narrowing his eyes.

"Why did you kill him?"

The Maiden's words took me completely by surprise. I lowered myself heavily onto the creaking bench and, in a dry, suppressed voice asked: "Are you kidding?"

"Couldn't be more serious."

"But what made you decide I did it?"

"What?" He smiled, raising his upper lip. "You're damn good at moving knights!" He looked sidelong at the board, touching the chesspieces with the tips of his fingers. "You're good at crooked moves, damn good."

"Listen," I said with a frown, "stop fooling around! What've those stupid moves got to do with it? If you know anything . . ."

"I don't know anything." He shrugged his shoulders. "That's just what it looks like to me."

"If that's what it *looks* like," I muttered, "better cross yourself, Maiden."

Suddenly someone spoke up from behind my back.

"Well, boys, how's it going? Who's ahead?"

I spun around and saw the Redhead. Small and round-shouldered, his bony face overgrown with copper bristles, he leaned on my shoulder.

"Looks like you've got the lead, Chuma," he said. "Sure does."

"That's not saying much." The Maiden stretched his lips into a grin. "It's not a very big lead so far. And luck, you know, has a way of changing sides."

We returned to the board, our former excitement gone. We both played a listless game now, each of us lost in his own thoughts.

The game ended in a draw.

That night I lay on my bunk, twisting and turning. There was a lot of elbow room now. The places once taken in our dim corner by Lenin and the Goblin were empty, and I was alone.

No, not alone. They were still with me. Now the terrible, dumb silhouette of the Siberian, now the face of Volodya Lenin, swollen, convulsed, and dead. And with despair I turned my thoughts from their fate to my own. It seemed to me that we had a lot in common.

What had happened to them was waiting in the wings for me. I didn't see any other way out of here. No hope and no choice. Under the circumstances I too would die, either by the knife or the noose or in a hospital ward.

I now experienced the same attack of depression that had first visited me in the Caucasus and persecuted me ever since. And every time it overtook me I'd plunge into an agony of helplessness and despair, wondering how I could ever live another day.

But, God, how I wanted to live! In peace, quietly leafing through my books, composing my poems. Dear God, I thought, when will I ever get out of this darkness, when will I ever be free?

Someone touched me on the shoulder. I turned with a shudder and saw the Maiden. He was smiling, as always, little dimples trembling on his cheeks. His upper lip raised in a sly, rapacious grin.

"You aren't sleeping, old man, are you?" he breathed into my ear.

"No," I said. "What is it?"

"Let's talk."

"You still on the same subject?"

"Yes. I just want to get it straight."

"What's there to get straight?" I leaned on my elbow, reached for some matches, and lighted up. "There's nothing to your suspicions. Nothing. You can't prove a thing!"

"Funny man," the Maiden whispered, bending toward me, "I'm not trying to prove anything at all. I'm not your enemy, believe me! I'm just—interested. Why?"

"What could it possibly mean to you?" I shrugged my shoulders. "You've been a professional killer all your life. Right?"

"Yes." He lowered his fluffy lashes.

"How many murders have you chalked up?"

"Lots." The Maiden brushed it aside.

"Exactly. Killing all those people without a second thought and now, all of a sudden—"

"Ah, but wait," he interrupted, "that's not what I'm talking about. If someone had been after me the way Lenin was after you, I'd have done him in, too. I'd have dropped him someplace, and that'd have been the end of it. Simple as that. But Lenin . . ." He fell silent for a second, knitting his brows. "Toward the end Lenin wasn't a danger to you anymore. Get it? He was through already, washed up. He'd lost all his authority, all his power."

"Right." I picked it up. "After his stay in the cell he was all washed up. I realized that, too. So you tell *me* what reason could I possibly have had for doing him in?"

"None?" the Maiden asked. And he looked at me expectantly.

"None," I said, looking good and hard right back into his clear, unblinking eyes.

For some time we just eyed each other in silence. Then he blinked and turned away. He was about to crawl back to his bunk when, suddenly, he turned around. And once again I heard him whisper: "Honestly now, the truth. It wasn't you?"

"It wasn't me."

"And if you really think about it?"

"No, damn it!" I said hoarsely and fiercely. "No, you hear me? No! It wasn't me!"

"All right, all right," he said with a little sigh. "No evidence, no trial. Go to sleep."

And with a soft, catlike movement, he leaped from my bunk to the floor.

I found my conversation with the Maiden unusually upsetting. At any moment he could share his suspicions with the others and then—well, I neither knew nor could imagine what might happen next. But just the thought of it was enough to make me feel a little sick.

If they'd only ship us out of here, I thought, and send me someplace far away—alone. If only they'd move faster!

I saw that as my only salvation. And before too long my wish came true. Even so, just before leaving I almost got involved in a dangerous piece of business.

IN THE ICE

Russia is a country of paradoxes—deprived from the dawn of history of her freedom and eternally drawn toward it; a country of slaves and dashing bands of freemen, both on a massive scale.

Once, long ago, the Cossack freemen had shaken the state to its foundations, holding sway over its outlying regions and rocking the throne itself. At times they had even overflowed the borders of the Motherland, darkening the skies above Persia and the bends of Siberian rivers with the smoke of smoldering ruins. Then the freemen had changed, gone underground, and turned into today's criminal world.

They had changed, but, in some essential ways, remained the same. As in the times of Stenka Razin and Pugachev, the society of freemen still stretched to the farthest reaches of the country, harboring runaways, taking the lost and the embittered to its breast. And, though hounded behind barbed wire into the camps, behind wire that, in the course of time, was to enmesh the vast expanse of Russia itself, it remained true to its violent style of life. The only laws it recognized were its own. As best it could, it opposed the regime, stubbornly striving to gain its freedom and break loose into the open, even when to strive was senseless and hopeless, even in the extreme conditions of the far north and the white deserts of Kolyma.

Escape in Kolyma means certain death. There is nowhere to hide, there are almost no major cities, and the sparse population centers are too dangerous to approach. For the local inhabitants, besides their basic industries of hunting and deer raising, have another pursuit: chasing escapees.

Any local discovering a prison escapee is fully authorized to kill him for a bounty. It's an easy job. He doesn't even have to drag the body into the commandant's office to get his reward: a severed right hand or ear will do just as well. As a matter of fact, along with the regular trade in furs and gold, a black market in human ears developed in the north and thrived for many years. The prisoners knew all about it. They also knew that any break for the "open" from the camp was practically impossible. There weren't even any railroads left in this part of the continent; they'd all been replaced by airlines and sea transport.

Still, the convicts persisted in their escapes, only to perish in the roadless woods, the marshy tundra, and the endless ice. The prisoners in Kolyma had a rather colorful term for the whole process. An escapee didn't break for freedom; he "headed for the ice."

It all began when two thieves from the neighboring barracks came to pay a business call. One of them was nicknamed the Snot, and had a rather original profession. He was involved in a delicate form of plunder thoroughly devoid of the coarseness and caddishness of most thief trades, a specialty confined mostly to large cities and major cultural centers. Settling down in a beer house or some kind of restaurant, he (working in tandem with the waiters) would pick a suitable client from among the patrons—a well-dressed man, usually—and would make his acquaintance. He'd start a conversation and then order a round of drinks on himself. At a sign, the waiter would bring beer; the client would toss it down the hatch and almost instantly black out. The fact was his drink had been laced with 180 proof spirits—an explosive mix almost imperceptible to the taste, especially in beer. The only way for the thief to distinguish the normal brew from the potion was by external signs: the shape of the beer mugs, the color and quality of the glass. Having already arranged which glass would hold which drink, he'd prime the unsuspecting *fraier* and then help him outside to some dark alley where, quietly, unhurriedly, and conscientiously, he'd strip him to the buff.

The Snot had successfully plied his trade for quite some time. Once, though, he made a mistake. He drank some beer out of the wrong glass too. He was able to lead the dazed client into the alley as usual, and even undress him, but when it came time to leave, he just couldn't make it. He collapsed in a dead heap under a fence, right next to his victim. Late that night a police patrol picked them both up and took them to headquarters. By the time the Snot came to, he was already behind bars.

His partner, the Hoof, was a well-known Caucasus house-breaker who had worked the great industrial center of Rustavi, not far from Tiflis. He'd also been a successful and talented thief. The Rustavian Criminal Investigation Department had been after him for a long time, but with little success. They just couldn't get the goods on him.

One fine day, though, his world came crashing in. No thanks to the police, either, but to a curious twist of fate. The Hoof was undone by his own love for souvenirs.

After a sensational apartment heist in town, the police came to his place to conduct a search. They were on the lookout for any kind of evidence, but to little avail. None of the stolen goods was uncovered. That's when the unexpected happened.

One of the men on the search noticed an amusing statuette on a bookstand in the corner—a white hen surrounded by chicks. He took it down from the shelf and, startled by its weight, dropped it to the floor with a thud. The policeman scratched the paint with his fingernail and, to everyone's amazement, discovered pure gold.

The statuette had no connection with the recent crime. Still, the Hoof had a lot of explaining to do. Twelve kilos of pure gold was no laughing matter. Where and how had the Hoof got hold of merchandise like that in the first place? Items like that just weren't for sale. And there was no passing it off as a family heirloom, either, not for a son of the proletariat and a professional rogue.

There are some pretty strict laws in the Soviet Union forbidding the hoarding of gold. The Hoof was well aware of that. He also knew that he might get a much heavier sentence now than the one doled out for mere theft. Without a moment's hesitation he confessed to everything.

He picked up the statuette, he said, on a night job at the apartment of a Secretary of the Rustavi Party Committee. He'd taken it, he confessed, when he was already halfway out the door with the rest of the loot, as a keepsake, for purely aesthetic reasons. He liked the way it looked. Indeed, until now he hadn't any idea how valuable it was.

His confession was met at first with a certain disbelief. It turned out the Secretary of the Party Committee had never mentioned a word of the theft to the police. And, under questioning, he continued to deny that it had ever happened. The interrogation lasted a long time and turned up some unexpected information. Apparently there'd long been a black market in Tiflis and Rustavi in foreign currency, stones, and gold, involving almost the entire local power structure.

Against that general background, the stolen hen was small potatoes indeed. Still, the little trifle blew the whistle on a lot of very big people, and some smaller ones, including the Hoof himself. The Department for the Struggle Against the Theft of Socialist Property took up the case against him, and since he couldn't prove his noninvolvement in the currency market, he got the "full bobbin" himself—twenty-five years of prison camp under strong quarantine.

Now he and the Snot spent all their time dreaming about heading for the ice and laying the groundwork for an escape.

Basically, they were victims of the same postwar prison conditions as the Goblin. The bitch war that had broken out on an unprecedented scale, the butchery and bloodshed and constant anxiety, produced a sharp and unrelieved sense of depression in every man there. There wasn't a single convict who hadn't experienced that feeling.

The Maiden, of course, was a fatalist. He looked at things with an eternally bemused grin. The Goblin was ready to go to extremes and had in fact already done so. I just languished and suffered. When the Snot and the Hoof came to talk to me, I found myself intrigued by their idea. Till then I hadn't even given a thought to escape. Now I suddenly saw it as the one solution to all my problems.

First of all, though, I had a request to honor. After deciding to escape, the two thieves started lining up their provisions. With that in mind, they'd found themselves a partner, a strapping Ukrainian boy in prison for embezzlement. The fellow (he had a classic Ukrainian name, Taras) had been specially designated for "meat." It was a common practice in the North. People picked a victim beforehand and ate him on the way.

Taras hadn't the slightest suspicion of what they had in mind. He was simple, naïve, and dreadfully homesick. This was his first time in prison, and all he wanted to do was get back home to the sunny Ukraine. They had no difficulty convincing him to come along. Suddenly, though, he'd done an about-face and become obstinate, sad, and strangely taciturn. He announced that he'd changed his mind and for the time being had no further plans to run.

He didn't want to give his reasons to the men, and he met all their attempts to find out what had really happened with the same mournful reply: "No need. I want to wait a while."

After hitting a dead end with him, the friends decided to send me on reconnaissance.

"After all, you've got culture," the Hoof told me. "You've got a knack with words. Talk to him heart to heart, find out what the hell is going on."

"The main thing, though," the Snot interrupted, "is find out why. Maybe he's on to us."

"Fat chance." The Hoof lazily brushed it aside. "He's just got doubts, the skunk. He's scared. He doesn't have the guts. It happens."

"So how long is he going to make us wait?" the Snot asked. "How long is he going to sit it out?"

"Let Chuma find out," the Hoof said, looking me imploringly in the eyes.

"You'll do it, won't you? Without meat, what can we do? It'd be impossible, you know that yourself, absolutely impossible."

"Sure you couldn't do without it?" I muttered. "I don't need grub like that."

"Listen," the Hoof said decisively. "What you do is your own business. Nobody says you have to touch it. Nobody says you have to go, even. But do us the favor, will you? We're all counting on you."

"Okay, okay," I agreed reluctantly. "I'll try."

And I did. I sought out Taras and made his acquaintance.

"Why so quiet?" I asked him, sitting next to him on the bunk.

"Home," he replied sadly.

He lay back, his powerful, thick-veined arms folded behind his head. His face was thoughtful.

"Home," he repeated and sighed.

"Who've you got back there?"

"Mama. She's alone." He sighed again. "How can she get by without me?"

"Must be hard for her," I said ingratiatingly.

"It sure ain't no bed of roses. She's alone, you know. And sick. She's been waiting years for a pension and still nothing."

"Hmm, yes," I said. "Sounds bad, all right. I'll tell you, if it was me, I'd tear right out of here."

"That's what I was thinking of, too, at first. But then I sort of had my doubts. Look, judge for yourself." He got up, leaning on his elbow, and moved his high-cheekboned, gloomy face toward me. "You're an understanding fellow, you got soul. You write such songs!"

"You know my songs?" I asked quickly.

"Sure." A vague smile crossed his face. "Beautiful songs, right from the heart. So, you tell me, won't my escaping hurt her?"

His words took me aback. It turned out the fellow knew me, valued me, trusted me. He liked my songs! How could I deceive him and condemn him to be eaten? I just didn't have it in me to do that.

Lighting up a cigarette and choking on the smoke, I said: "Look, if you really want my personal opinion, don't do it. It's not going to help anybody, least of all you."

And so I pitied the fellow, deceived my friends, and ruined the scheme. Actually, the escape still took place. I learned about it a little while later, after I'd been transferred to the farm camp at Tauisk.

Surprising as it may seem, Taras took off with the thieves anyway, right into the ice. How they managed it is beyond me. Probably they found themselves another smooth talker, some writer, some hunter of innocent souls. . . .

It was a daring undertaking. Hardly anyone had escaped from the deportation point till then. Ever since Karpunka had been created, there had only been three such attempts and none of them from the general zone, but from the labor units, where the prisoners were led out to work.

There were only three or four worker brigades on Karpunka, all of them widely separated, in an isolated sector of the camp. Somehow the boys had managed to connive their way into contact with the head foreman and get enrolled in one of the brigades, where they waited, working repairs on the route, till the time was right.

They escaped from the convoy relatively easily, under the cover of a suddenly breaking snowstorm. Then they left the route behind them and headed for the hills, where they vanished. A rumor eventually made the rounds that, in the taiga, not far from Okhotsk, Taras' body had been found.

The boy had been shot, but that was all. As for the Snot and the Hoof, they had totally disappeared.

What had happened out there in the backwoods? Had the roles been switched? Had those who dreamed of meat furnished a meal to the Ukrainian themselves?

Anything can happen in the taiga, from the unexpected to the downright miraculous. And, if you want to talk about miracles, imagine my sense of wonder the moment I arrived at Tauisk and learned the place was full of women!

MEAT IN MY SOUP

Tauisk is one of the southernmost population centers on Kolyma, located near the Sea of Okhotsk and protected from the northern winds by a ridge of unforested, gently sloping mountains called the Knolls. The climate is relatively mild, making it an ideal site for the auxiliary agriculture that supplies the main administration of Dalstroi with vegetables.

Several camp centers, consisting mostly of women, were involved in the growing and the harvesting. There were men in the local camps as well, of course, but not many. In the main they were invalids, the debilitated, the old; those rejected by the Selection Commission. The commission had immediately recognized I was temporarily unsuited for work. I'd never fully recovered from my Kharkov hunger strike and, although I wasn't as weak as before, I still looked pretty bad.

Frail and scrawny, with pale, peeling skin and protuberant ribs, I stood before the medics. One of them carelessly waved his hand: "To the Reduced Strength Camp with him," he said. And then I heard the word: "Tauisk."

The Redhead, who was standing beside me, winked and whispered with a smile, "Well, old man, looks like you finally got some meat in your soup!"

We arrived at the camp in the evening, during a lilac snowfall. There was another "goner" with me, an elderly wreck barely able to catch his breath. As usual, the escorts led us right to the bathhouse.

Fatigued and frozen from the day's journey, we took a long, languorous time scrubbing and drenching ourselves with hot water. We were alone in that dim, stuffy, spacious room. After washing, we splashed in our bare feet to the anteroom of the bathhouse and discovered that our underwear was gone.

"Damn it," my companion muttered, "don't tell me they got a bunch of wise-asses around here? It's a good thing they didn't touch my outside clothes. I got some coins there . . ."

He bent over his pea jacket on the bench, turned it inside out, felt the lining, sighed with relief, and calmed down.

Lighting up a cigarette, I said, "I don't know, they're pretty strange, whoever they are. If it'd been me, I'd have taken the outside clothes and left the underwear alone."

Suddenly, a low female voice interrupted us. "What is it, boys? Looking for your underwear? We've been giving it a little wash over here. It'll be dry in a second."

We turned around and saw a young woman in a robe standing in the doorway. Her arms akimbo, she leaned her round shoulder against the doorpost. A wily smile lighted her face. And, right behind her, we saw a multitude of other faces—all of them female—eying us with shameless intensity.

That's when my companion, Semyon was his name, gasped: "Brother, we've landed right in a pile of women!"

"Right in our hands." The woman nodded, screwing up her eyes. "Aren't you glad?"

"Sure," I muttered.

"Well then, all right," she said with satisfaction, turning to the women behind her. They exchanged whispers about something and, with an inviting movement of her hand, she said: "Come here and get your underwear. Don't be ashamed. There's nothing to it. Besides, you're ours now!"

And we went, stooping and covering ourselves as best we could, conscious of their unblinking eyes.

As we learned later, the incident was no accident. After

hearing about our arrival, the entire local elite had gathered in the linen room—cooks, forewomen, and workers in the Cultural Division—to arrange a bridal shower, so to speak, and decide who'd get whom.

Semyon was claimed by the head of the Industrial Planning Division, a lean, bright woman who took him firmly by the sleeve and led him off with a carnivorous glint in her eye and a flutter of whitish lashes.

I fell into the clutches of the head of the dining hall, a powerful woman a head taller than I and significantly broader in the shoulders. She smoked shag and swore in a husky bass. But she had a tender soul that had earned her the nickname of the Muse.

"My little tiptoe," she droned, pressing me to the heaving masses of her breasts. "My poor little wreck. Don't you worry, I'll fatten you up."

She lived in the Technical Personnel Barracks in a small niche apart from all the rest. It was a tight squeeze; we tossed and turned all night, shaking the trestle bed and rocking the plywood walls. Finally, I fell asleep, nestled on the Muse's breast, moored in her warmth and breathing the fragrance of her hot armpits. I dreamed of the sands of Turkestan all that night, of desert mirages and the salt-marsh steppes by the borders of Iran.

The next morning I ran into Semyon in the dining hall. We'd barely sat down at the table when the Muse set two steaming tureens of soup in front of us. "Eat," she said, a smile creasing her big, glossy cheeks.

"Well, how're things?" I asked, looking at my friend. He didn't look too good to me. His face was even sharper and more pinched than the day before.

"Guess for yourself." He shrugged his shoulders. "All night long, not a moment's sleep. I try to make her understand— wait, I say, hold off, give me a chance to get glued back together. . . ."

"What did she do?" I was getting interested.

"The snake, she doesn't have an ounce of sympathy. No understanding. And if that's not bad enough, she starts feeling hurt. 'You're in my power,' she says, 'completely. If I want to, all I got to do is give the word and back you go to the sludge detail.' And she can do it, too!"

"Well," I said slowly, "it's their show."

"Right, right," he took it up. "I just don't know what to do."

"Stay with it." I grinned. "Try somehow. You've got to, Syoma."

"I'll croak," he moaned.

"Better here than in some mine," I argued. "Better on a woman, in the warm. That's a holy business, brother."

He was silent for a moment, knitting his brows. Then, pulling the tureen toward him, he said: "Of course, it'd be stupid to leave. If you think about it, chances like this don't come more than once a lifetime. Can't say I like women that much, but the food's good. Just look at this soup, will you? Soup, hell! It's all meat!"

I lived in the camp till spring, with nothing heavier to do than chop wood for the kitchen. After working my appointed time, I'd take off and loaf about the zone, looking in on the barracks and getting to know the women.

Most of them, as far as I could tell, were much stronger than male prisoners. They were more stable and closer to the earth, and usually able to endure physical privations, like hunger and pain, a lot more easily. The one thing they couldn't take was separation from their families and loved ones.

I saw all kinds of women—hysterical, frenzied, embittered; I saw broken and estranged women, with empty, lifeless eyes. None of it was from excessive work (life on a subsidiary farm was like vacationing at a health resort, compared to other camps) and none of it from hunger (you're fed better in farm camps, too). It was depression that did it, and a longing for what was lost and gone.

I once happened by a barracks full of Lesbians.

I am no longer a young man. I've staggered all over the world, traveling hundreds of roads and gathering experience. I can judge and compare now with some insight. Take Lesbianism, for instance. Here it assumes a pathological dimension and undergoes monstrous transformations.

The same camp philosophy that separated men from women also gave rise to preposterous, abnormal characters here, such as the "male dogs"—Lesbians who imitated men in everything: habits, intonation, and dress. The entire population of the camp feared them. They swilled vodka, took narcotics, played cards, and pitilessly ordered their lovers about.

As a general rule, each of the male dogs had several lovers that they'd deal with in turn, keeping a tight hold on their harems. There were instances of monogamous love, though, and unusual alliances and strange weddings would occasionally be celebrated in the barracks. Oleshkovsky describes one such wedding in his well-known song, "A Prison Camp Lesbian":

> *Let them search us on the watch,*
> *Let them come into the barracks,*
> *Today we'll be singing and carrying on*
> *And setting a rich, festive table.*
> *My fiancé is a fine-looking woman,*
> *He treats me as nice as can be.*
> *He doesn't make himself up with lipstick*
> *He walks with the stride of a man.*
> *He looks like a man in every way*
> *Except that his beard doesn't grow.*
> *The young maidens dance the* tsiganochka *gaily,*
> *The old women shout, "It's bitter, so kiss!"*
> *While one little Lesbian sobs inconsolably*
> *In the arms of the unmarried girls.*

The song sounds happy enough, I suppose, but the truth behind it is frightful. I once saw something like it with my own eyes. A wedding like the one described in the song was just beginning in a barracks I was passing. Everything seemed perfectly in order: someone was singing, someone else was beating out the tight rhythms of the *tsiganochka*, and, in the midst of the general gaiety, a young redheaded Lesbian girl was sobbing by the dining table.

Right beside her the "bridegroom" (dressed in a man's embroidered Russian blouse, her hair cut short) looked at me suspiciously. Clearly, "he" took me for a potential rival, and all the time I found myself there I could feel his heavy look.

I soon wandered to the other end of the barracks and struck up a conversation with some girl. We were sitting in the corner, on a lower bunk, when I heard someone softly call me by my name. I looked around: the bride stood before me, the very same Lesbian who had been crying just a moment before.

"Why did you come?" she said breathlessly. "Get out quickly, I'm afraid!"

"What's there to be afraid of?" I asked her.

"I don't know. He's up to doing anything." She glanced around quickly. "Anything, anything. He might even kill you!"

"What?" I said with a laugh. "Don't talk nonsense. And calm down. Here, sit down. He's not going to do anything to me."

"Well, if he doesn't kill you," she whispered, "then he'll kill me. I'm sure of it. Go. I beg you!"

And I left, confused, puzzled, and depressed.

I had adventures of other kinds, too. One fine day in the middle of the spring, some lady thieves kidnapped me.

Here again I have to remind you of the matriarchy that prevailed. I'd fallen completely under the power of women, lost all my former privileges as a male, and begun to play a passive role that was completely alien to me. I wasn't my own master anymore. The right of choice no longer belonged to me, but to others. I simply swam along with the current, crossing from hand to hand, changing protectresses.

I didn't enjoy the warmth of the Muse's love for long. The head of the Industrial Planning Division, Yulia Matveevna, the woman who had once led Semyon off into the night, now took me away from her. As Semyon had feared, she'd finally made good on her threat to send him out of the zone. Thank

God, though, he hadn't ended up in a deportation. He remained in Tauisk, in a separate male sector, with all the other "goners." Strictly speaking, Semyon and I were supposed to have gone there ourselves after the bathhouse and had remained thanks only to Yulia Matveevna. Apparently, we'd charmed the ladies somehow or other, and Yulia had positively swooped down on Semyon. Now, after her disenchantment with him, she'd decided to start the game all over again.

Her conversation with the Muse was brief. The Muse grieved a little, wept, and yielded. Arguing with the head of the Industrial Planning Division was dangerous business, after all. Her powers were considerable. She was involved in the registration and disposition of the cadres. All kinds of appointments depended on her and in that sense the Muse, like the rest of us, was under Yulia Matveevna's thumb.

What more can I tell you about her? She was a specialist in planning who had once worked in the Ministry of Heavy Industry. Some kind of machinations with the office records had landed her in jail with a rather heavy term—ten years—but with all the privileges accorded anyone caught committing a crime in the line of official duty. The Chekists had a soft spot for people like that. After all, a similar fate might be awaiting them.

This was a predatory, perpetually unsated woman, with a personality as barbed as the wire surrounding the camp. I very quickly became convinced of that. But what was there to do? I endured.

And then, to top it all off, one fine evening, after retreat, the female thieves abducted me. I'd been wandering through the zone in the warm April darkness when some women suddenly rose up and surrounded me.

"Hey, you, stop!"

"What is it?" I asked.

"You come with us."

"Where?"

"You'll see."

"Why?"

"Come on, come on! We'll talk about it later."

"Forget it, ladies," I said exhaustedly, "I've had enough. I want to sleep. To hell with all of you."

"Don't move," they whispered ominously. "Do what you're told!"

Suddenly, I felt the icy touch of a knife at my throat.

Oho! I thought, that's something new! I was in another mess all right. I didn't want to fight it out with them (I couldn't have anyway, I was unarmed and all of them had knives) and calling for help was out of the question. It would have looked too comical. I had to resign myself and go.

And so I was delivered under guard to another barracks. As soon as I crossed the threshold, I realized it was a den of female thieves. The interior was pleasant, clean, and warm, decorated with gay little curtains that hung from most of the bunks and a patterned tablecloth that had been stretched from the doors to the table.

The table stood in the very center of the room and was covered with glittering bottles of vodka, a steaming pot of *chifir,* food, and a scattered deck of cards. An enormous, low-set bed heaped with pillows had been placed right beside the table and a woman in a short robe was lounging on it, puffing at a cigarette.

Her face was square and dry. A black strand of hair had fallen over her brow and the crimson slash of a scar coursed across her cheek from the edge of her mouth to her ear.

"Greetings," she said to me. "Sit down!" Indicating a spot right beside her, she extended her hand, mottled with the purple traceries of tattoos.

"Let's get acquainted. The name's Alyona, nicknamed the Cigarette Butt." And then, narrowing her eyes and smiling slowly: "You know where you are?"

"I can guess," I answered, pressing her moist and narrow hand. "I'd say you were all thieves."

"You got it." She nodded.

"It's no secret," someone chimed in from the corner. "We steal with our cunts and hustle with our asses."

"Where did you all come from?" I was amazed. "I've been

here a long time already and never heard a word about you."

"We just got here a week ago," Alyona said, "from Yagodny. Ever hear of it?"

"I've heard," I answered.

"All right. So, we got here and the only thing they talk about is you. You'd think it was a joke or something. A live male walking in the zone!"

Suddenly she giggled, exposing her black teeth.

"It's been three years since we've seen a man. So we decided to take advantage of the opportunity."

"What do you mean, you decided?" I asked gloomily.

"Simple. We drew cards. High one gets the prize."

"You mean me?"

"What else?"

"And who got the high card?"

"You're looking at her," she said, playing with her eyebrow. "Me, sweetpaw. Me!"

Alyona got up and stretched toward the table. Her robe (it rode way above her knees) opened a bit. Its flaps parted and I could see she had no underwear on.

"Let's have a drink," she said, taking a bottle from the table and pouring it into some glasses. "Take a pull," she said, handing one of them to me.

I drank the vodka slowly and wiped my mouth Then they offered me a little snack of smoked fish. I looked around as I chewed.

A strained silence reigned in the barracks, as in a theater before the opening curtain. Seated on the bunks, the women (there were about twenty of them here) were avidly watching Alyona and me, exchanging whispers and clearly waiting for something.

"Why so quiet?" I muttered in embarrassment.

"You want noise instead?" Alyona asked with a laugh.

"No." I shrugged my shoulders. "It just feels gloomy, that's all."

"It'll be lively soon." Alyona nodded.

She moved right up to me. Her robe flew open again and the dim light of the lamp slid along her belly and her thighs.

"How about a little music?" She winked at me. And, turning around, she snapped her fingers commandingly.

"Hey, Satan, where are you?"

"Here," came a voice from the bunks.

"Get your guitar. Play something fast."

"Like what?"

"Something about love. You ought to know." Alyona sharply waved her hand. "Do it!"

And there, in the quiet of the smoke-filled barracks, the strings shuddered and the melody of an old Rostov thief song filled the air:

> *"Don't stand on the ice,*
> *the ice'll break through;*
> *don't love a thief,*
> *a thief'll fall, too.*
> *A thief'll fall and land in jail*
> *and you won't like bringing him parcels . . ."*

Satan's voice was clear and strong, and the guitar in her hands quivered with a heart-rending sound.

> *"We'll drink, we'll love,*
> *and when misfortune comes, we'll despair."*

Listening intently to the song, Alyona fell silent, and moved close to me. Then she said slowly: "You see how they humor you? Just like a king at his saint's day. Now this, now that . . . I hope you appreciate it."

"I do," I said. "I do."

"Then let's have another, eh?"

She filled the glasses again. We drank them down and I felt a hot, intoxicating wave rise in my breast. I was getting light-headed. Without even waiting for the invitation, I reached for the bottle.

"Ah, Olenushka," I said, embracing her with one hand and holding a glass filled to the brim with the other, "you've got a nice name, just like in the fairy tales."

"It's nice," she agreed, "and you like me, too, right?"

My hand lay on her skinny little shoulder. The robe slipped

down and Alyona didn't bother to straighten it. I tossed off the vodka in a single gulp and, caressing her with my palm, said, "Of course I like you. Granted, you're a little scrawny and your bones stick out. But, no harm done."

"The nearer the bone, the sweeter the meat," she answered with a smile. She stared right back at me with dark, twinkling eyes full of longing.

"Well," I said, "all right, let's do it."

And, getting up, I looked around the barracks for a cozier nook.

"Let's go over there, in the corner."

"Why?" she said slowly.

"Why?" I was surprised. "Don't you want to do it?"

"Sure. But why in the corner? In the dark?"

"Where, then?"

"Here," she said, kneading the pillows with her behind.

"But we're in full view," I said. "They're looking at us."

"Let 'em!" She moved her little shoulder carelessly. "That's not going to bother you and me and, as for the girls, well, it'll be . . . interesting."

"You want to give them a show?"

"Sure," she said simply, "why not? Things like this don't happen every day. Let 'em get a look, at least. Don't be put out, my dear, don't pay any attention to them, just do what you're good at." She lay down nimbly and spread out on the pillows. "Do it!"

For an instant or two I was confused—but it passed. I was drunk, after all, hopelessly drunk. My head was spinning and my mind crumbling from the intoxication, the nearness of a woman, and Satan's heart-rending and plaintive songs.

What's the difference anyway? I thought. If they want to look, let 'em!

I bent down to Alyona and forgot everything. The sounds died away.

The following morning I crawled out of the barracks and stood shakily by the entrance, drinking in the sea breeze with its clean, chilling smell of salt and melted snow. I felt awful.

No, I reflected mournfully, dragging myself along on shaky legs, "I just can't go on like this. A half year more under these circumstances and I'm a dead man. I won't live out my term. I won't see freedom."

Yulia Matveevna met me with tears in her eyes. She asked me nothing about the night before and that, to tell you the truth, amazed me. Knowing her character, I'd been expecting a more stormy reaction.

"A paper came from the administration," she said, sniffling, "signed by the head of the Department of Operations. It's an order for your deportation. Immediately. And under double guard."

"Why?" I asked. "What happened?"

She shrugged her shoulders and raised her swollen, reddened eyes to me. "What did you do?"

"I don't know," I said. "You mean it doesn't say in the paper?"

"No. Just the order to ship you off, that's all."

"When?"

"Tomorrow," she said. "There's nothing we can do."

"So."

I reached for my tobacco pouch, rolled a cigarette, and lighted up, leaning against the table. "We'll have to part," I said.

"There's nothing to do," she repeated.

"I'd better get moving," I said. I got up and headed for the door. "I've got to get a few things together."

"And say good-bye to a few people here and there," she added, pressing her lips, "isn't that right? You've got a lot of girlfriends here, after all, don't you?"

"What girlfriends?" I brushed it aside with annoyance. "Don't be silly."

"I know," she said. "I know everything! I know where you were last night!"

"What could I do about it?" I protested. "I didn't stay there on my own, you know."

"Ah," she said with a sigh, "why do I love a dog like you? I know what you're like, and still it hurts to see you go. . . . All right." She bent toward the table and rustled some papers. "Go! We'll see each other this evening."

I did spend all that day parting with my girlfriends. I visited the Muse, looked in on the redheaded Lesbian, spent some time at a number of other places, and didn't get back to Alyona till late that evening.

The following morning they took me out of the zone under guard and put me in a large covered truck. The unexpected deportation, the truck, the size of the escort (three men armed with machine guns) were all beginning to make me feel a little uneasy. Yulia had said the order had come straight from the Department of Operations. What did they want from me? And where were they taking me now? The truck meant it was probably far away. But where? The Administration itself? The penal division, perhaps? And if so, why?

We traveled on the highway for quite a while. Finally the van shuffled to a stop and the little door flew open, letting in a burst of wind. There in the whitish, swirling damp of the fog the familiar features of the deportation point rose before me. The deportation point: the last thing I'd expected!

I got even more upset when I saw that they weren't taking me to quarantine or the general zone, but straight to the tight-security barracks, a squat stone prison right beneath the watchtower of the camp. As soon as I got there, they searched me thoroughly and pushed me into a cell.

I rummaged around in my pockets and came up with a few grains of tobacco. The second I arrived, they'd taken away my cigarettes and a bag of grub I was carrying. I lighted up and lay down on a low bunk with my shoulder to the icy cement wall. Suddenly I heard someone singing on the other side of the wall.

> *"You were a prostitute, I met you*
> *Beneath a willow in the square;*
> *A drunken wind whirled in your eyes*
> *And your cigarette smoked in the breeze."*

I'd written that song a long time ago, when I was still free and at large in Rostov, and now I listened to the familiar melody and words with surprise.

What amazed me wasn't the song itself (my compositions were well known and widely sung by then) but the fact that it was filtering through the prison wall. Suddenly I realized why. A dark crack by the corner window of the cell was winding like a snake from the ceiling to the floor (like everything built by prisoners, it was a shaky job of construction). That was where the song had been coming from. Huddling into the corner and putting my ear to the crack, I listened intently to the dim voice of my neighbor and realized it was the Maiden!

" 'And once again we've met, my dear,' " the Maiden was singing, " 'You're just the same as eight years back. / Those burning eyes, that whorish glint . . .' "

I called out his name. He fell silent. Then he asked in a hasty whisper: "Chuma, is it you?"

"Yes!"

"When did you get here?"

"An hour ago. What about you?"

"I've been here three days."

"Anybody else from the gang?"

"No, nobody. The whole den's at Indigirka now, under tight security. God, the things that're going on out there. . . ."

"Where were you all this time?"

"Same place as them."

I was amazed. "Why did they bring you here?"

"Same reason they brought you."

"But what's it all about?"

"You mean you don't know?" I could tell the Maiden was smiling. "You can't guess?"

"Haven't got the vaguest idea."

"Remember the Vanin deportation?"

"The deportation? What's—" I was about to go on when suddenly the whole deportation bathhouse scene rose in my mind—the swirls of steam, the hustling shadows, the bloody foam on the slippery floor. . . . I knew then what it was all about, but still unwilling to accept the bitter truth, I stalled:

"You mean that business? . . . The murder?"

"Of course," the Maiden replied. "What else?"

"But that investigation—they had wound it all up."

"So now they're unraveling it again. They're looking for the ones who started it in the first place. And that means us. You following me?"

That's when I said something I'm still ashamed of to this day. Not of the words so much, as of the tone in which they were said.

"Listen, Maiden, why me? I didn't have anything to do with it. I didn't lift a finger against anybody, you know that yourself. Tell me, you know it, right? Tell me—"

Something made me stop in mid-sentence. Inside me, I felt something abject and vile. The Maiden sensed it, too, and, after a little pause, he said: "I know, I know! Just don't bellyache, for the love of God! You'll clear yourself with the prosecutor and if it gets to me, I'll back you up. I haven't got any reason to drag you into this with me."

"And what about you?" I asked. "Don't you think you'll get off the hook?"

"Me? No," he said. "Things are looking bad for me."

"But they've called you already, haven't they?"

"Once. To the senior investigator."

"What did he ask you?"

"Nothing much," the Maiden said thoughtfully. "He just kept going around in circles. I've got a hunch he's waiting for something."

"Like what?"

"Probably some kind of supporting evidence. Maybe an order from the chief. I don't know, old man, what's the use of guessing? We'll all find out sooner or later."

And, soon enough, we did. It turned out the Godfather had just been waiting for the ships to start sailing again. And with the first passage he sent the Maiden and me off to "the big country," and the inquiry prison at Vladivostok.

A MEETING WITH THE GOBLIN

The Maiden and I weren't traveling alone to Vladivostok. There were two other prisoners with us in the dark compartment of the hold. They were being sent for questioning, too, but on another matter entirely. And, as we learned the following day, an old comrade was riding in the compartment right beside us: the Goblin.

It looked like he'd finally gotten what he was after. He'd faked them all out, including the chief doctor at the deportation hospital. No matter how hard the doctor had tried to expose his "patient," no matter what tricks he'd tried, he'd finally had to give in and sign the release papers. Along with a party of about fifteen other prisoners, the Goblin was sailing to freedom in Nakhodka Bay, not far from the main port of Vladivostok.

That's where our route ended, too, so we'd be having him for a neighbor, in the tight intimacy of the ship, for the many days of the journey that lay ahead. As a rule the prisoners on deportation met with the liberated passengers on the lower deck, at the rear of the vessel, during the exercise periods. They were transporting us on an old, remodeled ice ship called the *Tauisk*. The name seemed symbolic to me when I first saw it in port—a reminder of that unique period in my life, that blessed "matriarchy." And the farther we sailed, the greater my fondness for those bygone days.

Usually they led us out for a walk in the middle of the day, after lunch. The guards would position themselves on the sides, cordoning off the crowd of freemen and keeping them from any contact with us. No matter how hard they tried, though, they couldn't keep us apart from them. The freemen would wrangle with the guards and call to us, taking every opportunity to toss us bread and tobacco.

Once again—and for the first time in quite a while—I caught sight of the Goblin in that noisy, ragged crowd. God, how he'd changed! It looked as if he'd aged about ten years. He was bent and thin and dry. His shaggy beard and long hair, which was lying in tangles on his shoulders, were showered with a dirty gray that hadn't been there before. The past winter had brought it all out in him. He'd paid a high price for his freedom!

Word for word, that's what the Maiden said, and he spoke for all of us. "A high price, all right. To hell with freedom like that."

The Goblin was leaning against the bulwark, holding himself off from the crowd. He was taciturn and gloomy. The biting wind blew his already tousled gray mane and, for the first time, he really seemed to earn his nickname.

"Hey, Goblin!" the Maiden called out to him. "What's the matter, don't you recognize us? Over here, c'mon!"

The figure by the side slowly straightened up. The muddy, dilated eyes peered at us from beneath the bushy brows and something like a smile began to spread across that bony, wrinkled face. He walked toward us with a grin. The crowd instantly parted at his approach, giving him a wide berth and shying away from him, like someone stricken with the plague.

"Watch where you're going, you fucker!" a high-cheek-boned fellow in a wide-open quilted jacket muttered in disgust. "Don't you dare touch us, understand?"

Oddly enough, the Goblin took all the abuse with a kind of strange aloofness. Without a murmur or the slightest trace of anger, he slowly advanced as if he were the only person in the world. And, in fact, that's just what he was: all alone.

Someone else shouted: "Killing would be too good for him, the scum!"

The Goblin stopped and looked around. Stepping forward to defend an old comrade, I said reproachfully: "Brothers, brothers, why are you attacking him? Can't you see the man is sick?"

"What kind of man is that?" they barked back. "People don't eat shit."

"He did it on purpose," I answered, "and besides, that was a long time ago."

"I'm not talking about what happened before," the high-cheekboned fellow snapped back, "I'm talking about right now!"

I stopped short and turned, struck dumb, to the Goblin.

"That's right," the fellow confirmed. "He eats shit, you understand? As soon as he got on board he started right in. But why argue?" He suddenly smiled. "You're friends with him, right? Then go ask him yourself."

The Goblin was standing two paces away from us, shifting from one foot to the other, wheezing and twitching. The smile on his face gradually faded and set. There was something convulsive and wolflike about the grin that remained.

"Goblin," the Maiden called him softly, "do you hear me, Goblin? What's the matter with you?"

He didn't answer.

"All right, cut the gab," the chief guard shouted hoarsely. "What is this, anyway, a den meeting? Don't you know the rules? Beat it, parasites!"

He chased us away from the freemen (the Goblin among them) and ordered the guards to end the walk.

Later, off the shores of Japan, we ran into a line of storms and, as gales tossed the ship, sat out the final days of our deportation in the hold. "Laid out" was more like it, actually. As usual under such circumstances, I became depressed and took to writing poems. The Maiden slept. He could sleep for long stretches under any kind of weather. And when he'd wake, he'd just lie there, his eyes half closed, singing softly.

He knew a great number of thief and vagabond songs. His favorites were usually the sentimental ones. This time, though, all the songs he sang had one theme in common: death by firing squad.

There's a special cycle of songs on that subject. Take this famous one, for example, about the Tambov rebel Ataman Antonov, written by Antonov himself just before his own execution:

> *Somehow the sun isn't shining here*
> *There's a cloud above my head.*
> *Either the Commissar is near*
> *Or a bullet is aimed at my heart.*

> *At dawn the raven cries with a start,*
> *"Communist, open fire!"*
> *In the final, funeral hour,*
> *The home-brew smells of the dead.*

Then there's the anonymous "Wide, Wide World" song that I edited while still in the Caucasus:

> *Tomorrow they'll lead us out to be shot,*
> *The sentence cannot be reversed;*
> *The East is already turning blue.*
> *The shadows have started to swirl.*
> *I look at the sunrise and bid it good-bye . . .*
> *Aside from your hands, your lips, and your eyes,*
> *There's nothing I'll miss in this world.*

Prison folk music is full of similar examples. The Maiden knew them all. And now he sang them, with a kind of cheerless, monotonous, depressing persistence. I took it as long as I could and then finally spoke:

"Listen, what's the matter? Change the record, Maiden, it's depressing enough without that."

"Ah, old man," he replied with a little sigh, "depressing, you say. Well, what's there to be so happy about?"

"Give us something a little more pleasant anyway."

"My soul's in mourning," the Maiden muttered. "She can't sing. She wants to cry."

He said it pensively, hard little wrinkles gathering in the corners of his mouth. I'd never seen him like this before. I was used to his constant, lazy grin, to his mocking equanimity and bitter cynicism. I couldn't imagine the Maiden any other way. Of all the convicts I knew, he was the most true to type. An honest-to-God vagabond, a son of Gulag, with the soul of a thief!

But what did I really know about him? Only rarely, and usually under the influence of *chifir* or some other kind of drug, would he recall his past. And if he did, he'd no sooner start than stop, turning the conversation to something else.

The Maiden's life (what I could make out of it) was a mirror of our troubled age. In some particulars his childhood had been similar to mine. All his problems and misfortunes had begun during the years of the Stalinist terror, after the collapse of his family.

The Maiden (he did have a normal Christian name, by the way: Kirill) was born in 1928 in Angara, in the ancient taiga village of Boguchany. His father had been a political exile—one of those who, in the middle twenties, had sided with the Party opposition in Leningrad and been banished to a settlement in eastern Siberia. His mother was a native Siberian, a backward peasant of the taiga. The two of them had met soon after his arrival in the village. Before long they had a son, Kirill. But soon a new wave of repressions swept through the country, and all those who had previously been exiled (including the Maiden's father) ended up behind barbed wire with ten-year sentences in tight-security camps.

His mother was sentenced, too, her only crime being her union with a known enemy of the people. They shipped her off to the Arctic Circle, while her only son (then all of five years old) ended up in an Irkutsk foster home, an institution specifically designed for the abandoned children of convicts.

And so began the journey that finally led the Maiden straight to the bottom. For years he was shunted from one children's home to another. He was continually escaping and being caught and escaping once again. At the outbreak of the Second World War he was in Kazan, at a colony for juvenile offenders.

His first few criminal ventures weren't major—market thefts, mostly, and lifting "doves" (the term used for linen hung out to dry in the yard). Eventually he made some connections with professional thieves—a group of locksmiths working the towns and cities on the left bank of the Volga. As an apprentice, the Maiden performed every kind of petty errand you could think of: he was a messenger boy, a water boy, and on the rare occasions when he'd go off on night work, a sentry and "porter" for the loot. Until one fine night, in the middle of the war, when he did something that immediately changed his status and elevated him in the eyes of the thieves.

The incident is well known. The Maiden told me all the details himself. It happened in 1944 in Astrakhan, where he'd moved after leaving the juvenile colony. He came of age that year, got his passport and, having served his sentence, re-entered the world a free, grown man without any further need of State wardship. The young man took advantage of the opportunity at once.

The Archangel gang received him with open arms (in the criminal world everybody knows everything about you) and, after looking things over and getting used to the new town, he set right to work. One of his first major jobs was the famous burglary of the Astrakhan Military Trading Post.

It was a night heist, carefully researched. The man who had cased the site—a driver in the service of the post—was perfectly familiar with the arrangement of the depot and the procedures there. It was under tight military security. Three guards were posted there as a rule, one outside in a sentry box by the gates and the other two inside. The men took the outside guard out of action with one blow (muffled in a sheepskin coat, he was dozing with his arms around his rifle). They bludgeoned him with a cast-iron weight on a chain, a terrible weapon aptly named the Sleeper. With a twitch he dropped to the ground. Once inside the depot gates, the thieves rushed the other guards, a matter that took a little more doing, but that still went smoothly and without any extraneous noise.

Then, after a brief smoking break, the thieves got to work. The driver (a thick-lipped, fleshy-cheeked fellow in a camouflaged quilted jacket) poked about the depot, pointing out what to take. It was a princely haul: bolts of first-class burlap and of fine, imported English fabrics ("Churchill's gift," they called them), sweaters, leather raglans, and officers' box-calf boots—items well worth over several million rubles on the wartime market.

The riches had a hypnotic effect on the driver. He bustled to and fro, almost delirious, clicking his tongue, slapping his palms against his thighs, making an ineffectual stab at helping to carry the packages out to the waiting truck. All he really did, though, was interfere. He was the last to leave the depot. As soon as he got behind the wheel, he turned and said in a hoarse voice, "Hold on, boys, I'm worried about the guards. On my way out I thought I saw one of them move. Maybe he woke up and spotted me, eh? Hope to God he didn't, because if he did, I'm in real trouble."

"Cool down," they told him, "and stop twitching. People don't wake up from the bludgeon."

"But what if they do?" the driver objected. His teeth were chattering and he was trembling lightly all over. "And what if somebody saw, then what? It's just a joke to you, but I'm the one in the middle. No, we've got to check it out."

He leaped out of the cabin and crept back through the thinning darkness. It was already just before dawn. He didn't go alone: the Maiden went right behind.

A quarter of an hour later, the Maiden returned, crawled back into the cabin, sat in the driver's seat, and reached for the wheel.

"Well, what happened?" they asked him. "Was somebody moving?"

"Yep," the Maiden answered with a smile.

"Did you calm him down?"

"Sure did."

"Okay, let's go. Where's the driver?"

"What driver?" the Maiden replied. "There's no driver, and as far as you're concerned, never was."

"You mean you got him, too?"

"Right."

"But why?"

"Too nervous."

"But look what you did!" they reproached him. "Who's going to drive this thing now?"

"I will," the Maiden said, turning on the ignition. "I know a thing or two about it. Back at the children's home, in Kurgan, we had a group of drivers."

After this episode, the Maiden's reputation as a "business-like" fellow was strongly enhanced. Despite his age, he was quickly accepted, and even feared, among the thieves. Hardened old troopers and leaders would talk with him as with an equal. Others regarded it an honor—and even a comfort—to have him along on the job. Clearly, he was a man to be reckoned with.

He was usually employed on what were called "wet" affairs—killings. Murder is a far from popular art in the Russian criminal world. A wet affair is a dangerous affair, and a noisy one at that. The East Slavic Mafia, basically, has much less respect for brute power than for the skill, craft, and artistry of a clever theft.

For all that, the Maiden's authority was solid and incontestable, partly, perhaps, because of his style: he never acted in a fit of passion or without clear and sufficient reason. He was a model of coolness and imperturbability.

Somewhere behind that unruffled exterior one might divine a deep and hidden rage. Apparently, he'd been like this ever since he was a child; it was as if he were avenging himself on people for the bitter losses of his past.

Still, much—perhaps most—of this fellow remained a mystery to me, especially his present state of mind.

"Tomorrow we dock. It's the end of the ride. You haven't forgotten about our affair, have you?"

"No," I answered uncomfortably, "of course not. I remember everything."

"It's curtains, brother! They're going to lay the goods on us for sure. You just might come back, but not me. Can you imagine what they've got in store for me?"

"A stiff sentence. Maybe even twenty-five years. But not execution, anyway."

"Who can tell," he said evasively. "Who can tell?"

In Vladivostok prison we were immediately separated and led to different cells. All that time we saw each other only once, at a session in the investigator's office.

The investigator assigned to the case was a meticulous pest, hungry for every last detail of the bathhouse murder. In retracing the thread of events, from beginning to end and back again, he had come upon my name and the Maiden's. Now he was investigating our joint role in the affair.

My friend's participation in the murder was obvious and undeniable. He'd flung the washtub of boiling water into the victim's face, stopping him dead in his tracks. However, he'd received the tub from my hands. It was I, after all, who had filled it and handed it over to him—instantly and without protest. The way the investigator saw it, that could only have been by design. He considered me a direct accomplice to the crime and was stubbornly trying to prove it.

Just as stubbornly, I protested. Everything had happened accidentally, I argued, accidentally and suddenly. I had acted mechanically, in confusion, and without any malice afore-thought.

The Maiden supported me in all of his testimony. (Although the two of us were interrogated separately, the prison "post office," as always, kept us in touch.) The Maiden had kept his word; he was doing his best to defend me. And, as God is my witness, if it hadn't have been for him, I would never have pulled through in one piece.

The investigation dragged on for about two months. Fi-nally, we were summoned together and asked to re-enact the crime. The Maiden seemed his old self to me again: cool, calm, and sarcastic. Eagerly consenting to the investigator's request, he sat down on the floor and started to undress. He took off his shoes. He undid the button on his trousers. When the investigator asked him what kind of trick he was up to, the Maiden blinked his fluffy lashes and replied:

"I thought you said you wanted it just the way it was. Well, it was in a bathhouse, you know."

"All right, stop it." The investigator frowned. "That's all I need, an actor."

When the experiment was over and the Maiden and I were signing the examination record, my comrade turned to me and said: "So long, old man, I don't imagine we'll be seeing each other again. . . ."

He was right. His dark premonitions hadn't let him down. Those mournful "death" songs he'd been singing on the road had been forecasts of his fate.

I never saw the Maiden again and I know little of what happened to him after our last meeting. I did hear he'd gotten a twenty-five-year sentence and been dispatched to the Lensky mica mines. While there, he'd become involved in some new "bloody" affair and quickly received an additional term. In the course of time he piled up some eighty years of sentences.

When the death penalty was reinstated at the start of the fifties, people like the Maiden were among the first to fall under the *ukaz*. According to a rumor I heard, he was executed at Isketimsky Central, an outpost in the All-Union Penal Division. The story had it that at the meeting of the tribunal that pronounced the death sentence on him, the Maiden conducted himself with a calmness and a grinning, carefree air that surprised them all. In his final words he did not plead, as was the custom, either for mercy or for sympathy. The only request he made to the authorities had to do with food. He asked that, in remembrance of his soul, they feed all the prisoners of Central a good dinner.

I don't know if the story's true. It certainly sounds a lot like the Maiden to me.

I also heard about the Goblin. As soon as he'd arrived at Nakhodka, he'd drawn apart from the others and hidden in the portside crowd. Later someone saw him on the edge of Vladivostok—a filthy, ragged man wandering through the alleys and digging around in the garbage. Then he'd disappeared, only to resurface a month later in the local mental hospital. Apparently he'd gone there on his own. After that he sank without a trace.

DEPORTATION, DEPORTATION, CATTLE CARS . . .

At the end of the investigation, I was deported once again. Not to Kolyma, though. Dalstroi didn't take me back. A special mark on my official card (which, by the way, had never been there before) now identified me as a thief—a piece of business that labeled me in the eyes of the camp administration as a questionable and even dangerous figure. Apparently the investigator had seen to that. It was bad news, especially in view of the bitch war, which was growing wider and bloodier every day.

After its start in the south in 1946, it had spread to the farthest reaches of the continent, including the boundaries of Dalstroi. At the end of the forties, the authorities there had begun to screen out thieves and get rid of them as best they could. Those already at Kolyma were gradually quarantined and driven into the penal divisions. New ones were admitted with extreme reluctance. The administration had its own good reasons, of course. Kolyma didn't need thieves, it needed workers, men with any kind of service record, so long as it wasn't like mine.

In the summer of 1948 all the thieves gathered on the Vtoraya River, some three hundred in all, were sent to the new 503rd Construction Project at Krasnoyarsk. Only those still under investigation or awaiting trial remained. That included the Maiden. We didn't see each other, but he did manage on parting to send me a note and in it, among other things, he recalled Lenin's death.

"You still might get a whiff of freedom," he wrote. "You haven't got long to serve. I've got nothing to lose, brother, but for you the main thing is to take care of yourself. Just don't go asking for trouble. Especially with your own kind. You got lucky with Lenin. Another time you might not have had it so easy. Make it a lesson! Between you and me, though, I still can't understand why you did it."

They were the last words from a friend. I never managed to answer them.

"Deportation, deportation, cattle cars," I sang mournfully, leaning into the barred window from my upper bunk on the train. Outside, steaming and whirling, the endless evergreens flew by. The train was heading through eastern Siberia, following the same route it had ten months before, only in the opposite direction now, northwest.

We all knew what our destination was: the 503rd Construction Project. But what awaited us there? All we could do was guess. In any event, we had to assume the worst. "No change is for the better," says the old convict saying. The life of every convict, like any flip of a coin, depends on luck. But it's tails that usually comes up—tails, for prison bars, not freedom.

I'd long ago and more than once come up against this woeful consistency. And meditated on it a good deal. And the result of my reflections had been a song. To a certain degree it was autobiographical. However, in composing it, I was thinking not so much of myself as of my entire generation: of people like the Maiden and a hundred others. Here's the song, in its entirety:

> *I'm the son of a man from the underground,*
> *A worker, a Party man.*
> *My father loved me, I treasured him,*
> *But consumption laid him down.*
> *And so, without a father to support me,*
> *I left home and went to the street,*
> *And the street turned me into a thief,*
> *And I soon was behind prison bars.*
> *I began to wander, with a plan and without one,*
> *And five times I landed in jail.*
> *And in '33, with the canal completed,*
> *I decided to leave the thieves' life behind*
> *And cut all my criminal ties.*
> *I arrived in a town; I've forgotten its name,*
> *I decided on factory work.*
> *And they told me: oh, dear, a record. What's this?*
> *Please be sure to forget our address!*

> *I trampled that canal release underfoot*
> *And went out to the street again.*
> *And the criminal life took me back in its arms*
> *And once again I was back behind bars,*
> *And going the rounds of the camps.*
> *Bars and bunks, year in, year out,*
> *Year in, year out, the same.*
> *Ah, how hard it is to turn a new leaf*
> *When the State won't come to your aid!*
> *Deportation, deportation, cattle cars,*
> *Once again, we're bound God knows where,*
> *And with each day, and with each stop,*
> *The taiga grows drearier, and all my hopes drop.*

It was a long, depressing ride. What more can I tell you? It was business as usual. The closeness, the stench, the thirst destroyed us. Hunger tore at our bowels. The lack of tobacco was torture. I could give you painful details, lots of them, on the lives of the prisoners and the tyranny of the guards. But the principle of the thing has been dealt with before and clearly at that. A multitude of books have been written on the brutality that reigned in Soviet torture chambers. Besides the great Solzhenitsyn, the theme's been worked over by Dyakov, by Ginzburg, by Marchenko, and scores of other men of letters, Russian and foreign. On that level I couldn't add a thing. My intent is simply to show something of the world of the criminal underground. There are few who know anything about it, and none who has yet written about it as it really is, from personal experience.

In Krasnoyarsk we stopped for a river crossing. They took us out of the cars, held us for about three weeks in a deportation point, and then drove us to the river barges.

It was then, for the first time, that I saw the Yenisei. I saw its steep shores ("cheeks," the locals call them), bristly with pine, the frothy patches speckling the channel, the glints of sunlight on the wild, chilly rush of its waters, and the wide pools, rippled by the wind.

The river rolled along, massive and mighty and bracingly

fresh. Heavy, shaggy clouds hovered overhead, alternating here and there with spots of pure light blue. A cool sharp light poured from the gaps in the clouds and was reflected in the water. The Yenisei struck me with its sweep, its stern, Asiatic beauty. Squinting in the sunlight and looking at it flow, I felt a strange kind of jolt in my heart, an instinctive sense that here, from this moment on, something new had stepped into my life.

THE DEAD ROAD

The 503rd Construction Project was an extensive net of camps spread along the right banks of the Yenisei. The administration was headquartered in the village of Ermakovo, not far from the city of Igarka, right by the Arctic Circle.

They were laying the route for the Igarka-Norilsk railroad there which, when finished, would extend hundreds of kilometers to the Taymyr Peninsula, uniting the two largest industrial centers in the Arctic. Norilsk is a coal-mining center. Igarka, on the other hand, is a large port city and shipping base for all kinds of raw materials—precious woods, blubber oil, furs— headed to the West.

That, in short, was what the construction was all about. The trouble is that the permafrost zone begins just beyond the Arctic Circle. The soil there is subject to constant fluctuations and changes. In the spring, for example, it thaws and the Arctic tundra turns to marsh. In the fall, the viscous earth solidifies, swells, and cracks into a thousand fissures. Only a madman would think of laying track there. They said that Beria himself had put his hand to the project and I don't doubt it. After all, he wasn't a man to concern himself with incidental practical details; he simply gave orders and expected them to be carried out unquestioningly.

Whatever the case, the construction was underway on a massive scale and at full tilt, attaining a net gain of almost nothing. Everything they managed to accomplish in the winter was usually undone the following summer. And so the work would begin again: the embankment would be repaired, the subgrade fortified, and the cycle would repeat itself. Again and again.

About the time I arrived there, the project was already three years old and the route extended all of ten kilometers—a gain maintained primarily because the tundra in that part of Igarka wasn't really tundra, but a kind of wooded land covered with stunted "black" taiga. This secondary tundra thinned out toward the north and disappeared, finally yielding to the real, bare, frost-bound wastelands of the Arctic. And from this region the builders had yet to wrest a single inch.

Consequently, the track already laid served no purpose at all. Who'd want to use a railroad that went nowhere? By the time I left the area four years later, even that initial strip had gone to hell. The station buildings stood black and lonely, the telegraph poles creaked senselessly in the wind. The local Kerzhaks and Evenki feared the route and gave it a wide berth, calling it the "dead road."

I mention all this merely to be done with the subject of the construction itself. When I think about the 503rd Project, I see something far worse: the fierce skirmishes, the carnage, the faces of dead friends and foes. No wonder the term "dead road" has a double significance for me.

As soon as I arrived at the work site, I was sent to Ermakovo, one of the central prison camp points, where I met up with some old friends: Leo the Kike, the happy pickpocket; the Straw, the Rostov safecracker; and several others I'd known from the Caucasus and Central Asia. There were quite a few thieves here, all packed together in one barracks, living their very special and intricate lives. Here's how it went:

Morning. The silhouettes of the prisoners flash mournfully through the zone. The brigades hurry off to work, trailing one another to the watchtower.

The only two with nowhere to rush are the Straw and myself. We've been relieved of work—we're among the ill. The camp doctor, Levitsky, is on good terms with us. He has a warm spot for thieves, especially me. He likes my songs. He thinks I'm a man of real talent. He's spoken to me often about that, and he's always doing anything he can to help. So now the Straw and I laze about the barracks, smoking cigarettes and having a leisurely chat.

The Straw has a philosophical turn of mind. Tall and lean, with a long, bony face, he says, coughing from the smoke of the shag: "You ever notice that the camp is a kind of reduced copy of the entire country, the entire system? Climb up some morning on the roof: it's barely dawn, the muzhiks are on their way to work, groaning and dragging their tails. A little later the dummies tramp by: the bookkeepers, the barbers, the storekeepers—the intelligentsia, so to speak. They've got nothing to hurry about. Then there are the thieves, too busy as usual with their own affairs to work. And ringing them all are the guards. All of it, brother, part of the divine plan."

From behind the corner, a short, heavy-set man in a wide-open quilted jacket, a worker from the warehouse, waddles through the morning mist, singing through his teeth:

"What do I see, what do I hear,
  The Chief has climbed up on the roof . . ."

The storekeeper gives us a big grin and, making an obscene gesture, finishes the song:

  "Shouting to everyone, far and near,
    You want your freedom? Up your ear!"

Midday. I lie on the lower bunk, sipping *chifir*. (I'm too lazy to climb up to my own place.) The barracks are empty and quiet. I'm alone here: the Straw has left on business. We've stayed off work for reasons of the highest importance. Yesterday evening weapons were brought into the zone: ten pikes, some knives, and two bludgeons, manufactured at the central repair workshop, where several of the local brigades have been working. The messengers hid the weapons quickly and carelessly. Our job is to find a better place to put them. That, in fact, is what the Straw is seeing to at the moment.

And so I am alone. As always during my calmer moments,

poems are coming to me and I am trying them out, saying them out loud and listening to their caressing sound.

Suddenly, I hear the tramp of feet. The door of the barracks flies open with a crash and the figure of the Goose stands on the threshold, holding a pike.

The Goose! It has been so long I've completely forgotten about him. And one must never forget one's enemies. Once, in Kharkov, on Cold Mountain, he vowed to seek revenge on me, he promised a great "bloodletting." Now, here, in this damned construction site, he's come to keep his word.

Squat and stocky, with a face crisscrossed by dark scars, the Goose remains silent for a moment, savoring the effect. Then he advances slowly on me, letting in a noisy crowd behind him. Slowly, on squeaking leather boots polished to a gleam, the Goose approaches and our eyes meet. I jump back into the recesses of my bunk and stiffen with cold.

"Hello," says the Goose. He smirks, playing with the pike. "So, we finally meet. Or aren't you glad? You don't look too happy, I can see that. You're trembling. . . ."

He falls silent again for a moment. And then, his eyes open wide: "Say your prayers, you bastard! Your time is up. Can you feel it? You're caught now. You're mine!"

It's true. I'm trapped and there's nowhere to turn. I'm surrounded by bitches, front and side. Behind me there's a wall and above me the boards of the upper bunk.

How I curse myself now for my laziness, for my idiotic carelessness! If I'd been in my own bunk, everything would have taken a different turn. I'd have had the space for maneuvering up there, not to mention an excellent, razor-sharp knife in a crack between the boards.

Staring at the Goose, I hold my tongue, thinking feverishly of some way out. I have to break through to the bunk above. But how? I don't have a chance in hell. Still . . .

The moment the Goose finally bends toward me, raising his arm for the blow, I suddenly straighten out and slam my head through the upper boards.

Deafened by the blow, I almost lose consciousness. The pain takes my breath away. But the road to deliverance is open! Almost unconsciously, but rapidly, I climb through the breach. I rip half of a broken board from the upper bunk (it's heavy and covered with nails) and use it for a shield. I can catch my breath now, collect my energies, and retreat to the head of the bed where my blade lies hidden.

As it turns out, though, there's no longer any need. Startled by what's happened, the Goose mutters at my feet:

"You got away, you dog. No, wait . . ."

The Goose still wants to say something, but they cut him short. One of his pals outside the door says quickly, "Let's take off, brothers! They're coming."

"Who's coming?" the Goose asks, baring his teeth.

"Looks like that guy, what's his name? The Straw. Yes, it's him! And he's not alone!"

And my enemies leave. Hiding the pike in his trouser leg, the Goose turns to me and says: "All right, you got a lucky star. All the same, remember: I'm your hunter, you're my hare."

Evening. I'm sitting on my own bed again. My face is all cut up, my head is in bandages. It burns and aches, but my soul is at rest. I'm with my own people again.

There are two thieves sitting beside me on the upper bunk. One of them wears a pair of square, horn-rimmed glasses. They call him the Professor. The other goes by the name of Nikola the Chipmunk.

The Professor is comparatively young, not yet thirty. High-browed and thick-lipped, he lies on his stomach, writing something assiduously with a scratchy little pencil. He turns to me and shows me a picture of a walking man. It's like a child's drawing—a circle for a head, one long stroke for the torso, short, broken lines for the arms and legs. Beneath the man there's a signature, traced out in huge, clumsy letters. "Chyuma," it says.

It's a portrait of me. The Professor has been sweating over it since yesterday. The signature especially has cost him a good deal of effort, since he's illiterate. A thief by birth, he grew up in the dens of Moscow and a series of homes for retarded children. When he came into his own he specialized in apartment break-ins. The idea of getting an education, of learning how to read and write, never appealed to him. He more than made up for the lack, though, with a dignified, professorial appearance. He started wearing glasses a long time ago to correct a serious problem: he'd spoiled his own eyesight in one of the Moscow prisons by crumbling up an indelible pencil and sprinkling the poisonous powder in his eyes, a little trick called "the fix-up" that spared him from a bad deportation.

The prison doctors pulled him through and prescribed the glasses, thereby turning the retarded rogue into a Professor.

Now he lies back, his eyeglasses agleam, and dissolves into happy laughter. He's pleased with himself. His work has succeeded! He experiences the same sense of completion familiar to every artist.

Nikola the Chipmunk, sitting on the other side of me, looks just the opposite: quiet, introverted, and pensive. He's reading a letter from his wife back home. He furrows his brow and silently moves his lips. Nikola stops to reread several passages (they're places where his wife, Varka, writes about the children and the family). His lips soften and stretch into a smile. The old pickpocket is a family man, with a deep love for his wife and children. Here's the story of his marriage:

At one point during the Nazi occupation, the Chipmunk was plying his trade in the cities of the Donbass region of the Ukraine. As a rule, he'd work the trolleys and the local trains, a route also covered by a group of lady thieves, the oldest of whom was the notorious screen woman Varka.

Varka possessed an unusually ample figure—an immeasurable chest and a wide ("three armful" as they'd sing in the couplets), seductive behind. By the general admission of the gang, Varka was one of the most beautiful women in all the south.

The Chipmunk had heard quite a good deal about her, and was eager for a meeting. When it finally came to pass (in one of the village dens of Kharkov) he was smitten—deeply and forever.

He had dropped into the den on business, bringing a German officer's gold watch for the local fence. The sharpster knocked the price down so low Nikola was on the verge of picking up the watch and storming out when Varka suddenly appeared. One look at her and Nikola grew weak. "All right," he said, "go ahead and take it, Cain, but put your money on the table! And send for vodka. I'm going to have myself a good time today!"

They frolicked and swilled home-brew till late at night. Then they all lay down in a heap on the floor to sleep. Nikola woke up before dawn, dying of thirst. He drank his fill and then remembered Varka. She was lying by the wall nearby, snuffling in her sleep. He lay down beside her, settled in and, within a week, made her an honest woman.

Nikola hadn't given the slightest thought to marriage at first. He just felt obliged to do it on his honor as a gentleman, that's all. The fact was that Varka, to his great amazement, had been a virgin!

He'd made a perfect choice. She became a loyal wife and excellent homemaker. She abandoned her old line of work to devote all her time to her family. Varka had inherited a home from her parents on one of the outlying streets in the miner's city of Gorlovka, and that's where she and Nikola settled down. It was the start of a whole new life for this wandering man. In order to protect his family he didn't ply his trade in his hometown, but moved his practice a little farther away. Sometimes he'd vanish for weeks on end, but he'd always send the money home punctually by post. (He was "putting his pennies on the wire," as the thieves describe it.) He also became amazingly thrifty, thereby earning his unusual nickname. A chipmunk, as everybody knows, is continually storing all kinds of things away and never eating more than it can stash.

The Chipmunk always made his appearances in Gorlovka neatly scrubbed, in a new, ironed suit. He'd stroll through the streets, arm in arm with his young wife, shepherding their growing number of children. Varka, it turned out, was as fertile as a rabbit; she gave birth to a new child almost every year. The children grew, Nikola sent the oldest to school, and from time to time he'd sit in at parents' meetings, sometimes even stepping forth with a remark or two about the problems of pedagogy.

"Since I'm the working element," he'd reason, turning to the teachers, "I'd like to throw some light on the subject from the proletarian point of view. Children: what are they? The flowers of our lives and our helpers in the days to come. . . ."

All in all, Nikola earned himself the reputation of a staid and positive individual. He palmed himself off as a worker in one of the local shoe artels, who fulfilled his orders at home. Actually, he did nothing of the kind. Whenever the need arose, he'd simply buy his shoes from some private traders he knew at the neighboring markets.

He had the management of his artel on the take, and regularly passed them bribes. Nikola would hand over his official salary to the head of the guild. That way, no one at the artel ever gave him any trouble. What more can you say? The Chipmunk knew how to talk to the common man!

He didn't neglect the city authorities, either. Both the Bürgermeister (under the Germans) and the Chairman of the Executive Committee (under the Soviet regime) walked around in shoes Nikola had graciously given them.

This life of peaceful moderation continued for rather a long time, all through the war years, up to '47. During the entire period, Nikola didn't go to prison once. They caught him often, of course, but they'd always let him go. Here Varka proved to be an enormous help. A former pickpocket, she knew the score and, like a good businesswoman, had salted away several tens of thousands of rubles which she'd immediately put into action as soon as she learned her husband was under arrest.

Searching out the victim of the heist (who, let's say, had been relieved of a wallet with thirty rubles in it), she'd immediately offer him five hundred rubles by way of compensation. If the *fraier* still hesitated, she'd double the sum without a second's thought. There was no one in the world who could withstand an offer like that. Sooner or later, the injured party would withdraw the charges and the whole matter would be dropped. And if difficulties ever arose on the part of the investigators, Varka would buy them off, too.

However, all good things must come to an end, including the Chipmunk's prosperity and well-being. One time he traveled too far afield and was caught red-handed. They'd just introduced an *ukaz* at the time dispensing with most formalities and streamlining court procedures. By the time Varka found out about her husband's arrest, he was already in the deportation prison.

"Still," he mutters now, carefully folding Varka's letter, "I'm a lucky man. Thanks to her I had six good years on the outside. Six years, think of it. Six happy years! After that, being in jail doesn't hurt. It's like paying back an old debt."

The Straw bunks beside me, the "appreciator of Esenin and an old onanist." The terminology is apt. Not only is he a confirmed onanist, he's a professional at it. His bed is curtained off with blankets and there, in the deepest solitude, the Straw surrenders to his sin—persistently and with inspiration. In his hands, the activity acquires a whole new significance and becomes a kind of art form.

Usually, before swinging into action, the Straw summons up a colorful mental image of the object of his desire. Not an abstract image, either, but one firmly grounded in the most concrete detail. It might be a famous movie actress, for instance, or a queen whose picture he happened to see in a newspaper.

After defining the image and summoning the woman in the flesh, so to speak, he has his way with her and then, surfeited, tosses her aside for the next fantasy. Compared to him, Casanova is a mere child, a miserable dilettante.

Sometimes, though, he's short on concrete details. (He's a realist, after all, with nothing but contempt for abstractions and other modernistic influences.) In such cases, he'll usually glance out from under his curtain and call to me:

"Hey, Chuma! Remember the actress in that foreign movie? You know, the one in the scene with the automobiles? A real sharp sort of woman. Remember?"

"Not exactly," I answer. "Sarah Bernhardt, maybe?"

"What's Sarah got to do with it?" He brushes it aside. "What use have I got for an old hag like that? I can't even remember when I had *her*. Besides, what's she got to do with automobiles? No, I'm talking about something else. We discussed her just the other day. First she dresses in a man's suit and does something in the garage, then she shows up at the ball. . . ."

"Ah, I know who!" I finally remember. "Franceska Haal, the one in *Peter*."

"Right, that's the one!" the Straw says enthusiastically. "Franceska! How does she show up at the ball?"

"The way she's supposed to." I shrug my shoulders. "In a dress."

"Obviously. But what kind of a dress? A white one?"

"What else?" I say. "With all those little frills and flounces."

"Aha! Aha!" His bony, horselike face wrinkles in a smile. "Good, good, I've got it now. . . ."

And, bowing gratefully, he quickly crawls back to his kennel.

Another neighbor (also behind a curtain) is Seryoga, the well-known counterfeiter and Georgian prince. Seryoga's love of solitude stems from a somewhat different source. The Straw is a poet, a fantasist. Seryoga is the epitome of the pragmatist. Mere mental images hold no allure for him, no satisfaction. Deprived of the love of women, he consoles himself with the love of men. Or rather little boys. Seryoga has an entire harem whose ranks are continually swelling. As soon as a new deportation arrives in the zone, he goes prospecting, seeking out the youngest and most comely of the novices and winning them over.

He doesn't resort to fear or blackmail, he simply indulges them and coaxes them, sharing his stores of bread and tobacco. Next he proposes—for a price, of course—that they fulfill some petty work as a lackey, cleaning his shoes, for instance, straightening up the bunk. Not everyone accepts the offer, of course, but those that do invariably end up behind the curtain.

The boys leave Seryoga's lair fully transformed. In almost no time at all, they become coquettish and finicky, hopelessly vain and fond of adornments. They take on feminine names and from then on exist in the capacity of young girls in the camp.

We have quite a few such Katkas and Olkas in our barracks, about fifteen in all. They eat next to the thieves and serve them diligently. Besides their main sexual function, they have other responsibilities, including running errands and taking care of housekeeping.

They are on the very lowest rung of the prison camp social ladder and are relegated to sleeping quarters underneath the bunks where, rustling, romping, and quarreling shrilly, they are summoned as the need arises.

Compared to the simple "gray" workers, however, they live and look like belted earls, dressed in finery the thieves have given them. Leo and Vanka—also, like Leo, known as "the Kike"—our two best gamblers, are perhaps their most generous benefactors.

I've already acquainted you with Leo—a virtuoso pickpocket and tireless prattler. His partner Vanka is his complete opposite. In fact, despite the nickname, he isn't even a Jew, just a simple, snub-nosed fellow from Ryazan with a shock of whitish, strawlike curls and the calling of a village robber, or "forest bandit." How and why he ever got the nickname of the Kike is a mystery to me. Not that it bothers him: he responds readily to the name without the slightest objection. For, after all, there is no anti-Semitism in the world of thieves. All who enter its ranks are equals. (You can imagine how startled Vanka would be if he were to migrate, along with his nickname, into another world—the decent and enlightened society of the intelligentsia and the petty bourgeoisie, for instance.)

Simple-minded as he may seem, this fellow from Ryazan is a sharp and shrewd gambler, and as skillful a cardplayer as Leo himself. The two fellows are on excellent terms, as a matter of fact, and it isn't uncommon, after a night game among the gang, to find half the barracks sitting in its birthday

suit, clothes rising in a heap on the bunks of the two "Jews."
Vanka usually keeps quiet, grinning good-naturedly, while
Leo celebrates the victory in a constant flutter of movement
and gab.

"Hey, Katka," he calls, kicking the bunk with his heel.
"Come on, crawl out of there! Stand before me like a leaf
before the grass!"

Katka crawls out at once. His eyebrows are plucked, his
gaze downcast, his red, painted lips composed in an obsequi-
ous little smile, his every movement expressing readiness and
limitless devotion.

Leo bends over, playfully tweaks her on the cheek, and
indicating the pile of spoils with a generous gesture, says:
"Well, you little fool, choose! Whatever you like is yours. And
don't be shy! Today Leo is good. Today Leo is having a good
time."

Sometimes, out of sheer idleness, Leo and Vanka play each
other. Although they're friends and all their property is jointly
held, they play with a passion and for keeps!

It's quite a sight. Equal in strength and perfectly familiar
with each other's tricks, they understand one another with half
a word. No wonder the game that follows is so intense and
sometimes ends in a bitter clash.

I'm describing only one of the many days I spent on Dead
Road. Morning, midday, and evening have already passed.
Night now stretches over the camp, and here's how it ends.

The friends, as usual, begin to argue over their game. Their
remarks become more caustic and intense and, before morning, a fight erupts. They leap down from their bunks in a rage,
screaming and waking up the entire barracks. Leo is especially
frantic and out of control. He's snorted some cocaine and he's
all atremble, twitching and spewing saliva. His face is
contorted with malice. Even the good-natured Vanka is
passionately aroused. The gamblers have never gotten into
such a state before.

"So I'm covering up, am I?" Leo howls. "You got any proof
of that?"

"Proof? No," his partner snaps, "but I can feel it. I wouldn't put anything past you!"

"So you don't believe me?"

"No."

"Then it's all over! You aren't my friend anymore, understand?"

"That's okay with me," answers Vanka. "We'll split the same way we got together—fifty-fifty!"

And they start dividing all their property. The procedure drags on. They have a lot of things and they can't seem to divide them equally: three pairs of boots. What to do? Suddenly, Vanka has a brainstorm.

"I got it," he says. "We'll each take a pair and split the one that's left. You take the left boot, I'll take the right."

"What the hell do I want with one shoe?" Leo asks reasonably.

"To make it equal." Vanka grins. "You think I'd give you mine?"

"I don't want yours." Leo brushes it aside. "But I'm sure as hell not giving up mine, either."

"All right, then, let's do it the other way."

"But why should I get the left one?"

"Then take the right one, damn it!"

"All right. No, wait. The top on the right one's torn."

"Okay, then I'll take both the tops and you take the feet. Agreed?"

"It's a deal!"

"Let's start chopping!"

Leo takes an ax out of its hideaway. He tests the edge against his nail and chops the shoes in half.

"Ekh," he shouts, groaning and wheezing. "As long as we're splitting everything equally, let's do it to the rest. If we got to share, let's share for real!"

And with that he puts the ax to everything in sight: the jackets, the shirts, the raincoats. He's in a frenzy. There's no stopping him.

The entire barracks watches the mad work in silence. At long last, Leo calms down and walks out into the night, staggering, his legs tied up in rags, colorful little scraps hanging from his ax.

Before too long he reappears. His face is strangely tense, his eyes pale, dilated, and fixed. With a thud, he drops the ax to the floor. We can all see blotches of dark clotted blood on the gleaming blade.

"Boys," says Leo in a trembling voice, "I've just axed one of the bitches. Right in their own barracks, in front of everybody. Give me a smoke!"

"In front of everybody?" the Straw asks sternly, looking out from his hideout and passing a lighted cigarette to Leo. "Why the hell did you do that? You work dirty, my friend."

"I don't know," Leo says exhaustedly, "I don't know anything." And he draws his palm across his brow. "My head aches. . . ."

THE HEIR OF CALCUTTA

They took Leo away that night. Breaking into the barracks, the guards tied him up (he offered no resistance and was, in fact, in a state of exhaustion) and led him off in handcuffs to a cell.

He stopped for an instant in the doorway and looked around the barracks. Then, in a parting gesture, he raised his shackled hands, turned, and disappeared into the thinning darkness. A sharp frost came through the open door and a murky yellow spread over the black rooftops of the zone. A new day was dawning. Leo never lived to see it.

In the morning, during the breakfast handout, the jailer on duty looked into Leo's cell and discovered his body. It was still warm.

He was a shredded mess, his eyes gouged out, his face reduced to a bloody pulp, his chest and stomach torn with countless wounds. According to what Levitsky told me, the wounds had been inflicted by a thrusting, rather than a cutting, instrument—quite probably a pike.

I immediately suspected the Goose. The pike was his favorite weapon. Besides, only he could have entered the cell from the outside. As ringleader of the bitches, he enjoyed the confidence and cooperation of the guards, who let him go everywhere.

I'd guessed right. As it turned out, the Goose had been spotted that morning beside the cell. Surrounded by his friends, he'd been squatting and wiping his hands in the fresh, new-fallen snow, and muttering something.

One thing was absolutely clear to me: there wasn't enough room for the two of us, and my only salvation lay in turning as quickly as possible from a hare into a hunter.

From that moment on, I began pursuing the Goose as relentlessly as he pursued me. The hunt continued for some time. Once, just before evening, the Goose got the jump on me by the bathhouse and I was only saved by a miracle. A fresh deportation was being driven from the road for their wash-up and, seeing them, the Goose was forced to withdraw.

There were also two occasions when I had him within a hair's breadth of my knife only to have the bastard worm away. Not without blood, though. The second time I had him on the hook and added one more scar to his face. Small comfort, though: it did little more than decorate him.

Still, in the end he lost—though not at my hands. Others performed the righteous act. Others experienced the sweet triumph of revenge. And, to add the final touch of irony, the executioner was totally uninvolved in the bitch war and had nothing to do with the thieves.

In the past I'd had almost no contact with the political prisoners, and even less interest in them. Their lives, like those of all the other general convicts, flowed past me on the very edge of my awareness. That's the way it had been in the Ukraine and Kolyma, and all during the time of my deportations. That's the way it had been at the start of the 503rd Construction Project. It was only later that I began to associate with a few of the politicals and separate them from the general mass.

Little by little something was beginning to change in me. I was acquiring a desire to create that seemed to fill my soul to its limits. Yet the criminal world was entangling me more and more in its web, holding me back and weighing me down. I was desperate for intellectual company, for advisers and connoisseurs. These I found among the political prisoners.

One of them was Robert Shtilmark, a well-known Soviet man of letters these days, with several works to his credit, including the extremely popular *Heir of Calcutta*, a novel he wrote while in prison at the 503rd Construction Project. The whole thing happened right before my eyes, in fact.

Soon after Shtilmark arrived at the Construction Project he was summoned to the office of Vasilievsky, the chief dispatcher in the staff barracks. No longer a young man, with a broad, heavy peasant's face and whitish, darting eyes, Vasilievsky looked over the dossier lying before him on the table and asked:

"It says here you're a writer. Is that true?"

"In general, yes," Robert answered.

"What do you mean, 'in general'? Speak plainly. Are you or aren't you a writer?"

"The dossier isn't quite exact in that regard," Robert began to explain. "I was once head of the Literary Division in the theater. So it would be more correct to say I'm a literary worker. In principle, though—"

"But," the dispatcher interrupted him, "in matters of this sort you do understand a thing or two, don't you? Even if—in principle—"

"In matters of what sort?"

"Literary ones."

"I understand a thing or two, yes, of course."

"Aha." Vasilievsky nodded thoughtfully. "Good, good."

He sat, resting his fists on the table, frowning and biting his cigarette. Looking sharply at Shtilmark, he said: "Could you write something? Could you take something and write it up, eh?"

"It all depends on what." Shtilmark shrugged his shoulders.

"Well, a novél for instance," Vasilievsky said carefully and deliberately, pronouncing the word the way they do in prison, with the accent on the last syllable. "Well, could you? Tell me! Only don't get tricky. Remember!" He raised a finger with a thick brown nail. "I'm not to be fooled around with."

"Why are you talking like that?" Shtilmark asked him in confusion. "What's it to you whether I can write or not?"

"Ah, you idiot, can't you see what's to your advantage?" Vasilievsky stood up, frowning and stretching his wet, peeling lips. "If a novel comes out of this we could send it to the Main Camp Administration, to the Ministry itself! To Lavrenty Pavlovich, even . . ." (Beria, that is.) "Why, he might even pardon you for it and set you free!"

Coming out from behind the table, he walked up to Shtilmark and breathed right into his face.

"Let's give it a try. The two of us together, eh? I'll make up the story and you write it down. Only our names have got to be together, understand?"

"But what makes you think they'll free us for that?" Shtilmark expressed his doubts. "As far as I know, they aren't in the habit of pardoning writers these days. Quite the contrary."

"That's on account of their politics," the dispatcher said. "So they won't go messing around where they don't belong. But that's got nothing to do with us. What do we need politics for? We can do it about something else."

"Like what?"

"Well, like life in general, and not ours either. To hell with that! Try ancient times, for instance. The best stuff comes from there. Take something about the sea, for instance, something set abroad. Look, I've got it all worked out!"

Vasilievsky unclenched his meaty fist and extended a crumpled piece of paper to Shtilmark. Shtilmark was able to make out a few sentences on it; to judge by them, the dispatcher had worked out a whole plot with all the trappings of a traditional pirate romance: the treasures and the storms and the deserted islands; the skirmishes on board and the ships burning in the night. There was even a kidnapped youth from a noble family and a tame African lion.

"See?" the dispatcher droned, bending toward Shtilmark, "I've got everything done already. You don't have to think up a thing. Just sit down and start scribbling."

"Where did you get it all from?" Shtilmark was amazed, handing back the piece of paper.

"From the literature," he answered importantly. "I'm sitting out my third term already. Everybody should be so lucky!"

Shtilmark finally understood what kind of literature he was referring to. He knew how prison novéls were constructed. An experienced storyteller himself, he'd entertained the gang in his cell, creating monstrous mixes from Stevenson and Gaboriau and Haggard. But he'd never thought anyone would ever propose a book along the same lines. And not a prison novél, either, but the real thing.

"Well, what's it going to be?" said Vaselievsky. "Either or. Either you sit here in the warm, in the zone, and scratch away, or you go out and work with the rest of the stiffs."

Looking out through the dreary, frost-covered window, Shtilmark thought it over and agreed. The idea of going out into the cold on work detail seemed horrible. He thought it would be stupid to refuse. Fate had sent him a vain idiot and he'd be even more of a fool not to take advantage of it. Vasilievsky wanted him to scratch away? All right, then, he would.

He "scratched" for a long time. Almost two years, in fact. At first he simply dawdled, killing time. Where's a convict going to rush to, anyway? Then gradually he got involved in the work, developed a taste for it, and started writing in earnest.

The plot proposed by Vasilievsky started to jell and acquire definite features. In good faith Shtilmark hammered all the details into the novel that the dispatcher insisted on. The only thing he couldn't deal with was the tame lion.

"Listen," he'd say to the dispatcher, "what the hell do you need that lion for? Let's strike him out."

"Over my dead body." Vasilievsky would scowl. "Once I've said it, it sticks."

"But where am I going to put him?"

"Think of something! You're the writer. You telling me there isn't a place for him in the whole damned novel?"

After a long and tedious battle, the dispatcher finally was forced to yield. They scratched the lion and compromised on a kind of gigantic dog.

When the manuscript was completed, two experienced typists painstakingly copied it—they were former army clerks —and some prison camp artists made pencil drawings of the "coauthors." After that the novel was handed over to the authorities and went the rounds of the departments.

There was nothing left to do now but wait. Somewhere, in the depths of his soul, Shtilmark knew that there was really nothing to wait for. It wasn't the kind of creation that was going to set anybody free. Besides, miracles like that just don't happen in prison camps. He didn't share his thoughts with his "collaborator," though. It wasn't to his advantage to disenchant the dispatcher. He had a good life now, as one of the members of the inner-camp service force, where he fondly hoped to sit out the rest of his term.

Soon after, though, things began to change, especially with Vasilievsky. Every day the fellow became more and more unfriendly. One night Shtilmark set off to see some friends in a neighboring barracks. To fool the night guards in the event of a spot check, he fixed his bed (he slept on a lower bunk, by the stove) so it would look like a man was lying there with his head covered.

Returning just before dawn, Shtilmark found his bed in pieces. The blanket had been poked through in several places and his pillow had been chopped in half by an ax. Someone had tried to do him in as he slept. But why? A gentle, obliging man, Shtilmark generally associated only with people like himself—"dill tomatoes," they called them in prison—who were hardly given to murder. Even those with whom he wasn't on good terms or had quarreled would hardly have resorted to anything like this! Obviously, somebody else was involved. Who? Possibly just one person—his coauthor. The dispatcher had needed that book—and he'd gotten it. He wasn't as stupid as he'd seemed at first. He'd acted with calculation and guile.

As long as Shtilmark had been writing, he'd been necessary to the dispatcher; but no longer. In fact, he'd become dangerous. Vasilievsky couldn't afford to let out the truth about the way the novel had been written.

The only reliable method of getting rid of a rival was murder. Vasilievsky had done a little research among the prisoners and found himself some professional killers. He didn't have far to look. The carnage that had been going on for so many years had spawned a multitude of murderers. Never a man to care that much about criminal affairs, Shtilmark now began to take a very keen interest in the thieves.

Robert Shtilmark and I met halfway, in a sense; we were both groping our way slowly toward each other. And finally, like two men in the dark, we collided and met. A bibliophile and scholar, a connoisseur and lover of poetry, Robert was the first person ever to take a professional interest in my verse and give me practical, intelligent advice. He did me an invaluable service.

In my own way, I returned the favor. In the bitch conflict (as in any real war) the opposing sides were as much involved in fighting as in spying on each other's activities. We had a reliable secret agent of our own among the bitches. It was he I now turned to for help.

Many of the convicts in the Goose's barracks were simple workers. One of them (a former front-line soldier who'd spent some time at Buchenwald) hated the bitches with all his heart and soul, finding them little different from the German prison camp "kapos," who'd also recruited prisoners into their ranks. He'd suffered a good deal at their hands in the past and considered thieves who crossed over or who were in complicity with the authorities to be no less loathsome and vile than their employers. Not that he felt any special tenderness for us, except, perhaps, as he termed it, for our "pure style." It was enough, however, to earn us his support and continuing services in the struggle.

I gave him the job of finding out all the details concerning the night assault on Shtilmark's barracks. The following day he reported that two fellows had been sent out to do the job—the Rhino and the Brunette. Vasilievsky had apparently been in their company just a short while before. Shtilmark's suspicions were borne out in full.

"What can I do?" he asked despondently. "Vasilievsky won't leave me in peace. Now that he's decided to get rid of me—"

"Then we'll have to forestall him," I said. "You'll have to get rid of him first. We'll give him a scare and see what happens."

I summoned the gang (I already held a prominent position at the 503rd Construction Project as one of the "authorities," or members of the Central Committee, so to speak), and chose a number of the most keen-witted young thieves.

Late that night, as Vasilievsky returned to his place (he lived in a small wooden structure near the staff barracks), he saw a note pinned with a knife to the head of his bed.

"Listen, scum!" it said. "We know everything you're up to, messing with decent folks. If anything happens to anyone on account of you, the same thing'll happen to you. As it is, you're already living on borrowed time. Don't expect any mercy. This is your first—and last—warning!"

The threat worked. The dispatcher got the message: his coauthor had protectors among the thieves. There were no further attempts on Shtilmark's life.

Robert and I spent a lot of time with each other after that. He not only discussed literature with me, but supplied me with valuable books. (Like the thieves, the politicals sometimes managed to get their supplies from the outside. The only difference was that while my friends went for liquor and narcotics, Robert's friends preferred spiritual food.)

There was one book that I got from Shtilmark that especially interested me and was later to serve me well. It was called *Newspaper Design and Production.* In handing it to me, Robert had drawn his dry, sunken cheeks into a smile and said: "Read it carefully. There's a lot of useful information for you there. When you get outside, it'll all come in handy. Believe me!"

THE BURDEN OF FAME

I met a lot of interesting people through Shtilmark. Besides him, there was another political prisoner involved with literature, Sergei Ivanovich, a professional translator who'd worked at one time at the State Publishing House. Then there was an art critic, a former professor at Kazan University, who told me a good deal about the development of the Russian Renaissance and the work of Dionysius, Rublev, and Feofan the Greek. There was an old sybarite and aesthete, too, a connoisseur of French poetry, named Prince Obolensky. During the nineteenth century his ancestors, the Decembrists and the Masons, had been exiled in hordes to Siberia. Now that there were no more lands available for exile, the Soviet regime had perpetuated the family tradition by putting Obolensky behind bars. There was also Konstantin Levitsky, the prison doctor—the man who'd long since regarded me and the thieves with a decided sympathy.

It was with Levitsky that I had the closest ties of all. He not only honored me with his conversation (he was a brilliant talker) but helped me by freeing me from work. There was even an occasion when he saved me from the inner-camp prison cell.

I had landed there for a rather ridiculous reason. It had to do indirectly with my growing popularity among the local thieves, a popularity due in large measure to my poems and songs. The thieves loved them, knew them by heart, and sang them everywhere. Even the camp authorities were aware of them. In fact it was here, at the 503rd Construction Project, that I received my first acclaim as a poet and, along with it, my first understanding of the fact that every honor has its negative side.

In the eyes of the Chekists I was, after all, no simple prison-camp versifier. They saw me as a kind of home-grown thief ideologist and spiritual leader (an exaggerated notion, needless to say). And the more prominent my creative efforts became, the greater the suspicion with which the authorities regarded me.

I felt their gaze on me constantly; they made use of any pretext to frighten me, isolate me, and land me behind bars. I was now being held responsible for everything—for every incident, every disturbance, even for compositions that weren't my own.

There's a well-known song from Revolutionary times which was once popular among the anarchists and sailors of St. Petersburg. It began with these lines:

> Down with the Marxists, the USSR,
> Down with the Bolshevik cells;
> Down with them, down with them, shout the woods
>   and the steppes,
> Down with them, down with them, thunders the surf,
> This is our final struggle, men,
> To break all the Communists' chains!

Someone had written these lines in coal on the white stove in the center of the barracks. The inscription appeared before dinner and, a little later, during the evening check, all hell broke loose.

As soon as the supervisor entered the barracks and took a look at the stove, he trembled and said in a voice tense with rage: "All right, who's the poet?"

His only answer was silence.

"Who's the poet!" he barked, turning a deep red.

"We're all poets here," the Straw replied lazily from behind his curtain.

"So that's all you got to say, is it? All right . . ." The guard fell silent for a minute or two, taking us all in with a look from beneath his brows. Then, in a booming voice, he shouted:

"Day guard!"

The day guard of the barracks, a bright, shortish old man, leaped forward.

"Yes, sir!" He reached for the inscription. "Wipe it off?"

"Just the opposite," the guard said sternly. "Let it stand!"

"Yes, sir!" the day guard replied.

"You stay here till I get back and make sure nobody lays a finger on it!"

A quarter of an hour later the guard re-entered the barracks with the head of the regime, the senior guard, and the Godfather.

The Godfather, apparently, had been called directly from his private quarters. He was still yawning and smacking his lips. His face was glossy, the collar of his tunic was unbuttoned, and his overcoat hung carelessly over his shoulders.

"So," he said, carefully reading the lines written on the stove and turning sharply to the guard. "So, they're all poets here, you say?"

"Who knows what that stuff means?" The guard shrugged.

"Doesn't matter." The Godfather smiled. "We'll figure it out! It's really not that hard. And as for the poet, well, we've known who that was for a long time now."

He wiped his lips with the side of his hand and slowly buttoned up his tunic. Then, softly but distinctly, he called: "Hey, Chuma! Where are you hiding? Or do you want to play hide and seek with me? Come out, come out . . . all right, on the double!"

While they were leading me off, I caught his husky, muffled voice behind my back: "We'll have to draw up a report. It's a clear case of agitation. Look at the kinds of poems he's been writing."

"But that isn't mine. Ask anyone you want. . . ."

"Come on, come on." The Godfather pushed me in the back. "Keep it quiet. You'll get your chance to answer. You'll answer, all right, you'll answer for everything!"

They gave me ten straight days of solitary, starting that evening. Solitary's no joking matter. During the years when I'd been shuffled from one prison camp to another I'd had my taste of every kind of solitary: I'd frozen on the damp cement floors, I'd received my three-hundred-gram ration of bread and my glass of water every twenty-four hours (under a tight regime they give you hot food every third day). Now it was all staring me in the face again. But the hardest thing of all to bear was the fact that my punishment was only beginning. The authorities weren't limiting themselves to jail. They were planning to stick me with an extra sentence, as the one responsible for all the inner-camp agitation.

And if Levitsky hadn't come to my aid in time, that's undoubtedly how it would have all turned out. He came to my cell after I'd been there four days. The prisoner in the adjoining cell had had an epileptic seizure and the guard had been forced to call for a doctor. I heard a vague commotion in the corridor, leaned my ear to the door, and made out Levitsky's high thin voice (he was scolding the medics and ordering them to do something). I started knocking and calling for the day guard and when he finally looked in on me, I declared that I was sick and demanded help.

Levitsky didn't betray any surprise at seeing me. He simply knitted his brows, looked me over, took my temperature, and announced to the guard that, in his opinion, I was an extremely sick man.

"I'm afraid it's highly infectious," he said, painstakingly dipping some gauze in ether and wiping his hands. "Spotted fever, I suspect. It'll have to be verified, of course, but the symptoms are menacing."

And so I landed in Levitsky's infirmary with a diagnosis of "spotted fever."

THE DARKEST HOUR'S JUST BEFORE THE DAWN

At the doctor's orders I was placed in quarantine in a small room at the back of the barracks, by the storeroom. The storeroom was run by Valka, a sprightly hospital chambermaid with a round, freckled, dimpled face and ample breasts firmly laced into her little dress. She bent down to make my bed and I involuntarily jerked back.

"Don't stare," she said quietly. "You'll go blind."

I turned around and lighted a cigarette. And felt the warm touch of her palm on my cheek.

"Hey, what's the matter," she said gently. "Don't get upset."

"I'm not upset," I muttered.

"No?" She screwed up her eyes.

"No."

"Oh, I'm going to have trouble with you." Valka smiled lazily. "Always the same thing. Well, so what, it's normal."

After making the bed she straightened up, looked around the room, and pressed her lips.

"I see you and Kostya are big friends."

"Where'd you get that idea?"

"Come on! He's never set anybody else up like you. A separate bed and all the rest."

"Then you're a little fool. I'm—highly infectious."

"Go tell that to somebody else." Valka brushed it aside. "Kostya's explained the whole thing to me."

Again she brushed my cheek lightly with her hand.

"Lie down, my dear. If there's anything you need, let me know. My room's right next door."

"Even at night?" I asked, chewing my cigarette and squinting from the smoke.

"Depends on what you're after." She slowly raised her shoulder.

Late that night (I'd already begun to doze off) the door squeaked open and, like a gust of wind, blew the sleep from my eyes.

Valka! I thought, sitting up in bed and looking avidly into the darkness. The light switch clicked on and I saw the thin figure of Konstantin Levitsky.

"Did I wake you?" he asked, sitting down heavily on the edge of the bed.

"Of course not." Disappointed, I settled down on the pillow and stretched out with a sigh. "What's up?"

"I just decided to sit for a while and have a chat." He yawned, rubbing his face with his hand: "I'm dog-tired, but I can't seem to sleep. Depressed, too. It's that damnedest time of all, just before the dawn. The Buddhist monks used to call it the 'hour of the bull,' when the forces of evil and the demons of the dark hold complete sway over the earth."

"That's odd," I replied, "all the books I ever read said the worst time was midnight. In Dumas, for instance, midnight's the hour the murderers strike. The same with Conan Doyle and the others. That's the way it seemed to me, too."

"It may suit murders," Levitsky said. "I don't know. That's more up your alley. But I'm talking about something else. Mystical things. Darkness oppresses a man. The most agonizing hours don't come in the middle of the night, but at the end. The ancient Romans knew it, too. They had an excellent saying about it. Listen, it goes like this." And raising a finger, he recited slowly and melodiously: "*Dolor ignis ante lucem.* 'The fire's bite before the light.' The darkest hour's just before the dawn."

"The darkest hour's just before the dawn," I repeated in a whisper. "That's a line already!"

"What?" He moved toward me.

"A line of poetry," I said, "an iambic pentameter."

"Take it, it's yours," he said courteously. "Maybe you'll put it somewhere. The main point is that the demons hold sway just before the dawn, you understand? Their power's not unbounded. Sooner or later, the darkness ends and yields to the light. And the fiercer the depression, the nearer the light—and liberation."

"That's a different department altogether, my friend," I said. "That's politics."

"Why are you so afraid of politics?" Levitsky asked slowly.

"What's there to be afraid of?" I shrugged my shoulders. "I've just always kept away from it, that's all."

"That's what you think," he said. "Nobody's free of politics. Nobody, you understand? Your entire life's been a direct corroboration of that. Anyway, how can you escape it? Look, here we are, you and I, in a prison camp. The direct result of politics. And the night's all around us. And the forces of evil. In hordes. Ordering us around, standing guard over us in the watchtowers. You understand?"

Levitsky looked at me and then drew his eyes away, and I suddenly realized his visit hadn't been accidental.

"Listen," I said, recalling Valka's words (the memory of her, by the way, hadn't left me for an instant), "let's be straight with each other. Why did you set me up here anyway? Out of friendship?"

"Well, not entirely"—he hesitated—"not entirely. I have the highest regard for you, you know that. And I deal with you sincerely, as a friend, the way I do with the other thieves. The real ones, I mean."

"Why do you have such a high opinion of us, by the way?"

"If you let me, I'll tell you." He moved slowly. And again from beneath those heavy brows, he fixed me with his gaze. "If you really want to know . . ."

"Of course I do!" I answered.

"The fact is," he began, lowering his voice, "you thieves represent a real force—" Suddenly, he got up and walked to the door, threw it open, and looked out into the hall. Then, turning back and sitting down beside me, he continued: "The very force we so desperately need. Desperately! Without you, I'm afraid, we won't be able to manage."

"Who's 'we'?"

"The Committee of Resistance," he said. "Have you heard of it?"

"No."

"All right. Anyway, it exists. And is extremely active."

"Doing what?"

"In this case, preparing for an uprising."

"Oho!" I said in surprise. "So that's what you're up to! No wonder you need the thieves. But, old man, you aren't serious, are you?"

"Absolutely," he said. "Tomorrow you can see for yourself."

"You're going to revolt tomorrow?"

"Of course not." He laughed. "We're still a long way from

that. Tomorrow we have a conference, that's all. Right here, in this room. In fact, the committee will be meeting on account of you!"

"You mean you got me here specifically for that?"

He nodded. "Of course. It's quiet here. You're on the quarantine list, remember. What could be better than that?"

"And how long am I going to stay here?" I wanted to know.

"Not for long." Levitsky frowned, biting his lip. "The tests will come and that'll be the end of it. But we've got a week, in any event. And by then, I hope, we'll have settled all our problems!"

The underground committee (all five members) met at the appointed time, on the evening of the following day. To my considerable surprise, they were all familiar faces. They included Sergei Ivanovich, the former worker at the State Publishing House, and Prince Obolensky.

"Prince," I said, "I hardly thought I'd be meeting you here! You're a refined individual. What're you messing around in the underground for?"

"You're right, my dove, of course." The Prince smiled, looking down at me from the height of his splendid six-and-a-half-foot frame. "But how could I destroy a family tradition? As far as I know, there has never been even one more or less reputable underground in Russia my forebears haven't participated in. This 'mess,' as you call it, is my legacy. Although, of course," he added, "my contribution's quite small. I'm no warrior, just a humble statistician. I draw up the lists and keep the minutes."

What kind of minutes? the thought crossed my mind. I quickly became distracted, however, talking with the others, and forgot all about it.

One of them was nicknamed the Beard, a thickset man of advanced years with a wrinkled face, straight shoulders, and a knobby, shaved skull. Although his brows and beard were shot with gray, he still looked amazingly powerful. You could divine the traces of a hardened soldier in the way he moved and talked. As I soon discovered, the Beard had served as an

artillery corporal during the war. He'd been wounded somewhere in the south and had fallen prisoner. Then he'd deserted
to Vlasov's troops till the end of the war, when the English
handed him back to the Soviets.

His comrade, a former Baltic navy antiaircraft gunner and
gun crew petty officer, had never fallen prisoner and had
served his time honorably in the fleet, where he'd been
wounded twice and decorated four times. None of that had
kept him from prison either, though. On the eve of Victory
Day he'd been arrested by an informer for anti-Soviet
attitudes and received the same sentence to the day as the
corporal. And so the law and the stern fate of the convict had
made them brothers.

The two of them were inseparable. They worked in the same
brigade and went everywhere together. Here, at the meeting,
they also sat side by side: the gray, stocky Beard and his huge,
taciturn companion (Vitya they called him) with the bony
chest, long, apelike arms, and small head. Vitya greeted me
with a smile, baring his huge, flat, bluish teeth and silently
squeezing my hand.

The Beard also looked me over, took me in with an
appraising glance, and, looking sideways at Levitsky, said:

"So that's your little Makhno, eh?"

"Makhno?" I wondered.

The Beard screwed up his eyes. "Your roles are alike, aren't
they? You're here in the same capacity as Daddy Makhno,
when he was still on good terms with the Bolsheviks, that is.
Makhno represented his bandits in the staff of the southern
front the same way you're representing your rabble in our staff
right now."

"Perhaps," Levitsky agreed. "The scale's different, though."

"But the proportions are the same," the Beard quickly
replied. "The ratio of forces, roughly, is exactly the same."

He got a light from someone's cigarette and, waving away
the smoke with his hand, continued: "And speaking about the
alignment of forces, isn't it about time we got down to
business? There are a lot of undecided questions and time

won't wait. We have to assign specific sectors once and for all and stop this perpetual muddle we're always getting into. But that's for later. Right now, in regard to the appearance of our new comrade—"

"Daddy Makhno," someone burst in, laughing.

"Wait a minute, my friends," I said. "Let's get one thing straight. I'm not Makhno. First of all because thieves, unlike Makhno's men, do not and never have had any chiefs. Besides, nobody authorized me."

"You may not have any chiefs," Sergei Ivanovich interrupted me, "but you do have some kind of leadership all the same, a kind of high soviet, don't you?"

"Yes," I agreed.

"Which you belong to, isn't that correct?"

"To a certain degree."

"Don't be modest, my friend." Levitsky slapped me on the shoulder. "Don't belittle yourself. Besides, no special powers are required in this case. Our committee simply decided to establish contact with the thieves. We gathered here to get acquainted with you and ask some questions. And to explain the situation."

"So go ahead and explain," I said. "I already know a little something. What are your goals, though? How many of you are there? What are you counting on?"

"We have the same goal," Levitsky started to speak quietly. Suddenly, though, Vitya stood up. "Stop," he said (it turned out he had a low, toneless voice with a kind of heartbreaking hoarseness to it). "Stop, wait a minute!"

"What's the matter?" Levitsky turned to him.

"You've just started right in on our goals. You think that's a good idea?" Vitya raised his brows in my direction. "Can you vouch for him?"

"Ah, that's what's bothering you," Levitsky said and smiled sparingly. "Don't worry. He's been under surveillance for a long time. Like with an X-ray machine. We've investigated him through and through."

Oh, Kostya, you *fraier*, you, I was thinking. So that's what these poetry lovers are really all about. Like an idiot, I'd assumed they liked my poems and, it turned out, they'd simply been checking me out.

"If that's the case—" Vitya muttered.

"Now sit down." The Beard pulled him impatiently by the sleeve. "Don't ever leap up like that without damn good cause!"

The sailor made for the corner and sat down obediently. Levitsky spoke, looking me straight and hard in the eye. "Don't look so surprised, my friend. Of course we checked you out."

What I then heard came as a considerable surprise. The underground insurgent organization, it turned out, had been active at the 503rd Construction Project for quite some time. It embraced almost all the local camp centers, including even Igarka and distant Norilsk. The central staff was located somewhere near there, in fact, in the far north. The uprising was to take place simultaneously all along the route, at a predetermined signal to be given from the outside. Special clandestine "outside" connections chosen from among exiled settlers, of whom there were a large number in the area, existed for that purpose. They maintained unbroken contact with the center of the conspiracy and provided a periphery of essential information and weapons.

"So, there you have it," Levitsky said in conclusion. "That's the general picture. It's sketchy, of course, but I trust you don't need to know all the details."

"Of course not," I replied. "What for? There's only one thing I don't understand, though. Why is the center so far away? That only complicates matters."

"Simply because our ultimate goal is to seize the Norilsk radio station," Levitsky said slowly. "We'll burst onto the air and get in touch with America and the West. . . ."

"You think anybody's going to support you?" I expressed my doubts. "Ah, brothers, you aren't too familiar with the history of the camps, I'm afraid."

And, as briefly as possible, I told them the famous story of the Solovetsky insurrection—about the massive escape of prisoners from the islands and their betrayal by the Norwegians, who sent them all back under guard. I also informed them of the uprisings in Vorkut and Solikamsk. Some of them had been relying on the support of the local population, too, and the natives had betrayed them. As a result both of the uprisings had been crushed with all the brutality the Chekists were capable of. In fact, the very same locals had even helped chase the prisoners down in the taiga.

"So what do you propose?" the Beard asked after a moment's silence. "In your opinion, it seems any struggle is doomed to failure. Must we lay down our arms, then? Is that what you're saying?"

"Absolutely not," I answered. "You couldn't do that now if you wanted to. You've already stuck your necks in the noose, so you've got to act. But don't amuse yourselves with illusions. That's what I'm getting at. No one on the outside is going to help you. You have to rely completely on yourselves and your own power. And instead of thinking about that idiotic radio station, think about how to get as far away as you can. The main thing is to get the hell out in time."

"Brother, you're reasoning like a professional thief," said Levitsky, turning his head.

"How else can I reason? That's exactly what I am! And if I'm going to speak in the name of the gang, then let me assure you here and now we'll help you. To smash the guards and to take the zone—without question. But after that our paths diverge."

"What do you mean, diverge?" Levitsky asked sharply. "And when?"

"After the slaughter. After the guards've been liquidated. You probably plan to stick around and hold a defensive position. But for thieves that's pointless. An uprising isn't a goal in itself for them, just the quickest route to freedom. You understand, old man? To freedom—to escape! That's the only reason they'd ever agree to anything, and it's the only basis on which I can give you any guarantee you want."

"Any?" Sergei Ivanovich asked, narrowing his eyes.

"For God's sake," I answered, "don't hold me to every

word I say. In principle, I know how thieves think. I could be mistaken, of course, on some points here and there. But, regardless of that, most of my boys will go along, I'm completely sure of that."

"Allow me to make that more precise." The Beard's voice resounded. "Translated into numbers—'most'—how many would that be? Roughly speaking, that is."

"Sixty men," I answered, giving it some thought. "Maybe even a few more. You've got to remember there's always a lot of small fry and novices hanging out near the thieves. 'Beetles,' we call them. There's another category, too: women. 'Sixes,' we call them. But they don't count. The beetles are an active force, though, and a big one. You can't overlook them."

"So," the Beard strained through his teeth, "that means that, counting those beetles of yours, there'll be, shall we say, something like a hundred?"

"Say eighty," I replied. "That's for sure."

"That's wonderful!"

The Beard gave a broad smile, quickly wiped the top of his head, and shouted: "Make a note of it, Prince: eighty men—against the tower. From the left—don't forget!—from the left. The other group can now fully concentrate on the western sector."

I looked at Obolensky. During the general discussion he'd been sitting quietly in the corner, rustling his papers, and I'd completely forgotten about him. Now, with mounting alarm, I noticed he'd been writing all the time.

"Prince," I asked, "are you really keeping minutes?"

"Why, yes, my dove." He raised his faded, light-blue, innocent eyes. "Of course. Which brings me to my next question. There's something I'd like to ascertain. Eighty people's not a small group. It's not worth enumerating them by name, of course, but I'll need to register some of them, the main ones, the leaders. After all, you won't be heading up the entire operation on your own!"

"You mean you've already written my name down?"

"Of course. Under 'T'—for 'Thief.' "

"Oh, God," I moaned, "who the hell have I gotten mixed up with?"

Walking over to Obolensky I bent down and said angrily: "Cross out my name! You hear me? Cross it out this instant!"

"But—" the Prince muttered in confusion, "the system—"

"To hell with your system!"

"Please, please!" Sergei Ivanovich started to get excited. "Let me point out to you this system has been in existence for quite some time and is entirely in accord with Russian revolutionary underground practice. You're still young—an elemental being. But we're exemplars, worthy models. Yes," he finished in a falsetto, "models!"

"I don't give a damn what you're guided by"—I shrugged my shoulders—"but if you ask me, you've all gone crazy! I told you already you're sticking your necks in a noose. I meant that figuratively. Now I'm not so sure. Can you imagine what would happen if those minutes of yours fell into the wrong hands?"

"I hope that would never happen." Levitsky smiled sullenly.

"So do I." I fell silent for a minute, measuring my breath and trying to get hold of my temper. "All the same, I won't give you any names. And as for my own, cross it off, too. I beg you. No, I insist! Otherwise we've got nothing more to talk about."

"All right, all right." The Beard raised both his hands in a conciliatory gesture. "There won't be any names."

"Still," Sergei Ivanovich drawled thoughtfully, "we've got to designate them somehow."

"Then make up some kind of code, for God's sake," I said, "use numbers or something. I don't know. I'm not a specialist."

"We could do that." Levitsky nodded in agreement. "So the boy won't feel nervous."

He lowered his thick shaggy brows and bit his lip. "You say there are eighty men in your group?" he asked. "All right, let's designate it with an eight. You don't object to that, do you?"

"All right," I said. "Let it stand."

"And you'll go under the same cipher yourself, all right?"

"Agreed."

"Aren't we overdoing it a bit?" I suddenly heard Vitya's leisurely bass. "We're playing up to him like a pretty girl. There's nothing we won't do to indulge him. First one thing, then another. It's enough to make me sick."

I turned on him quickly but before I could reply, Obolensky entered the conversation. "I have a question for our young colleague. In thief parlance, unless I'm mistaken, isn't there also a kind of system of numerical symbols?"

"There is," I said. " 'To six,' for instance, means to worm your way into someone's favor. 'To eight' means to be cunning and wily."

"So what's the problem?" Levitsky started to laugh. "Everything coincides then. No number could suit you and your group better."

"You saying I'm conniving?"

"I don't mean just you. I'm speaking about the wiliness of the whole caste. You only look after your own interests."

"So does everybody else." I waved my hand exhaustedly. "That's our damned life in a nutshell! Some people have caste interests, some have party ones. What's the difference?"

SNOWFALL

We talked and argued right up to retreat that evening. The underground met several times more after that in my room, to discuss details and work out a plan of action. The deadline for the uprising was near; it was supposed to begin sometime in the middle of the winter, and it was already December—the last gloomy month of 1950.

Late one evening I went outside to obey a call of nature and to cool off (I'd been squabbling with Vitya again). Standing at the corner of the barracks, I breathed in the fresh, intoxicating smell of the winter. I lifted my face to the large, slow snowflakes as they fell, whirling and sparkling through the chilly darkness, landing heavily on my eyelashes and sending waves of cold up and down my body as they melted underneath my collar.

Suddenly I heard a rustling sound around the corner. The snow had squeaked as if someone was shifting his weight from one foot to the other. Then, describing a semicircle in the darkness, a cigarette briefly glittered and went out with a hiss.

There were two windows, Valka's and mine, on the rear wooden wall of the barracks. Maybe someone was paying a call on the sly. I smiled. But the windows had been locked shut behind double storm frames. Besides, I recalled that Valka wasn't in the storeroom, but in the general ward helping to carry medicines and give treatment. Whoever he was, he hadn't come on her account.

At that thought my heart skipped a beat. I looked round the corner and saw a short, bulky male figure in the cascading snow. And even though he stood half-turned from me with his face against the windowpane (mine, incidentally, and not Valka's) I recognized the Goose. I would have recognized him in pitch darkness with my eyes blindfolded. I'd have sensed him instinctively.

Leaning against the wall and hooking his nails into the window frame, the Goose was looking intently into the room. Most likely he'd come after me and accidentally stumbled across our meeting. Sounds of voices filtered indistinctly through the frosted glass. Standing on tiptoe, stretching his neck, he'd been trying to make some sense out of what was going on. He'd even cocked his fur cap to one side so he could hear better.

I had no idea how long he'd been there or exactly what he'd managed to see and hear, but one thing was clear—our heads were on the block!

Returning to the hospital, I dashed to my door and was on the verge of opening it when I suddenly realized that it would be risky coming into the room; after all, the Goose was on the outside watching everything that happened. I heard Valka talking and giggling with someone down in the hall. Of course! I called her softly.

She was a reliable woman. She idolized Levitsky and obeyed his every word. She even had a soft spot for me and had often come to visit me in the night.

"Listen, my dear," I told her. "Listen very carefully. Go into my room right now and call Kostya. But do it carefully, so that nobody notices or pays any attention. Find some kind of excuse. Say a patient is calling for him. Think of something! I have to speak to him urgently. Do it quietly, without any fuss."

"All right," she said, blinking in confusion. She disappeared behind the door and returned almost at once with Levitsky.

"What are you doing out here?" He was surprised to see me. "They're waiting for you."

I turned to Valka. "Leave us now, my dear, go. . . ." When Kostya and I were alone I continued: "I'm afraid we're all in trouble, old man. You realize they're spying on us?"

"Who?" Levitsky asked, his face turning dark. He grabbed me by the collar of my robe and pulled me to him. "Who's spying?" He was breathing heavily now, his nostrils flared. "Is this some kind of joke?"

"Hell, no! I just saw a spy. Right beneath our window. I know him, too."

I briefly explained to Levitsky who the Goose was and added, spreading my hands in distress: "The bitch of it is, I don't have anything on me. No feather, no pike. I came here straight from solitary. But we can't let the Goose out of here alive. Listen, old man, have you or one of the boys got anything? Lend it to me, just for the time being, and I'll take care of everything."

"No, wait, let's try something else," Levitsky said hoarsely. "The main thing right now is to keep him from going away, to keep him interested. . . . You'll be the bait!"

"How?"

"Go right back into the room as if nothing had happened. And start talking about him. Loudly, distinctly, as if the Goose was right out there listening. That'll be sure to get him interested. Don't worry about the rest. We'll take care of everything ourselves. By the way, whisper to Vitya on the way in that I need him out here."

"So you want Vitya to—"

"What does it matter to you?" Levitsky pressed his lips into a smile. "You've got your own role to play, so go and play it. Don't worry about Vitya. The man bends horseshoes like they were made out of cardboard. He doesn't need any weapons. You're still a child. What do you really know about our people? We don't earn our living with petty terror, as a rule, but if there's no choice . . ."

This dialogue didn't last more than a minute. I threw myself into the room, stood by the window, and started talking at the top of my voice, denouncing the bitches and mentioning the Goose, their ringleader. The unexpected speech had the gathering dumfounded. Obolensky laid down his pen and lifted his brows. The Beard raised his shoulders in a shrug and kept them there, without taking his eyes off me. And Sergei Ivanovich, stammering and visibly upset, said:

"What is this? What are you talking about? Please, please . . ."

I was inspired. I chattered and wailed and gesticulated incessantly, keeping my eye on the window all the time. A soft, smoky strip of light fell from the window to the snow outside, illuminating a small patch that seemed to be shaded by snowflakes. Still, I could see him, or rather his shadow, through the shimmering, light blue grid. He was riveted to the window, trying avidly to catch every word.

Then something happened: the shadow was flung to the side. Another immediately appeared beside it. Both of them fused and intertwined, turning into one formless spot. The spot seemed frozen for a moment and then it split and fell apart. The next instant Vitya's face pressed against the frosted windowpane. He knocked on the frame with his nail, winking slowly at me and drawing his dry, thin lips into a smile. Wiping the perspiration from my brow and looking at my dumbstruck conspirators, I said: "Okay, brothers, figure it out for yourselves."

The event seriously agitated the members of the committee. They decided to stop all meetings for the time being and quickly left. Then Levitsky and I went outside to the site of the skirmish.

The Goose had been strangled. "Our sailor did a good job," Levitsky said, looking the body over. "He's a master, all right, no denying it. Take a look at this: not only did he break his neck, but the cervical vertebrae too."

"There's only one thing that bothers me. It was Vitya that did him in and not me," I said.

"But, my boy, you couldn't have done it like this."

"Doesn't matter. I'd have taken care of it somehow. I'd been on his trail for more than a year. It shouldn't have turned out like this."

"God knows what you're talking about." Levitsky smiled. "Listen, if it matters that much, why not take his scalp? That'll be some comfort, at least. Better hurry, though, there'll be a check within half an hour." His smile faded. "We've got to put him somewhere else."

"Listen," I said quickly, "we're right next to the bathhouse. There's a big stack of firewood nearby. We'll put him in the pile, put some snow on top, and that'll be the end of it."

"Maybe," Levitsky agreed. "It's an idea. . . . Forget the snow, though, it's coming down fine without us."

The weather really was getting worse. The snow was falling even harder now. We could act calmly without worrying about onlookers. After dragging the dead man to the bathhouse we crept back to the hospital. I'd barely managed to undress and get into bed when I heard the slow, distant pealing of the bell—the signal for the evening check.

Later that night Levitsky came to see me. He sat down heavily on the bed, lit a cigarette, and wrapped himself up in smoke. Then he said with a yawn: "I was just talking with the Godfather about an hour ago. He confides in me, you see. After all, I treat his wife. God knows what kinds of medicines I push on that hysteric! Anyway"—Levitsky moved, making himself more comfortable—"we talked. He told me they'd found the Goose's body. You should have seen how infuriated he was at losing such a valuable fellow. Besides, and this is the funny part, they don't suspect the thieves at all, but one of their own boys. It turns out one of the bitches works in the bathhouse, chopping wood. He'd had a big argument with the Goose at one point. The Godfather knew about it, and figures it was all a matter of settling personal scores. They've already taken the fellow away. The Godfather told me his nickname, only it's gone clear out of my head." Kostya frowned and chewed on the end of his cigarette. "Something preposterous."

"The Rhino, maybe?" I suggested indifferently, looking at the peeling paint on the ceiling.

"Yes, yes, that's it! Wait—" He fell silent and lowered his eyebrows. "You knew he worked there?"

"I'd heard something of the sort. What about it?"

"So you didn't just happen to remember about the firewood, did you? You cooked up the whole thing!"

"What difference does it make?" I replied, repeating what Kostya himself had told me not so long ago. "You have your own role to play, so go and play it. And I'll play mine."

"You're a fine little fellow," he said slowly in amazement. "Explain something to me, will you? Where does a simple Soviet boy like you learn this stuff?"

"Kostya," I said, "beat a rabbit on the head long enough and you can teach it to light a match."

"Yes, yes, of course," he muttered. "Come to think of it, you're not so Soviet—or so simple."

"And just who *do* you think I am?" I was clearly interested in the answer.

"It's not that easy to define, right off the bat, like that. Of course, you're a shady character. . . ."

"Don't overdo it, friend," I said.

"Think about it yourself," Kostya said. "You're a tramp, an adventurer, one of the leaders of the thief Mafia. But, on the other hand, you've got a real intellect and talent. You're a creative individual. Take it all together and you've got one hell of a bouquet!" He lightly patted me on the knee. "One thing's clear. We weren't mistaken about you—you'll do. We need people with character and imagination. And that's exactly what you've got. I'd hate to be one of *your* enemies."

"By the way," I said, "the Rhino isn't just an enemy of mine. He's the one who made the attempt on Shtilmark's life. Tell Robert that, the next time you see him. He'll be pleased to know."

"I won't have a chance," Levitsky said slowly, stubbing out his cigarette. "Robert is gone."

"What do you mean, gone?" I got up, resting on my elbow. "What happened to him?"

"They sent him off on deportation."

"When?"

"Day before yesterday. I thought you knew."

"What?" I said, feeling hurt. "He didn't even say good-bye."

"He didn't say good-bye to anybody. It all happened suddenly. They called him out of the dining hall during breakfast, led him off to the watchtower, and that's the last anyone ever saw of him. They didn't even let him gather his things. A guard ran into the barracks to get them later."

"Where did they send him, do you know?"

"Some kind of penal camp, they say."

"Vasilievsky's mixed up in this, for sure," I concluded gloomily. "He had to get rid of his rival, the skunk! He couldn't bring off killing him, so he shoves Robert into the whirlpool with the penal types. The senior dispatcher can do a lot! If he knew I'd helped Robert then he'd do the same to me, especially now that I'm in trouble. It'd be easy. I'm hanging by a thread as it is. The Godfather's accusing me of agitation, you know."

"Oh, by the way," Levitsky said, "the Godfather and I had a little talk about that." He got up and stretched with a crack. "He was really nervous this time, and absent-minded. He hung around for a long time, starting in on one thing and then jumping to another. Suddenly he remembered you and asked how you were doing."

"How thoughtful of him," I grumbled. "Maybe he guesses something?"

"I don't know. In any event, you fascinate him. You and your songs. It was the songs we talked about. In particular, the one they got you for."

Levitsky fell silent, fighting to keep from smiling.

"Well, what happened?" I said impatiently.

"I turned the Godfather's attention to one highly significant detail. There's some mention in the song of 'Bolshevik cells,' isn't there? Well, I pointed out that that was an antiquated expression, used only in pre-Revolutionary times. Nobody talks about the Party that way nowadays. The author of that song could never have been a green kid like you."

"Kostya," I said, deeply moved, "as God is my witness, I'm in your debt forever. How can I pay you back?"

"Stop it." He waved his hand. "What kind of debts could there ever be between us?" He turned toward the door. "Be true to our cause, that's the most important thing. True," he stopped in the doorway and looked at me over his shoulder, "if they were to send me off tomorrow, if I were to lose all my prestige in the eyes of the authorities, then . . ."

I fired a question as if I were shooting him right in the back: "Tell me, Kostya, where do you get your prestige, anyway? Who are you?"

"A doctor," he said. "What else? A doctor of medicine."

"Where did you work before?"

"In a German army hospital."

"The whole war?"

"No, just toward the end. I served the first years in different places in East Prussia. A good training from excellent professors! I have a blood tie with the Prussians."

"What are you, a German?"

"No," he replied, "not entirely. I was born in Minsk. My father is a famous Minsk surgeon. My mother, it's true, was from an old Prussian family, but her ancestors moved east two centuries before and were thoroughly Russified."

"So that's it," I said. "And where did you serve in Prussia?"

"What difference does it make?" He worried the corner of his mouth. "In any event, I went through a good school."

Kostya was still standing in the doorway, picking at the doorknob. His fingers trembled; apparently the conversation was upsetting him. Suddenly he walked up to me, bent his lean, high-browed, sharp-cornered face, and said: "I am a famous specialist, my friend. And if I ever get burned, it'll only be on account of people like you."

"Which means?"

"Do you think you're the first person I've ever put in the hospital with an idiotic diagnosis? How many people do you think I've had to free from work detail under different pretexts? God, I'm amazed they haven't kicked me out yet. There's only one thing that's saved me so far, the naïve faith of the Chekists in the might of German medicine. It's an amazing thing! They hardly ever go to their own civilian doctors. They turn to me instead. . . ."

I had a hard time getting to sleep that night. I turned in my bed. I smoked. The hospital was quiet; only the windowpanes trembled and rattled mournfully as the storm grew stronger and fiercer outside. The snow wasn't falling straight down anymore, but at an angle. It looked like furious, flying torrents of frothy water, swishing and splashing against the windows, submerging the surrounding area and letting out a whistle that seemed to search the night to the marrow. The darkness was threatening and impenetrable. Once again, I recalled the line, "The darkest hour's just before the dawn."

Reaching for my notebook on the night table, I hastily wrote down the first, still unpolished lines of a poem:

The darkest hour's just before the dawn,
No stars, pitch dark, between the storm's white tresses;
But if I read it right: all hope's not gone,
For, after all, the day is born of darkness.

GUNFIRE AT NIGHT

I was soon discharged from the hospital and returned to my usual surroundings with the thieves. There'd been some changes in my absence. New faces had appeared and old ones, like Vanka the Kike, the Professor, and the Georgian prince (the one with a taste for little boys) had all gone off on deportation, along with Shtilmark, somewhere toward the Far North. But what really unnerved me was an incident that had happened to a friend of mine, Nikola the Chipmunk, the husband of Varka, the legendary beauty. Thanks to her, he'd lived for six happy years in freedom. Some of the recently arrived thieves had had a conversation on that very subject and, at a noisy night gathering, had given him a vote of no confidence and chased him out of the den. The man responsible for the whole affair was a new arrival named the Agitator. Hunched and emaciated, with an apelike, twitching face, he was continually sticking his nose into other people's business and causing trouble. Once, during a card game, he'd had a disagreement with Nikola that had quickly developed into a heated quarrel.

Twitching and spewing saliva, the Agitator had declared that Nikola was an unclean person with a dark soul. Nikola demanded proof and the Agitator gave it. His argument went like this: Thieves call prison their "home ground" because they usually spend about half their lives there—a fact especially true of pickpockets. Any screen man, no matter how much of a virtuoso, always lands behind bars at least once a year—once every two years if he's particularly lucky. But six? Unheard of! There had never been anything like it. The only way you could pull something like that off would be with the help of the police, and the nature of contacts like that was clear. However regrettable it might be, the Agitator did have a point. To believe in Nikola you'd have had to know all the details of his family life, and there was hardly anyone left in the camp who could vouch for that. Some of the boys had perished or vanished, others had been sent off on deportation and I'd been away in a hospital bed. The only one to raise his voice in Nikola's defense had been the Straw, but to no avail.

The Straw told me the story right after I'd returned. "I feel sorry for the Chipmunk," he sighed. "What a thief we've lost! A real aristocrat he was."

"Where is he now?" I started to get upset.

"Another barracks," the Straw said. "He doesn't live here anymore, he didn't want to. Can't say as I blame him."

"And this damned Agitator," I said, "who in the hell is he? Point him out to me."

"Over there, in the corner," the Straw said, leaning from his bunk. "Making a row, as usual."

A minute later I was standing beside the Agitator. Surrounded by youths, he was railing away. "You're all small fry," he was shouting. "What do you know about Belozersky Central? I was there back in '34, before the lot of you could even crawl. I'm an old tramp, I've seen a thing or two, I know! I got a beard that hangs down to my thing."

The Agitator delivered the last sentence with special emphasis, even though he was beardless and absolutely bald. It would have been difficult to determine his exact age. He didn't look like an old man to me, but he didn't seem young either. Looking him over closely, I said, "I don't know what kind of beard you've got or what it hangs down to, but you sure talk a lot."

He turned swiftly to me, his face twitching.

"What do you mean by that crack?" he asked slowly.

"There's a parable. Two guys are standing up to their necks in shit and one of them says to the other, 'Hey, don't make waves!' That's what you're making right now. Waves. And not for the first time, either."

As always, during an attack of rage, I felt a momentary sense of suffocation. I stopped for a second to regain my breath. Then I added, "I'm warning you, be on your guard. One false step and I'll swallow you like a boa constrictor, understand? Get it?"

"I get it," he said hoarsely. "Seems you must be a friend of this Chipmunk fellow."

"So?" I said.

"What are you after now?"

I smiled. "I just thought I'd take a look at you and get acquainted."

"And give me a good scare?"

"I'm not trying to scare you, I'm warning you to make sure you know what you're talking about. Call it good advice."

"Well, I'll get by without it." He made a wry face. "I wasn't the only one involved in that. There were a lot of other thieves at the meeting. You planning on defying them, too?"

I realized I'd lost the first round. I'd spoken too much and shown my hand. The Agitator turned out to be a strong rival, dodgy, resourceful, and far from stupid. He reminded me a bit of Volodya Lenin—another man who hadn't been that easy to deal with.

All right, I decided. I'll wait for the right time.

A week later I was sitting in the neighboring barracks with Nikola. An outcast, deprived of all his privileges, he'd crossed over to the ranks of the simple workers among whom he now lived in a repairmen's brigade. He was settled on a lower bunk not far from the entrance, right in the middle of a steady draft. The place was a pigsty.

Wrapping himself up in a torn blanket, Nikola said: "What's there left for me to do? What am I living for?"

"Don't panic," I said. "You can still play it all over again. It's not evening yet."

"Evening, hell." He smiled. "It's the middle of the Arctic night!"

"Don't panic! There'll be another meeting, I'll raise the issue. Look, I heard about you and Varka a long time ago, way back on the Don. The Straw will support you, and so will the rest of them. We'll set things straight, you'll see!"

He looked at me strangely, somehow, from the corners of his eyes. Then he said with a sigh: "But should we? Is there any sense to it now?"

"What?" I didn't understand. "Wait a minute—"

"I was just thinking," he said slowly, tonelessly, "on this earth nothing happens in vain. Whatever the Lord does is for the best. How did I botch it up in the first place? On account of my family. And that's where I have to return. Home, to a quiet life! I've wandered enough. It's time to get used to a *fraier*'s fate."

"And will you?" I asked.

"I don't know." He hesitated. "I haven't yet, anyway. I go out slogging with the workers, I dig around, take a firm stand, and there's all this darkness in my soul. It drives me crazy."

"You're mixing me up, Nikola. Look, if you want your rights back . . ."

"I'm telling you I don't know myself. Sure, a *fraier*'s fate is lousy, but it's quiet. Here on this bunk"—he slapped his hand against the rough, dirty boards—"I live more quietly and more safely than before. And I'll live to see freedom faster, too, than I would back with you guys. Here I'm hungry, there I'm full, here I'm bored, there I'm happy—but do you know the price you have to pay for that happiness?"

He searched for his tobacco pouch at the head of his bed, rustled a piece of paper, and began to roll a cigarette. While he smoked, I looked at him and realized he was the second person I knew to arrive at the same conclusions as I had. First there was the Goblin, and now Nikola—both of them tired of the life, disillusioned with it; and determined to make a break with the thieves. And here I was still vacillating, unable to build up the necessary determination in myself.

Nikola took a few drags and extended the glowing butt to me. Holding it in the tips of my fingers and squinting from the smoke, I said:

"It's a mixed blessing, this happiness of ours. Laugh, hell, it makes you want to wail like a wolf."

"That's it," he agreed, "especially nowadays! You know how it is with the thieves. Here today, gone tomorrow."

I wanted to say something else, but I didn't have the chance. There was a sudden burst of gunfire behind the door. Someone shrieked. Then silence and a new burst of gunfire. Apparently, the shooting was coming from somewhere very near in the zone.

My first thought was the uprising. It can't have started yet! I said to myself. It's the wrong time. Besides, why didn't anyone give me any advance warning?

I was already on the run. As soon as I got outside into the darkness, I realized the shooting was coming from my "happy" barracks!

The door was wide open and a man with an automatic weapon was standing on the threshold with his back to me, firing short bursts into the barracks.

This was no soldier, or guard either! He was dressed in the gray pea jacket of a prisoner.

"A bitch!" Nikola shouted hoarsely, slipping out suddenly from behind my shoulder. He'd run toward the noise without thinking, still half-dressed, his blanket on his back.

"A bitch!" he shouted, looking sideways at me. "You understand? Oh, God, look what they've started in on now!"

His shout coincided with a short pause in the gunfire. The man apparently heard Nikola's voice and wheeled around sharply. It was the Brunette, the Rhino's friend. His face seemed frozen in a strange convulsion. His eyes were glassy, deprived of all expression. I'd run across eyes like that before. The Brunette was clearly doped to the gills, in a strange half-sleep where all his feelings were bared and sharpened to the extreme. He was standing in the light; we were in the cover of darkness, just two steps away. He couldn't make us out, but, reacting instantly to Nikola's shout, he swung the barrel around and squeezed the trigger.

I ducked and pulled my knife out of the top of my boot. The bullet flew over me. One little bullet! But it was enough. I heard my friend wheeze, his voice suddenly turning into a low, gurgling scream.

Nikola staggered and sank. With a weak gesture he threw up his hands to his throat. The blanket slipped down from his shoulders. The same instant I flung my knife at the Brunette.

The throw was off. The bluish blade spun, flashed, and struck the barrel of the submachine gun with a ring. I was disarmed now and defenseless. I stepped back cautiously and waited for the gunfire. It didn't come. The Brunette leaped from the porch, ran off toward the opposite barracks and, swearing furiously, threw the weapon in the snow. Apparently, he'd run out of ammunition. Maybe he'd simply been in a hurry to hide. The whole camp was already on alert. The spotlights were tossing over the zone and you could hear the rumble of voices and rushing feet coming our way.

I bent down to Nikola. He was dying. His lips were blue and almost lifeless. They moved with difficulty, whispering something. I leaned my ear toward them and caught the light puff of his words:

"Still . . . I'm dying a thief. . . . You said you can play again . . . so do it! For the sake of my soul. You see what's happening. Could I do anything else? And get even with the Agitator. Okay? Do it?"

"I'll do it," I muttered. "I'll do it all, brother. I'll get even. Rest easy!"

But there was no getting even with the Agitator. He had died that night, mowed down by machine-gun fire, along with the other inhabitants of my happy barracks.

A SEQUEL

These were the circumstances behind the attack:

After the death of the Goose, and especially after the Brunette's friend, the Rhino, had been pinned with the rap, the bitches went into a panic. The Brunette vowed to seek revenge on the thieves—all of them at once. And he soon got his chance.

The bitches enjoyed the support of the administration and some of them, as members of the prison camp self-protection squads, had access to weapons. One midnight, with the help of one of these "vigilantes," the Brunette got his hands on a submachine gun. Hiding the weapon under the flap of his pea jacket, he'd stolen out of the staff barracks, burst into the thieves' quarters, and opened fire from the threshold.

There was a big game in progress; all of the players (several pairs of them) were settled on the floor near the stove, surrounded by a crowd of onlookers with the Agitator, as usual, in the middle, wriggling and prattling away.

All of them were cut down by the bullets. The only thieves to be saved were on the other side of the stove at the far end of the barracks. One of them, by the way, was the Straw, the well-known onanist. Living as he did in solitude, behind a curtain, he took no part in the general amusements, having more than enough of his own.

Thirteen bodies in one night—a record of its kind. Although the authorities had gotten rather used to bloodshed in the camps in recent years, a massacre of this size had them all worried. The matter went as far as Moscow. A commission from the Ministry arrived at the 503rd Construction Project to undertake a massive investigation.

The Brunette and all of his vigilante friends were immediately sent in chains to the inner prison at Krasnoyarsk. All the guards on duty in the zone that fateful night were put under arrest. Generally speaking, the commission acted decisively and with dispatch. The prison camp administration was reshuffled and the top levels completely replaced.

Then it was our turn. A rumor went the rounds of the zone that a massive deportation was in the works. One fine morning, during the mounting of the guards, the senior dispatcher read a list from the watchtower of those who were to get ready to be shipped out. It was a long list, with my name right near the top.

When the deportees were already wandering toward the gates of the camp with their things, I dropped into the hospital to see Levitsky.

"So long," Kostya said, knitting his brows, "I'm sorry, of course. It couldn't have happened at a worse time."

"Right," I agreed. "Still, who knows? Like my old pal Nikola the Chipmunk once said, 'Whatever the Lord does is for the best.' "

"Nikola? You mean the one who got killed by the door to the barracks?"

"That's the one." I nodded.

"So much for his philosophy." Levitsky smiled. "Besides,

my dear, it's hard to count on the best. Don't forget our old arrangement, though. It's still in effect."

He gave me a piercing look from under his shaggy brows. "You understand? At the first signal. We're counting on it."

"But I haven't got the vaguest idea where they're sending us."

"It doesn't matter. If you're within the boundaries of the Construction Project."

"Okay." I nodded, and, lowering my voice, asked: "Tell me, only be straight about it, do you really think it'll work? Do you really believe in it yourself?"

"And you?" he shot right back.

I silently shrugged my shoulders.

"Have you talked with your boys already?" Kostya wanted to know.

"Only with some, my closest friends."

"Reliable people?"

"The best," I said. "But you haven't answered me yet."

"What can I tell you?" He made a wry face. "It all depends on the main staff, and they're far away. But, yes, if you want to know, I think it's all workable. The latest incident helped prove it."

He moved toward me, his eyes gleaming with a strange, dark fire.

"You know how long it took from the start of the shooting to the time they sounded the alarm?"

"Who the hell knows?" I hesitated. "Not much, probably."

"More than twenty minutes!" Levitsky announced triumphantly. "Almost half an hour! It turns out all the guards were asleep in the staff barracks. Even one of the guards in the tower was asleep. And when another guard got so confused he called headquarters, they were sleeping there, too. You understand what I'm saying? Sleeping like logs! They'd all been drinking that night."

"But," I objected, "now it'll be different. A new broom . . ."

"Nonsense." Kostya brushed it aside. "People are people wherever you go. They get used to things and everything goes back to where it started. Anyway, it's not such a new broom. The Chekists who arrived with the commission are old northerners. They worked in the neighboring administration in Labutnang, and they're just the same as the others. The new Godfather, as I've already discovered, loves to drink. He'll be needing me for sure. And the head of the camp is a ladies' man. We'll take care of that, too. For a start, of course, we'll ship him Valka."

"Yes, Valka." I drew a long sigh. "A good woman. I'll miss her. Where is she, by the way?"

"In the main depot. Run, maybe you'll have a chance to see her."

For an instant, with a kind of bitter-sweet yearning, I summoned the image of that woman in my mind: the sound of her breathing, the smell of her skin. It was better to leave like this, without seeing her. Otherwise, the memory of her would overpower me on the road and make my life even more miserable than it was.

"Give her my regards," I said. "Tell her not to forget me! And say good-bye to all the others, too. To Obolensky and the Beard and Vitya. Even though he can't stand me. I never did understand, by the way, what he had against me."

"He's not against *you*," Levitsky said. "It's thieves in general he doesn't like. What are you going to do? Still, he started treating you pretty well. Especially after I showed him your poems."

"Which poems?"

"The ones you copied into the notebook, remember?"

Once, while lolling in the hospital, I had decided to write some new poems down to keep from forgetting them. I'd asked Levitsky for a notebook and then left it behind on the night table in my room. Besides, the latest developments had been so catastrophic that I'd lost my taste for poetry. Now, remembering the poems, I said carelessly: "Nonsense, old man, it's all nonsense. Although I'm glad Vitya liked them."

"Not just Vitya," he answered. "Me, too. Please don't belittle yourself. There are some memorable things there, especially among the miniatures. You're very good at lyric landscapes. Take this one, for instance." And, wrinkling his chin with concentration, he quoted: " 'An excavation. The frost crackles. A trail of hoofs in the dawn. Some goats come at night, it seems, to warm themselves by our fire.' Or this one: 'Darkness looks down on my planet. The trunks of three pines are ringing like three arrows shot from Mars.' Not bad at all. So don't blaspheme your gifts."

He fell silent. And then:

"I kept the notebook. Will you be taking it?"

"I don't know," I said. "There'll be a search at the penal camp—they'll take it away anyway. But, yes, give it to me, I can use it for rolling cigarettes on the road."

"If that's the case," he said, "I'll keep it here myself. You know what I'd do if I were you?"

"What?"

"I'd send the poems to some publishing house."

"Are you kidding? Who'd be interested? They've already got a million rhymers of their own."

I argued and objected, but it was all for show. The very mention of a publishing house took my breath away. Still, I controlled myself and asked him in what I hoped sounded like an indifferent voice:

"Just where would you send them?"

"Wherever you like. Krasnoyarsk, for instance. To the regional newspaper, to the local office of the Writers' Union. There are plenty of possibilities!"

"You think they'd be interested in poems from a prison camp?"

"Why from a prison camp?" Levitsky was surprised. "I have friends on the outside, they can send them. All right?"

"Okay," I said. "Try it if you want. You realize, don't you, we're both sitting on a volcano."

"Well, my dear, that's better left unsaid. Live like a soldier! Don't look ahead. If you're fated to fall, you'll fall. But while you're still in one piece, do your own work, take advantage of every opportunity, and break through to success. And leave the rest to fate."

We embraced and I rushed outside. The deportation had long since gathered at the watch and as soon as I appeared the column wavered and began to buzz. The escort ran up, cracked his bolt, and started to wail.

"Fucking around, you bastard? Make us wait, eh? Take your stand!"

THE EDGE OF THE KNIFE

Eight days and nights they drove us through the tundra and the sparsely wooded lands, to the lower reaches of the Yenisei. A string of sledges accompanied the column: machine gunners ahead of us, four other sledges with provisions, medical supplies, and our property bringing up the rear.

It snowed every day; the ground winds coiled and rustled at our feet; and all around us, in the snow and haze, loomed the shaggy, jagged pines. Stumbling through the snowdrifts, tripping over the rock scree, and bedding down at night in the snow by the campfire, I once again recalled my father's verses and repeated the line from his ancient convict's cycle: "The lash of fate drives us, through wild, uncharted places . . ."

Where were we going? No one knew. But it was sure to be a God-forsaken hole. There was nothing but the Arctic wastes, untouched and untroubled by a single dwelling or the scent of man.

And when on the ninth day of the journey, the outlines of the camp rose before us, I shuddered with a dark premonition.

The penal camp was constructed on a steep and bare riverbank, without a single dwelling in sight. The only building near the watch had a clearly barrackslike appearance. A truck dusted with snow stood by the entrance. A series of electric power lines stretched around the corner, ringing mournfully in the wind and disappearing behind the edge of a distant crest of pines. A sentry in a sheepskin coat paced back and forth by the barracks. A second sentry was on the roof, overlooking a little square with searchlights and a pair of machine guns, all of them trained on the zone where, behind a double row of barbed wire, a crowd of convicts now thronged and wailed.

They met us with shrieks, hoots, and howls. "Hold on to your hat, boy." The Straw winked at me. "This is the place where ninety-nine weep for each man that laughs!"

I spent about a year there, from that winter through the following autumn. It was a miserable, barren, and terrible life. They fed us substandard rations, when they bothered to feed us at all. The kitchen and other vital services were located outside the perimeter of the camp—behind the woods—about five versts away. Grub was brought in by sled, and when the weather was bad and the snowstorms closed down the road, the supply would be completely cut off. Hundreds of people wild with hunger would gather by the watch (as they had the day our deportation arrived). It was a frequent occurrence. During my own stay at the penal division there were three serious clashes with the authorities: the machine guns would open fire from the watchtowers and the barracks, covering the zone in a cross fire, scattering the crowds and restoring order. That, in essence, was the administration's only job. They neither interfered with our internal affairs nor drove us off to work. We were completely left to our own devices.

The physical campsite was small, but packed to the rafters. Thieves swarmed there like spiders in a jar. Desperate and famished, completely cut off from the rest of the world, they gradually lost their former cohesion and were transformed into a fierce rabble. The den fell apart. The traditional ties were destroyed. Mutual enmity and fights that often led to bloodshed were common, everyday occurrences. Once the Straw and I (and that famous old bear hunter was universally respected) called a special meeting and made an attempt to bring the men to reason and to remind them of the sacred traditions. But the enterprise failed; they simply didn't want to listen.

With things this bad, I thought despondently, how can you

talk about supporting an uprising? You need an organized force to seize control and with scum like this, what can I do? Even if I *were* to get the signal, it wouldn't do any good. They can't see that they've got anything in common.

I had no idea when or how I'd get the news of an uprising. And to be honest, I didn't very much believe in one. Still, I waited for the agreed-upon signal. And I often thought of Kostya Levitsky and his friends. During those last few months I'd grown close to the politicals. What a joy it would have been to see Levitsky again, or Shtilmark! (Luckily for him, incidentally, Robert had not ended up at our penal camp. As I later learned, the party that he, the Professor, and the Georgian prince were in had been sent to a different camp: a tight-security one as well, but not quite so terrible as ours. They'd apparently settled in there and adjusted pretty well.)

The only remembrance I now had of my friends was the book Shtilmark had given me at the start of our acquaintance. Under the title, *Newspaper Composition and Production*, Robert had signed his name. And in the lower corner of the page, in the Professor's hand, was a drawing of a stick figure with spread arms and bow legs. "*Kanai!*" he'd scrawled in huge, tumbling letters beneath it: "Go!"

Strange as it may seem, they hadn't taken the book away during the search. Apparently, the guards were confused by the fact that it was a journalism textbook and journalism is, of course, a particularly Party affair!

And so I brought the textbook into the zone. Lounging on the bunk in the musty barracks amidst the abuse, the swearing, and the turmoil, I finally read it through and, for nothing better to do, assiduously learned all the newspaper terms.

Robert had said that journalism was the main road to literature and this came strongly back to mind. So did Levitsky's parting words: "While you're still in one piece, do your own work, take advantage of every opportunity, and break through to success!" Both of them had been talking about the same thing. They believed in me. For that I was grateful.

I was waiting for some kind of news from Levitsky. And finally, toward the end of the winter, right after Shrovetide, it came.

We celebrated Shrovetide, by the way, with the usual hunger strike. This time the snowstorms weren't to blame, but the holiday itself. The administration had gotten drunk and forgotten all about us. Once again a crowd raged and wailed by the watchtower, and once again the machine guns rang through the zone. For a long time afterwards the bodies of the prisoners—five dead and twice that many wounded—lay heaped in the pre-zone area like firewood. And yet, despite the fact that our camp—to all appearances—was a camp of the condemned, they did finally give the victims the help they needed. (Apparently, some kind of special instructions existed on that score.) From somewhere, doctors and orderlies materialized and, in the course of a week, a medical center was in operation in the zone.

One of the doctors I turned to was a dentist. Recently, my teeth had been tormenting me. Several times before I'd made a row trying to get a doctor, but to no avail. Now, finally, the dentist—a short, thickset fellow with wire-frame glasses—conscientiously wrote my first and last names, sat me down on the bench, and opened my lips with his fingers.

"It's not your teeth that're giving you the trouble, my friend," he said, "it's your gums. A pronounced case of scurvy."

"That's all I need! What do you treat scurvy with?"

"Vitamins." He smiled. "And fresh fruit, vegetables . . ."

"Are you laughing at me?"

"What else is there left?" He twitched his shoulders. "If you really want to do something about it, I'd advise you to take conifer broth. It's not hard to prepare. I'll order it. It's not very pleasant, but it's absolutely essential. Several of your teeth have already started to come loose."

"Probably the ones that've been aching," I said. "How many?"

"Quite a few." He looked in my mouth again and dug

around in there. "Here . . . and here, too. . . . All in all, six!"

"A round figure," I muttered, groaning and spitting with disgust.

The orderlies had been lounging in the room. As soon as they left and the doctor and I were alone, he drew right up to my face and said distinctly:

"There's another round figure—eight!"

"Eight?" I repeated, suddenly tense and rising in my chair.

"Sit down, sit down," he whispered sharply. "I send you greetings from Levitsky."

"How is he?" I rushed to say. "How are things in general?"

"As usual," the doctor answered evasively. "I'm not authorized to tell you much, but there is one piece of news he asked me to give you." He looked at me, screwing up his eyes. "Your papers have already been sent off. They left for Krasnoyarsk!"

"What papers?" I didn't understand. Suddenly I realized he was talking about my poems. "This news—it's from Kostya?"

"Yes, yes, from him."

"And he didn't want to tell me anything else?"

"For the time being, no. As for the rest, we'll see when the time comes. Wait!"

"Listen," I said, "isn't there any way of setting up some kind of permanent connection? You can see for yourself what the situation is here. You and I got lucky, so to speak. But it'd be absurd to count on coincidences like this. You mean to say you don't have any reliable means of communication?"

"We do," he replied, "we do!" He looked back at the door and pressed his lips tightly together. "The driver who brings the produce here is one of us. Whisper your code to him. Call out the number, understand?"

And, changing to a different tone of voice (strangers had once again come into the room), he said, wiping his instruments with a little rag:

"Conifer broth! But remember, use it regularly, and no tricks. That's imperative! Otherwise, we simply won't treat you next time."

It was some time before I got the next piece of news. It was the head of the camp who brought it. Accompanied by a large retinue of supervisors, all of them plainly under the influence of alcohol, he appeared late at night in the zone.

They drove the prisoners out of the barracks and gathered them by the watch. And there, wheezing and shouting, the chief announced that a group of prisoners accused of underground anti-Soviet activity had recently been sentenced by a special conference to the highest measure of social defense: death by firing squad!

They handed him a piece of paper. Knitting his brows and shielding his eyes from the slanting rays of the sun (it was summer already and the flat, sleepless Arctic sun rolled over the horizon) he read the names of the accused.

Among them were all of my friends from the committee: Levitsky and the Beard and Vitya and the old translator and the descendant of the disgraced Obolensky princes, and the dentist—the same one I'd seen just the other day. The reading took some time. At the end the chief added in a drunken wheeze:

"The sentence has been carried out! Period. Draw your own conclusions."

The entire camp had a hard time calming down that night. The news had upset them all. What struck the thieves most was the fact that an active political underground had even existed in our construction project in the first place. Aside from the Straw, myself, and three other reliable thieves from the committee with whom I'd managed to talk in my own time, nobody had known about it.

While the gang animatedly discussed what they'd heard, the five of us retired to a quiet corner and met on my bunk. How had it happened? And why? Probably someone had betrayed them. Maybe, though, what had happened had been what I'd forecast from the start: somehow the list of all their names had fallen into the wrong hands.

"That's how it happened, most likely," I concluded gloomily.

"But are you sure?" the Straw asked. "Are you sure our names weren't there?"

"If they had been, we wouldn't be here right now!"

"That's true." The Straw nodded thoughtfully.

"Besides the only one mentioned in the lists was me! Not under my own name, it's true, but under a number. Thank God I didn't give them either a name or a nickname. I almost broke with them on account of that."

"Better be on your guard anyway," one of the thieves, nicknamed Gray, grumbled. "If somebody suddenly broke. . . . *Fraiers* don't hold up too well under torture."

"You didn't know these boys. No, I'm sure of them. Anyway, what *can* you do to be on your guard around here?"

"Well, don't respond to your number at least," the Straw said. "Forget about it, understand? And don't even think of dealing with that driver. The investigators may not know your name, but they've sure got a number for you."

"Damn it," I moaned, "why have I got such lousy luck? They've been at my heels from the beginning, now with a bitch's knife, now with a new article in the criminal code. And my term's going to end soon and yet . . . and yet. . . ."

"It's true," the Straw drawled. "You'll be free soon, my boy. How much time have you got left?"

"Not much." I brushed it aside. "I'm afraid to talk about it. Nikola dreamed of freedom and ten minutes later a bullet cut him down."

"Yes," Gray muttered. "Chuma's right, of course. Our life's a goddamn rabbit hunt, without a ray of hope."

"Or a kind of fairy tale," someone added. "The farther you go, the worse it gets."

"Or like a plane ride," the Straw said. "No matter how sick you get, you can't crawl out."

"Or like a potato," I concluded. "If they don't eat you on the spot, they stuff you back in the ground."

There really was little time left to my term—just a year. Freedom was getting nearer, glimmering more and more brightly. Still, with a kind of superstitious obstinacy, I avoided talking or even thinking about it. I knew what Levitsky had meant when he said to me: "Live like a soldier, don't think about the future." What was there to hope for in my position? I was always walking on the brink of disaster. At any moment I might stumble and fall.

At the end of September our penal camp was suddenly and strangely transformed. The Arctic aspen had already blazed into flower and shed its seeds, the sparse birches glowed crimson and the swans stretched and melted in the blue over the floodlands of the Yenisei.

If earlier they'd been starving us, now they began to stuff us till we popped. They eliminated the three-hundred-gram bread ration and started giving us half a loaf apiece. The food changed, too. Instead of the former watery bran mash, we were flooded with barley and kasha. One look and you'd have thought the extermination camp had changed into a sanatorium.

Swelling from the food and inactivity, the thieves loafed about the zone and wondered exactly what was going on. Had Stalin decided to declare a general amnesty and was this the first sign of the impending changes for the better? Had power changed hands in the country? Had Stalin died and a new government come in? Endless conversations raged on that score, and some of the most fantastic guesses were ventured. The majority was inclined to the idea of a new government, and only the experienced thieves refused to share in the general elation.

"You'll see," the Straw prophesied. "None of it's for the better. There's something fishy here. Some kind of dirty trick. There's never been a government that would feed you for no good reason! These oats are going to give you the shaft, boys." And lifting the spoonful of kasha to his mouth, he gave it a distrustful look.

One fine morning the penal camp was evacuated: we were led down to the river and loaded on closed barges. A week later we arrived at the port of Dudinka, near the Kara Sea, where we finally realized what the story was. Our deportation had been designated for dispatch to the coal mines of Novaya Zemlya, an island in the Arctic Ocean above the 70th parallel, with brutal conditions only the strongest could survive. A special commission had been appointed to choose the people for the mines and, apparently, we'd been fattened up for the inspection.

Once again I was feeling the ground slip away from under me; I was falling, falling, and there was nothing to hold onto.

We were all in a panic. Novaya Zemlya was the end! Those who landed there would never be coming back. Somehow, we had to save ourselves. But how? I didn't know. My friends, though, quickly hatched a scheme.

The only reason the commission might reject any of us (despite our sated appearance) was illness. Especially an infectious illness. And so, in short order, the thieves started changing themselves into consumptives and syphilitics.

Generally, it was an easy thing to do. To get "syphilis," for instance, just sear the proper place with a burning match or cigarette. That gives you the sore. The rest is entirely up to your skill as an actor. This was the means the Straw immediately resorted to. I took pity on myself, though, and chose "tuberculosis." (I'd suck blood from my fingers and then spit it up in the presence of the authorities, while wheezing, gasping for breath, and clutching my chest.) A few of the thieves impersonated epileptics. This worked well, too, as long as you remembered to bring a little bathing soap with you and foam at the mouth.

Of course, if the commission had had more time, it would certainly have looked into the whole thing a bit more carefully. But they couldn't wait for the results of the tests. Autumn had ended. Low gray snow-laden clouds were rolling in from the Kara Sea. The prewinter gales for which the latitudes are famous were rapidly approaching.

As a result, almost half of our deportation was saved and remained on the mainland. Soon I was sitting in the closed and stinking hold of the barge again, surrounded by the gang. Once again I was lost in thought, wondering where fate was taking me, anticipating new nightmares and neither daring nor wanting to believe that freedom was at hand. Only when our caravan landed at the deportation point in Krasnoyarsk did I begin to relax.

I spent my final months there in comparative peace and quiet. Having lost all my old friends, I no longer reached out for any new ones and kept to myself. All during that time the only person I really saw much of was the Straw. Late one night I told him over a cup of *chifir*:

"You know, old man, I've had enough. With my first step to freedom, I leave 'the life' behind."

"But what are you going to do?" He frowned.

"I'll try to write. Maybe it'll come off."

"And if it doesn't?"

I didn't answer that. What could I have said? I wasn't sure of anything myself.

"Well, and if it doesn't," the Straw said insistently, "then what? Literature is a shaky business. A lot depends on luck there and on the kind of card you get dealt. It's not easy to come out from under there! Take Esenin—"

"He came out from under."

"But you're not Esenin."

"Who knows?" I smiled. "Anyway, that's not the point. Fact is, I just can't go on like this anymore. I don't want to. I haven't got the strength."

"So you're going to tie up, is that it?"

"Yes."

"Have you told anybody yet?"

"So far only you."

The Straw nodded. "Keep mum. Until the bell's sounded, don't say a word."

"But why?" I got indignant. "Why should I be quiet? According to the law every thief's got the right to tie up, as long as he does it cleanly."

"The law!" He mournfully waved his hand. "What's the law! Times aren't what they used to be. The way things are today, whoever isn't with us is against us. They could accuse you of renouncing the faith when the going got really tough.

Or of betraying us all. And what will you have to say against that?"

"It's hard to say anything." I hesitated.

"Right! That's why I'm telling you, don't be in a hurry. When the time comes, I'll announce it to the thieves myself."

He was silent and thoughtful. He looked into his cup, took a noisy sip, and lifted his eyes to me.

"Besides, we still have some unfinished business. Have you forgotten Nikola the Chipmunk? You remember his last request?"

"What do you mean?" I muttered in embarrassment. "Of course I haven't forgotten. I remember everything!" (The truth was that, to my shame, I had forgotten.)

And so, up to the last day, till the very "bell," I remained in the den. Restoring Nikola's rightful place turned out to be no easy task, but, all the same, I did it, in memory of his soul. There were other matters to tend to as well, and we discussed them at the noisy general meetings. And I stayed there right to the end. Finally, in January of 1952 (a day before my liberation) there was a meeting I couldn't attend—the talk was about me. My fate was being decided. And, while the discussion was going on, I loitered beneath the windows of the thieves' barracks, listening with trepidation to the voices inside. The meeting was long and stormy and it ended unexpectedly.

The dry, stooping figure of the Straw appeared on the threshold. He knitted his brows and his long face broke into a smile. Beckoning me with his finger, he said:

"Come into the room, my dove."

When I entered, he pointed toward the corner.

"There, take a look. It's for you!"

In the corner, in a heap, was a pile of clothes: suits, shoes, sweaters. And, beside it, a stuffed bag tied with a string. I looked at it and asked in confusion:

"Why all this?"

"Why? Because you're not a thief anymore," the Straw said.

"You said so yourself. 'My first step.' . . . So, let your first step be a peaceful one."

"But how am I going to take it all?"

"If you don't want to wear it, sell it. You can get a good price on clothes these days. The main thing is to avoid temptation on the way, and not get pinched for trifles. There's no way you can get burned now."

And apparently noticing something in my face, the Straw added sharply, almost threateningly: "Don't you dare refuse. Take it all! The gathering has decided. . . ."

"Decided what?"

"Decided that you're going to be a poet!"

(*Paris*, 1969–71)

A NOTE ABOUT THE AUTHOR

Mikhail Dyomin has taken his writing name from the forged identity papers he was forced to use while in hiding within the Soviet criminal underground. He was born Georgy Trifonov in 1926. His mother belonged to the pre-revolutionary nobility; his father, a top Red Army commissar in the Civil War, fell into disfavor and was persecuted during the Stalinist era. Dyomin was first arrested in 1942, at the age of sixteen, for disobeying a compulsory work order. Sentenced to two years of hard labor in a Moscow foundry, he was finally given a medical discharge. He worked for a while as an advertising artist, until an office-wide investigation by the secret police sent him fleeing, without identity papers, into the underground. There he lived for several years, working with a pickpocket gang and "riding the rails." After his arrest, he spent six years in some of the most notorious Arctic camps—as a member of the criminal elite—and during this time earned a name for himself as a "scribbler" of prison songs and poems. Dyomin's first literary scholarship was earned upon his release from the Siberian camp, when his fellow inmates took up a collection to see him through his first book. In the fifteen years following his release, he published six books; he became a member of the Writers' Union and was by all measures a successful, popular author. Yet, he was dissatisfied with the restrictions imposed by state censorship, and during a visit to France some years ago, he quietly defected. He now lives in a small apartment in Paris, where he continues to write.

A NOTE ABOUT THE TYPE

The text of this book was set by use of Cathode Ray Tube in a face called TIMES ROMAN, *originally designed as a linotype face by* STANLEY MORISON *for* The Times *(London), and first introduced by that newspaper in 1932.*

Among typographers and designers of the twentieth century, Stanley Morison has been a strong forming influence, as typographical adviser to the English Monotype Corporation, as a director of two distinguished English publishing houses, and as a writer of sensibility, erudition, and keen practical sense.

In 1930 Morison wrote: "Type design moves at the pace of the most conservative reader. The good type-designer therefore realises that, for a new fount to be successful, it has to be so good that only very few recognise its novelty. If readers do not notice the consummate reticence and rare discipline of a new type, it is probably a good letter." It is now generally recognised that in the creation of TIMES ROMAN *Morison successfully met the qualifications of this theoretical doctrine.*

This book was composed by The Colonial Press Inc., Clinton, Massachusetts, and printed and bound by American Book-Stratford Press, Saddle Brook, New Jersey.

Typography and binding design by Camilla Filancia